Sorry Kid, I Don't Much Feel Like Playing Today

Sorry Kid, I Don't Much Feel Like Playing Today

Kelly D. Cleaver Sr.

iUniverse, Inc.
Bloomington

Sorry Kid, I Don't Much Feel Like Playing Today

iUniverse books may be ordered through booksellers or by contacting:

iUniverse
1663 Liberty Drive
Bloomington, IN 47403
www.iuniverse.com
1-800-Authors (1-800-288-4677)

ISBN: 978-1-4620-1719-5 (sc)
ISBN: 978-1-4620-1720-1 (dj)

Library of Congress Control Number: 2011906776

Printed in the United States of America

iUniverse rev. date: 05/16/2011

Acknowledgements

I would like to take the time to thank the following people who helped immensely to this project. My Pop Hunce Cleaver, who taught me the meaning of sports and how to love it. My nephew Johnny Cleaver Jr., whom I must have drove nuts with late night phone calls. Thanks Meat, for everything! I would also like to thank my niece, Tara Barnes who also provided invaluable information especially the 1919 Chicago Tribune articles regarding the World Series. A special thanks to my wife Linda, for all the typing and giving me the support to finish something I never thought I'd finish, and for three beautiful children, and well, everything you do! I love you more Pookie, everyday. Just wait til tomorrow. Big thanks to my computer guy, Caleb McNail in Arkansas. And also to my daughter Katie boo-boo, who gave up the use of her laptop for over a year while I worked on this book. Thanks also to my boys Kelly Jr. and Maxwell, who gave me constant encouragement to finish this project.

I would also like to thank my Mother Joan Cleaver, not just for everything but for all the sacrifices she made raising six boys with a terminally ill husband. I love you MOM. And thanks to my big brother Hunce Jr., who would take time from his Christmas painting to check facts for me. Thanks Ben (not just for this). I would also like to mention my nephew Mike Cleaver Jr., who wanted to see his name in my book. Along with: Bill Cobb, Steph and Harry Balls. Also Steve Jr., Craig, Jason, Richie, Nicky-poo (I see you) and Robby. Let's not forget Joan (so proud of you, way to go Jo-Jo!), and Johnny Jr. I can't leave out Raoul, Kenya, Becky, Mikey, Vanessa and Jordan. I'd be in big trouble if I didn't mention Jimmy Jr., Dandan the piper man (our all-stater, so proud), Molly, and the dude-man Christian. I'm so proud to be to all of you, you're Uncle Kel. Also my brothers wives and my sisters (in-law doesn't apply here), Rosa, Jodie, Shelley, our newest member to the family Gail, Francis, Elisa and Lib. I'd also like to thank my Father-in-law Harold Daniels.

Dedications

For my Pooky: For whom the sun rises and sets.

To Mom and Pop: For everything.

To my brothers: Hunce Jr., Teets, John, Mike, and Jimmy

To my children: Katie, Kelly Jr., and Max: What life is all about.

To Bill Schlerf: For always being my friend.

To Mike Riley: If it wasn't for you, I wouldn't have met Linda

And to Oscar Pierson and Billy Farrell, where ever you may be.

In Loving Memory

To my Pop, Teets, Mike, Jimmy Coco,

Tom Fucci, Uncle Steve, Nanny and Pop Pop,

Raoul , Grandma Nancy, Crazy Aunt Gail

And my mother in- law Esther Daniels.

"Regardless of the verdict of juries, no player who throws a ball game, no player that undertakes or promises to throw a ball game, no player that sits in conference with a bunch of crooked players and gamblers where the ways and means of throwing a game are discussed and does not promptly tell his club about it, will ever play professional baseball!"

- Kennesaw Mountain Landis

"I don't know what's the matter, but I do know that something is wrong with my gang. The bunch I had fighting in August for the pennant would have trimmed this Cincinnati bunch without a struggle. This bunch I have now couldn't beat a high school team."

- Sox manager Kid Gleason after game five

"Boys, I want to give you a sailor's farewell, goodbye; good luck; and to hell with Ban Johnson."

- Chick Gandil after the acquittals

"Swede is a hard guy."

-Joe Jackson

Contents

Introduction

Prelude to a fall from grace.

When the Chicago White Sox started out the 1919 World Series as 8 to 5 betting favorites, most people thought that the Cincinnati Reds should not even have bothered to show up. But when the odds shifted dramatically right before the first game making the Reds a 3 to 1 favorite, things just didn't seem right (and they weren't). But this book is not about gamblers and betting, as every baseball fan old enough to care about the history of the game knows why and who were involved in the World Series fix. This book is about how the Chicago players went about throwing these games. The 1919 Chicago White Sox were one of the greatest teams ever to put on a baseball uniform. In my opinion, at the very least the Sox have to be in the top ten of all time. Led by a player whom Ty Cobb called "The best natural hitter I ever saw," Shoeless Joe Jackson was the Sox leading hitter in 1919 with a .351 batting average. There is no doubt Joe would have landed in Cooperstown someday, most likely on the first ballot with the rest of the immortals. Also playing for the Sox that season were eventual Hall of Famers, 2nd baseman Eddie Collins, catcher Ray Schalk and pitcher Urban " Red" Faber (Faber hurt his ankle late in the season and was not available in the Series), along with three other probable hall members, 3rd baseman George "Buck" Weaver, and pitcher Claude "Lefty" Williams. Last but not least, one of the best right-handed pitchers in the game, Eddie Cicotte. That made seven ballplayers off of one team that were of Hall of Fame material, and how many teams can make that claim?

Playing only a one hundred and forty game schedule in 1919 because of the end of World War 1, and the fact that the owners were uncertain about the money end of their business (although baseball set a new attendance record of 3,654,236 in 1919 and scored a financial windfall), the White Sox were involved in a tight pennant race all summer, eventually edging out the Cleveland Indians by only three and a half games. With the pre- Babe Ruth New York Yankees seven and a half games behind and Ty Cobb's Detroit Tigers eight games back. The White Sox ended up with an 88-52 record (.624 winning percentage), compare that to their 100 – 54 record (.649) in 1917 when they defeated the New York Giants 4 games to 2 to win the World Championship, with basically the same team, show the Sox were a very consistent winner. The Cincinnati Reds on the other hand had a much easier time in the National League that summer, edging out John McGraw's New York Giants by nine games with a 96-44 record (.686). So sports writers were sadly mistaken when they thought the Reds were a push over. Cincinnati was led by Hall of Fame center fielder Edd Roush, the 1919 National League batting champion with a .321 average, and the great 3rd baseman Henry "Heinie" Groh, 2nd baseman Morris "Morrie" Rath, and the speedy right fielder and future college and professional Hall of Fame football coach Alfred "Greasy" Neale. Throw in the formidable pitching of Walter "Dutch" Ruether who was 19-6 and led the National League in winning percentage with a .760 and also with a league leading 1.81 earned run average, and twenty game winners Horace " Hod" Eller (20-9 2.40) and Harry "Slim" Sallee (21-7 2.05). The Reds were far from pushovers and would have matched up well against any team in American League. The White Sox did have something special about them, and it would have been great to see up-and-up best five out of nine contests between them. What would have resulted in a square contest? Only the baseball Gods know for sure, although I believe the White Sox win the Series in six games (nobody would have beaten Hod Eller in game five). Perhaps somewhere in the Heavens they still play today.

What you're about to read is a statistical play by play, inning by inning, breakdown of the tainted and not so tainted White Sox players (some players not involved in the fix, just had a terrible World Series). From the obviously dropped balls, booted grounders, slow running, missed cut offs, and double plays that just couldn't be turned, not to mention the pitched balls a high schooler could have hit, to the not so obvious. When the Sox player's statistics are looked at in the box score a person could say, "Oh, those things could have happened to anyone." But when these eight games of a World Series that history tells us was thrown, I think you'll see only four players on the White Sox played like they were really trying to win, and the great Hall of Famer Eddie Collins was not one of them. The four players being Buck Weaver, as I will get into later, who had an injustice done to him that will make a baseball fan sick to his stomach, Ray Schalk, Little Dickie Kerr, who won two games in spite of his teammate's ineptitude, and John "Shano" Collins. Excluding Fred McMullin who only had two at-bats in the Series (and had one base hit) but received $5,000 of the pay-off money and was eventually banned, and the relief pitchers along with bench players, who's role's in the Series were too insignificant to mention in depth. Although this book is about the Chicago White Sox, the reader will get to know the Cincinnati Reds players really well through their at-bats in the Sox pitching section and their pitchers and fielders in the Sox hitting section. Also the reader will learn about White Sox field manager Kid Gleason throughout the chapters, and his peculiar way of running a ballclub that was intent on losing. When you are finished with this expose', I believe you will agree that there should have been only seven White Sox players that should have been banned from baseball, and the one who shouldn't have been was not the great Joe Jackson.

The rest of the team had no other excuse other than to say, "Sorry Kid, I don't much feel like playing today".

Section One

The White Sox Pitchers and the Fielders

Chapter 1

Edward Victor Cicotte

But you started this Mr. Comiskey.

Edward Victor Cicotte was born June 19, 1884 in Detroit, Michigan. On September 3rd, 1905 at the age of just 21 years old, Eddie made his Major League debut with the Detroit Tigers. Cicotte went 1-1 with a 3.50 ERA, appearing in just three games. After being released by the Tigers after the season, Eddie re-appeared in the bigs in 1908 with the Boston Red Sox. After four and one half seasons in Boston where Eddie won 51 games with 46 losses, he was sold to the Chicago White Sox (for an undisclosed sum), in mid season on July 22, 1912. Cicotte pitched his remaining eight and a half years in Chicago. Nicknamed "Knuckles" for his famous pitch, Eddie was also a shine ball expert.

Eddie was always a dependable hurler, but really started to blossom in 1917, going 28-12 with a league leading 1.53 ERA, also throwing a no-hitter against the St. Louis Browns on April 14. From 1917 until his suspension on September 27th, 1920 Eddie was 90-48 for a .652 winning percentage. Though Eddie lost eighteen games for the Sox in the war torn season of 1918 (when most of the Sox regulars were away from the club, working under the work or fight order), Cicotte's greatest year was 1919. Knuckles won twenty-nine games with only seven losses to go along with a 1.82 ERA, putting Eddie on track to maybe being someday enshrined in Cooperstown. In Eddie's final season of 1920 which ended prematurely on September 27th when he and seven teammates were suspended by club owner Charles Comiskey, was a year in which Eddie was 21-10 with a 3.26 ERA (which wasn't too shabby for the beginning of the live ball era). Even though Cicotte was one of the game's greatest pitchers, Eddie's salary for 1919 was only $5,500. Compared to the Reds opening day Series pitcher Dutch Ruether, who made $11,000 a year, Eddie felt cheated. Plus he also felt cheated out of a supposed $10,000 bonus if he would have won thirty games in 1917, by owner Charles Comiskey. But to an owner like Comiskey, twenty-eight wins were not thirty, and twenty-eight wins did not merit an extra dime although most historians believe this bonus story to be a myth. What is not a myth though is that Kid Gleason started Cicotte twice in the last week of the 1919 season, including on the 28th of September, two days before the series began on October 1st, when the pennant was already wrapped up (an example of Kid's managerial skills).

The opening day starting pitcher of the World Series is a dream every baseball player dreams of. Eddie Cicotte was no different. Eddie had a dark secret though, under his pillow before game one was $10,000 cash. With the cheapest owner in either league Charles Comiskey, who paid one of the best pitchers in baseball the lowest salary, the $10,000 must have felt like redemption to Knuckles Cicotte. Eddie was to be paid an additional $10,000 dollars before each loss after the first game, for $30,000 dollars total. The winner's share of the series was $5,207.00, losers share $3,254.00. The temptation must have been too much, throw a few games in the Series and collect almost six times your annual pay? Cicotte claims he wanted to pay off the mortgage on his farm, which he did. At what price did he pay when the devil came to collect? In less than four innings (three and two thirds to be exact) his reputation and eventually his career came to an end.

Knuckles pitched well for three innings of the opener, giving up only one run, but the fourth inning will forever be remembered as batting practice for the Cincinnati Reds. Five runs, six hits in only eight batters was the end of Ed's and the White Sox's day. This one inning of baseball ruined a stellar career and immortality among the baseball greats. I always wondered how Eddie Cicotte explained this to his wife and two daughters when they asked "why?" After seeing the $10,000 pay off before game one, Eddie went out and did more than his part. Most people believe that Eddie threw game four also, but after reading the results of that game the reader will probably change their mind. Cicotte got paid off to bag the first game and he did, but when no more money came before his next start, so did Eddie's will to lose.

Eddie Cicotte played alongside other former teammates, after he was banned from baseball for a few years in the outlaw leagues. Done with baseball, Cicotte returned to his home in Michigan outside of Detroit and became a game warden for the state. Eddie died May 5, 1969 at the age of 68.

Here are the play by play results of Cicotte's three games pitched in the 1919 World Series, as if we were sitting in a box seat at field level.

Game One

Cincinnati, OH

October 1st 1919 Redland Field

Bottom 1st inning

It doesn't get any better than this, as 30,511 baseball loyalists turned out today to witness the opening game of the 1919 World Series. The Reds left-hander Dutch Ruether (19-6 1.81) taking on the White Sox 29 game winner, right-handed Eddie Cicotte (29-7 1.82). In one of the most significant at bats in the history of Major League Baseball, left handed hitting 2B Morrie Rath, of National league champion Cincinnati Reds with a .264 season batting average, leads-off the bottom of the 1st, after the Sox failed to score in the top half. Chicago ace Eddie Cicotte pumps a first pitch strike, called by home plate umpire Charles Rigler of the National League. Cicotte then drills Rath with a pitch (HBP) to the right shoulder. Nothing unusual about a hit batter, other than it was the signal to gambler Arnold Rothstein that the fix was on. I always wondered how Rothstein would have felt if Morrie would have popped that first pitch up or grounded out.

With Rath on 1st base and no outs, next up for the Reds is 1B Jake Daubert, with a season average of .276. Daubert another left handed hitter delivers a single (1B) to right center field, sending Rath all the way to 3rd base.

Now coming to bat with runners on the corners and no outs is 3B Heinie Groh, a right handed batter with .310 season average and the Reds top power hitter. Groh hits a deep fly ball to Joe Jackson in left field for an RBI sacrifice fly (SF-7), scoring Rath with the first run of the Series, and putting the Reds up 1-0.

With one out and one run in, the great Cincinnati Hall of Famer (1962), left handed hitting CF Edd Roush with a NL leading.321 season average, steps up to the plate. Before Roush can do any damage though, Jake Daubert is thrown out trying to steal 2nd base, C Ray Schalk to SS Swede Risberg (CS 2-6) for out number two. Roush then draws a base on balls (BB), and he promptly steals 2nd base (SB).

Cicotte then entices .269 right handed hitting LF Louis "Pat" Duncan, to ground out to Swede Risberg at short stop (6-3), ending the 1st inning.

Cicotte's Pitching Line

INN	H	R	ER	BB	K	HBP	WP	E
1	1	1	1	1	0	1	0	0

Bottom 2nd Inning

Chicago tied up the game 1-1 in the top of the 2nd inning. SS Larry Kopf, a .270 switch- hitter, leads-off the Reds half of the 2nd. Batting left handed against the right handed throwing Cicotte, Eddie strikes-out Kopf on three straight pitches (K), for the first out of the inning.

Next up for the Reds is Alfred "Greasy" Neale, a .242 hitting right fielder. Greasy, another left handed hitter, bounces a routine grounder to future Hall of Famer (1939) 2B Eddie Collins, who throws to 1B Chick Gandil (4-3), for out number two.

Now with two down, Reds left handed hitting C Ivey Wingo, a .273 hitter, lofts a high lazy fly ball to straight away center which CF Happy Felsch gloves (F-8), ending the bottom of the 2nd inning.

Cicotte's Pitching Line

	INN	H	R	ER	BB	K	HBP	WP	E
	1	0	0	0	0	1	0	0	0
Total	2	1	1	1	1	1	1	0	0

Bottom 3rd inning

After giving up the 1st inning run, Eddie seems to be settling into a groove. Leading off the bottom of the 3rd inning, Pitcher Walter "Dutch" Ruether, a hard hitting (.261) left handed batter; works Cicotte for a base on balls (BB).

Now back to the top of the order, Morrie Rath drops down a nice sacrifice bunt back to Cicotte, who throws to Chick Gandil at 1st base (SAC 1-3), moving Ruether into scoring position.

With one out and Ruether on 2nd, Jake Daubert lifts a fly ball to left field that "Shoeless" Joe Jackson takes care of (F-7), for the second out of the inning

With two away and Ruether still on 2nd base, Heinie Groh for the second time in as many at-bats, fly's out to Jackson in left field (F-7), putting an end to the bottom of the 3rd.

Cicotte's Pitching Line

	INN	H	R	ER	BB	K	HBP	WP	E
	1	0	0	0	1	0	0	0	0
Total	3	1	1	1	2	1	1	0	0

Bottom 4th inning

The Reds 4th inning started innocently enough, as Edd Roush leads-off in a 1-1 ballgame, with a rather deep fly that CF Oscar "Happy" Felsch hauls in (F-8), making the first out.

With one out, Pat Duncan lines a shot over 2B Eddie Collins head for a base hit (1B).

Next batter Larry Kopf, lays down a bunt that Cicotte quickly pounces on to force Duncan out at 2nd base, Cicotte to Risberg (FC 1-6), with Kopf taking 1st base on fielder's choice.

Now with two down and Kopf on 1st base, the inning and Cicotte's day goes completely down the drain. Greasy Neale bounces a ball up the middle that Swede Risberg knocks down but he could not make the play on Kopf, going for an infield single (1B). Could Risberg have made the play? Only he and God know for sure. But what is for sure is that if Swede could have come up with the play, the 4th inning would have been over with no runs scored and the game still tied at one apiece.

With runners now on at 1st and 2nd base and two out, Ivy Wingo lines a single (1B) into right field scoring Kopf and sending Neale to 3rd. When RF John "Shano" Collins' throw to the plate trying to nail Kopf was too high for Chick Gandil to cut off, Wingo takes 2nd base.

This brings up the Reds pitcher Dutch Ruether, with runners on 2nd and 3rd base. Still with two out, Dutch smashes a vicious liner up the gap in left center field scoring Neale and Wingo. Ruether making it into 3rd base with a stand-up two run triple (3B), giving the Reds a 3-0 lead.

With three runs already in, Morrie Rath next doubles (2B) over 3B Buck Weaver's head down the left-field line, for an RBI scoring Ruether. The Reds now hold a 4-0 advantage.

Jake Daubert then sends Cicotte's next pitch into right field (1B), scoring Rath with the fifth run of the inning. Daubert also taking 2nd base on yet another RF Shano Collins throw to the plate that allowed a runner to move up into scoring position. Right-hander Roy Wilkenson (1-1 2.05) then comes into the game replacing Cicotte, as his day ended in a loud Cincinnati applause. For the record, Wilkenson got Heinie Groh to fly out to Happy Felsch (F-7), to finally end the frame. All five of the Cincinnati runs scored with two outs.

Cicotte's Pitching Line

INN	H	R	ER	BB	K	HBP	WP	E
2/3	6	5	5	0	0	0	0	0
Total 3 2/3	7	6	6	2	1	1	0	0

After retiring 3rd baseman Heinie Groh to end the disastrous 4th inning, Roy Wilkenson worked the next three innings, giving up two runs (one earned); with the Reds taking an 8-1 lead. White Sox fielding plays of note with Roy Wilkenson pitching- Swede Risberg made a great stop on Larry Kopf's grounder (6-3), to end the bottom of the 5th inning. In the 6th, Swede snatched Morrie Rath's liner and turned it in to an inning ending double play (DP L-6-4), catching Greasy Neale sleep walking off the bag. In the 7th, Chick Gandil made a huge error when he dropped Buck Weaver's throw, on a sacrifice bunt by Edd Roush (SAC, E-3), allowing Heinie Groh to take 3rd base. Groh scored making the score 7-1, when Risberg and Eddie Collins couldn't turn a double play (FC 6-4). Still with only one out, Swede and Collins then turned a double play (DP 6-4-3), to end the 7th inning.

Wilkenson's Pitching Line

INN	H	R	ER	BB	K	HBP	WP	E
3 1/3	5	2	1	0	1	0	0	1

Right-hander Grover Lowdermilk (5-5 2.78) then came in to mop-up the 8th, giving up the 9th and final run, to make the final score 9-1. White Sox fielding plays of note with Grover Lowdermilk pitching- None.

Lowdermilk's Pitching Line

INN	H	R	ER	BB	K	HBP	WP	E
1	2	1	1	1	0	1	0	0

WP- Ruether (1-0) LP- Cicotte (0-1)

Game One Summary

No doubt he bagged it.

Being the opening day starting pitcher of the World Series is something every pitcher dreams of; and Eddie Cicotte was no exception. Unfortunately for Knuckles, when he hit Morrie Rath with the second pitch of the game, he set in motion a set of circumstances that would lead to the downfall of seven other ball players, all of their own doing with the exception of one player (Weaver). The Cincinnati Reds jumped out to a 1-0 lead after one inning, and they would not get another hit until the dreadful 4th inning. The next eight batters would seal the fate of the Chicago White Sox and the career of one Edward Victor Cicotte.

But it could have been a whole lot different. If Cicotte had been a little quicker getting the ball to Swede Risberg (or Risberg a little faster on the pivot) on Larry Kopf's sacrifice bunt, the 4th inning might have ended in a 1-6-3 double play. Instead Kopf was safely on at 1st base as the inning continued. The very next batter, Greasy Neale hit a ball up the middle that Swede probably should have made the play on, instead going for an infield single. That too would have ended the 4th still tied 1-1. After that the inning went right down the drain. Ivy Wingo singled in Kopf from 2nd base, Shano Collins poor throw to the plate allowing Wingo to go to 2nd base. Dutch Ruether, who was a decent hitter, then cracked a two run triple. Morrie Rath also lined an RBI double to left, and Jake Daubert brought in Rath with a single to right, ending Eddie's afternoon.

Down 6-1, the White Sox would not recover. By all accounts Cicotte was pitching so much differently in the 4th inning than the first three. Eddie was paid $10,000 the night before and he certainly earned his money in the 4th. Swede Risberg didn't disappoint his benefactors in the 4th either. But Like Joe Garagiola said, "Baseball is a funny game," and after game one there were six other White Sox players laughing like hyenas. I would bet my life though, that Buck Weaver was not laughing. Not even a giggle.

Game Four

Chicago, Ill

October 4th, 1919 Comiskey Park

Top 1st inning

By the time the fourth game of the 1919 World Series rolled around, Chicago find themselves only down two games to one, after the Sox Dickie Kerr's three hit shut-out win (3-0) yesterday. Eddie Cicotte is sent back out to the hill today to redeem himself, after he got pounded in the Series opener. Cincinnati counters with Jimmy Ring (10-9 2.26), a 6' 1" right hander. Ring will try and give the Reds a three games to one lead in the best of nine Series. Cincinnati's Morrie Rath leads off the game before 34,636 mostly Chicago fans with a sharp single (1B), to left- field. After losing game one with a monumental beating in only 3 2/3 innings of work, word was out that Ed's arm was shot. But was it?

Cicotte comes right back by getting Jake Daubert to ground to 2B Eddie Collins, who flips the ball to SS Swede Risberg forcing Rath at second, then throwing to 1B Chick Gandil for a very welcomed (and rare) double play (DP 4-6-3).

Knuckles next gets the hard hitting Heinie Groh to pop-up to SS Risberg (F-6), for the final out of the 1st frame. A very different Eddie Cicotte is on the mound today for Chicago.

Cicotte's Pitching Line

INN	H	R	ER	BB	K	HBP	WP	E
1	1	0	0	0	0	0	0	0

Top of the 2nd

National League batting champion Edd Roush steps into the batter's box to face Cicotte, leading off the top of the 2nd inning with the score still tied 0-0. Roush lifts a soft fly ball out to left, which LF Shoeless Joe grabs (F-7) for the first out of the inning.

Next up for the Reds is Pat Duncan, who hits a short fly into right, which "Cocky" 2B Eddie Collins races back on, making a fine catch (F-4) for out number two.

Cicotte dispels all rumors that his arm is shot by striking-out Larry Kopf swinging (K), ending an extremely quick 2nd inning. Eddie is pitching right now like a man on a mission.

Cicotte's Pitching Line

	INN	H	R	ER	BB	K	HBP	WP	E
	1	0	0	0	0	1	0	0	0
Total	2	1	0	0	0	1	0	0	0

Top 3rd inning

Locked in a 0-0 early pitcher dual, Cincinnati's Greasy Neale starts off the bottom of the 3rd inning by grounding out to Buck Weaver at 3rd base (5-3).

After retiring six straight batters Cicotte faces Ivy Wingo, who raps a sharp single (1B) into center- field. Eddie next fans pitcher Jimmy Ring for the second out (K), bringing up the top of the Reds' order. But before Morrie Rath can do any damage, Sox's catcher Ray Schalk cuts down Ivy Wingo trying to steal 2nd base (CS 2-4), ending the top half of the third inning.

Cicotte's Pitching Line

	INN	H	R	ER	BB	K	HBP	WP	E
	1	1	0	0	0	0	0	0	0
Total	3	2	0	0	0	1	0	0	0

Top of the 4th

In the inning that ruined him in game one, Knuckles starts out the 4th with the score still tied 0-0, retiring lead -off hitter Morrie Rath with a fly out to Joe Jackson in left field (F-7).

Next up for the Reds, Jake Daubert tries to drag bunt for a base hit. But quick footed catcher Ray Schalk, with cat like reflexes, pounces on the ball and throws a strike to 1B Chick Gandil for out number two (2-3).

Cincinnati great Heinie Groh then lines Cicotte's offering right at second baseman Eddie Collins, putting an end to the fourth frame (L-4). Cicotte is working on a nifty two hit shut-out, but Reds pitcher Jimmy Ring is matching Ed pitch for pitch.

Cicotte's Pitching Line

	INN	H	R	ER	BB	K	HBP	WP	E
	1	0	0	0	0	0	0	0	0
Total	4	2	0	0	0	1	0	0	0

Top 5th inning

Eddie Cicotte for sure has the command today that won him 29 games during the regular season. Edd Roush leads -off the top of the fifth inning, tapping a swinging bunt out in front of the plate, which Catcher Ray Schalk quickly grabs bare handed and throws to Chick Gandil (2-3), for the first out of the fifth inning.

Pat Duncan next rips a ball back to the mound. Cicotte knocks the ball down with his glove, but it squirted toward 3rd base. Eddie has plenty of time to make the play but hurries his throw past Chick Gandil at 1st base. By the time catcher Ray Schalk, who was hustling down the line to back up the play gets the ball; Duncan is standing on 2nd base (E-1).

Next a very curious play occurred which has conflicting reports. Larry Kopf drills a sharp single (1B) to left field which Joe Jackson fields cleanly and fires home to try to nail Duncan at the plate. Cicotte tries to cut-off Jackson's peg even though Schalk was ready to make the play on Duncan. Kopf is credited with an RBI as Duncan scores putting the Reds in front 1-0, and makes it to 2nd base on Cicotte's second error (E-1) of the inning. Here is where the conflicting report of the play, as reported by the Associate Press wire service confuses everyone.

As quoted by the Associated Press:

"Duncan was safe when Cicotte threw his drive wide to first, the ball going to the stand and Duncan reaching 2nd. Kopf singled to left and Duncan stopped at 3rd, but scored when Jackson threw wild to the plate. Kopf reached 2nd. - correction the official scorer gives Cicotte the error for muffing Jackson's throw."

What is really puzzling is if Jackson made a good throw home and had a chance to get Duncan at the plate of a 0-0 game, Cicotte is totally at fault and deserved the error, for allowing Kopf to reach 2nd base. But on the other hand if Duncan was stopping at 3rd as the AP wire suggested, and Jackson's throw was wild, Cicotte should have tried to cut off the ball to hold Kopf at 1st.

What also is odd is what was Cicotte doing there in the first place? The cut-off man should have been 3rd baseman Buck Weaver, because Cicotte's play was to back up home plate with a runner on 2nd base on a base hit to left. What exactly Swede Risberg was doing on this play was not recorded either, but he should have been covering third base as the throw was heading towards the plate. Weaver should have screamed at Cicotte to get his but behind home plate where he belonged and taken the throw himself, bad or not from Jackson. Since the first regular commercial radio broadcasts didn't exist until mid 1920 and moving pictures were few and far between, what really happened on this key play is lost to the memories of the working press, and like witnesses at a trial, everyone sees things differently. Who you believe is strictly up to the reader. What is not lost is that the Reds now have a 1-0 lead, and the Sox are not hitting Jimmy Ring.

For some reason, with Larry Kopf on 2nd base with one out, LF Joe Jackson was playing extremely shallow. Greasy Neale hits a ball to not so deep left field that finds its way over Jackson's head for a run scoring double (2B). Did Joe lose the ball and not see it until it was too late? The fifth inning of game four is one example of how Joe Jackson could have done his part in the payoff. It will not be the last time Joe's fielding on a key play would come into question.

With two runs in and still only one out, Ivy Wingo grounds to 2B Eddie Collins for the second out (4-3), moving Neale over to 3rd base.

Pitcher Jimmy Ring also grounds out to 2B Eddie Collins (4-3), ending a very strange inning, leaving Greasy Neale stranded on 3rd base. Instead of the game still tied 0-0, Cincinnati takes a 2-0 lead. For sure Cicotte and Jackson had a poor inning in the field. Chicago would not recover.

Cicotte's Pitching Line

	INN	H	R	ER	BB	K	HBP	WP	E
	1	2	2	0	0	0	0	0	2
Total	5	4	2	0	0	1	0	0	2

Top 6th inning

Finding himself down 2-0 after the goofy 5th inning, Cicotte goes back to work in 6th by getting lead-off hitter Morrie Rath to ground out to SS Swede Risberg (6-3), making out number one.

Jake Daubert next chops a ball that 2B Eddie Collins scoops up (4-3), for the second out.

This brings up Heinie Groh, who grounds to his counterpart, 3B Buck Weaver (5-3), to end the easy 6th inning for Cicotte.

Cicotte's Pitching Line

	INN	H	R	ER	BB	K	HBP	WP	E
	1	0	0	0	0	0	0	0	0
Total	6	4	2	0	0	1	0	0	2

Top 7th inning

Chicago still trails 2-0 as Edd Roush starts the 7th frame by grounding out to 2B Eddie Collins (4-3), one future Hall of Famer being tossed out by another future Hall of Famer.

With one out Pat Duncan smashes a hard grounder to 3B Buck Weaver, who makes a sensational stop and throw to 1B Chick Gandil (5-3), for the second out.

Unlike his last at bat when his single (1B) resulted in the key play of the game, Larry Kopf's routine grounder to SS Risberg (6-3) ends another one, two, three inning. It is the eighth straight batter Cicotte sits down after the 5th inning fiasco.

Cicotte's Pitching Line

	INN	H	R	ER	BB	K	HBP	WP	E
	1	0	0	0	0	0	0	0	0
Total	6	4	2	0	0	1	0	0	2

Top 8th inning

For a man supposedly pitching to throw a ball game, Eddie Cicotte was fooling everyone. With the Reds holding on to their 2-0 lead, Greasy Neale leads-off the top of the 8th inning by hitting a bouncer back to the box (1-3). Cicotte is now on a roll, retiring nine Reds hitters in a row.

With one out Ivy Wingo breaks up the streak, rapping a base hit up the middle (1B), his second knock of the ballgame.

This brings up pitcher Jimmy Ring, who taps back to Cicotte; Eddie turns and throws to SS Swede Risberg, who relays the pill to 1B Chick Gandil for a (DP1-6-3) double play ending the 8th inning. Chicago proving that they could turn a double play on a ball hit back to the pitcher.

Cicotte's Pitching Line

	INN	H	R	ER	BB	K	HBP	WP	E
	1	1	0	0	0	0	0	0	0
Total	8	5	2	0	0	1	0	0	2

Top 9th inning

Still giving the Chicago White Sox their best chance at a victory but down 2-0, Cicotte induced lead-off hitter Morrie Rath to foul out to C Ray Schalk (FO-2), to start the 9th inning.

With one out Jake Daubert finishes his day at the plate, flying out to Joe Jackson in left field (F-7), for the second out.

Heinie Groh also fouls out to C Ray Schalk (FO-2) to end the 9th. Unfortunately for Eddie, Chicago could not muster a single run off Cincinnati's Jimmy Ring, losing 2-0.

Cicotte's Pitching Line

	INN	H	R	ER	BB	K	HBP	WP	E
	1	0	0	0	0	0	0	0	0
Total	9	5	2	0	0	1	0	0	2

WP-Ring (1-0) LP-Cicotte (0-2)

Game Four Summary

He pitched to win.

History has taught us that the Chicago White Sox threw the 1919 World Series. History has also taught us that Eddie Cicotte almost single handedly threw game one. History taught us that Eddie received $10,000 dollars under his pillow the night before the Series opened in Cincinnati. Now it is time for a little math. Cicotte thought he was going to get paid $10,000 before every game he threw for $30,000 dollars total. When the money was not coming in after the first game, Eddie must have sensed something was not kosher. Was the $10,000 placed under his pillow worth intentionally losing more than one game? Eddie Cicotte must have been ashamed of his game one performance, but there is no way he pitched to lose in game four. He was just too good this day. The boys playing behind him though is another matter. Were they really trying their best or was Jimmy Ring just too good this day? It would be real easy to say that Cicotte knew the Sox were not going to hit today, and only pitched well enough not to lose as badly as he did in game one. If that were the case, a two run Cincinnati lead was hardly a cushion.

Remember, Chicago was the home team and had the last at bat. A three run 9th inning to win the game was not impossible.

Although Jimmy Ring was only 10-9 during the regular season, he did have an ERA of only 2.26. And although the White Sox had only three hits off Ring, they also had three walks, two hit batsmen and two runners by way of errors. In the 2nd inning Jackson led -off with a double and moved to 3rd base on Hap Felsch's sacrifice bunt. After Chick Gandil hit a weak pop-up to 3rd baseman Heinie Groh in front of the plate for the second out, two straight walks loaded the bases. Unfortunately, Cicotte worked a full count before grounding out to 2B Morrie Rath to end the inning. The Sox left also left two more runners on base when Hap Felsch's grounder to Heinie Groh ended the third inning. Any one of these players getting a clutch hit might have won the game for the Sox, tying the Series at two apiece, instead of them being down three games to one. But then again, look at who the batters were who came up in these clutch situations- Gandil, Risberg and Felsch.

The two unearned runs in the fifth inning were directly attributed to two Cicotte errors. The first error was definitely Eddie's. On Pat Duncan's come backer, Cicotte's bad throw to 1st base flew over Chick Gandil's head. The second Cicotte error, after Larry Kopf's single to left, would be another question. Was it really Eddie blowing the game or was it Joe Jackson helping out the cause? As you've read in the fifth inning, there are two very different accounts of the play. Baseball historians and the public alike have given Joe a free pass in this Series. I can't! All this doesn't really matter though, except in the historical sense, because Chicago didn't score. But on the other hand, if Duncan did stop on 3rd base and Weaver not Cicotte had been the cutoff man, Buck would have fielded, or at least let the ball carry to the plate, and Duncan probably would not have scored. Then if Jackson had been playing Greasy Neale at normal depth in the outfield, Neale's fly ball probably would not have been deep enough to score Duncan (at the very least, Jackson would have had a play on Duncan at the plate). With two outs Ivy Wingo would have ended the inning with his ground out to Eddie Collins and no runs would have scored. But that is strictly hypothetical. The game could have been 0-0, heading into extra innings. Who knows what would have happened then? History might have been rewritten.

Game Seven

Cincinnati, Oh

October 8th, 1919 Redland Field

Bottom 1st inning

A funny thing happened in Cincinnati today, only 13,923 people turned out for a potential Series ending game. Was it the misty drizzle? Was it boredom with a not well played Series? Was it all the rumors of a fixed Series? Cincinnati hadn't won a real Championship since 1882 while they were playing in the American Association, and the Reds had averaged 30,738 spectators in their first three home games. The low turnout is very puzzling. With the Cincinnati Reds holding a four games to two lead, after the Sox won yesterday in an exciting 5-4 ten inning ballgame, Eddie Cicotte takes his turn on the mound, trying to give the Sox a two game sweep in Cincinnati and send the Series back to Chicago. The Reds will send game two winner, left-hander Slim Sallee (21-7 2.05) to the hill, to put the fork in the Sox and close out this year's World Series. The White Sox took a 1-0 lead in the top of the 1st inning, and Cicotte trots to the mound for the bottom half.

Morrie Rath leads-off for the Reds and smacks a grounder too hot for 2B Eddie Collins to handle (E-4). Not the start Chicago was hoping for.

With Rath on at 1st base, Jake Daubert pops Eddie Cicotte's next offering up to 2B Eddie Collins, which he handled this time, for the first out (F-4).

Heinie Groh next comes up to the plate with one out and Cicotte bares down for a strike-out (K), making out number two.

Cicotte pitches out of potential trouble by enticing Edd Roush to hit a bounding ball up the middle, which 2B Eddie Collins snags and flips to SS Swede Risberg (FC 4-6), forcing Rath out at 2nd base to end the inning.

Cicotte's Pitching Line

INN	H	R	ER	BB	K	HBP	WP	E
1	0	0	0	0	1	0	0	1

Bottom 2nd inning

Slim Sallee held Chicago scoreless in top of the 2nd inning; with the score still 1-0 in favor of the Sox. Leading off the bottom of the 2nd, Pat Duncan pelts a fly ball to RF Hap Felsch (F-9), for the first out. If you're wondering why Felsch is in right field instead of center, Kid Gleason moved him over because of his poor play in the field yesterday.

Next up for the Red Legs, Larry Kopf lines a sharp single (1B) to left center field.

With Kopf on at 1st and one out, Greasy Neale fouls to 3B Buck Weaver (FO-5), who makes the catch near the 3rd base dug-out. While next Reds batter Ivy Wingo waited for a pitch he could handle, Larry Kopf is thrown out trying to steal, C Schalk to SS Risberg (CS 2-6), ending the 2nd inning.

Cicotte's Pitching Line

	INN	H	R	ER	BB	K	HBP	WP	E
	1	1	0	0	0	0	0	0	0
Total	2	1	0	0	0	1	0	0	1

Bottom 3rd inning

The White Sox took a 2-0 lead, scoring one run in the top of the 3rd inning off Slim Sallee. The way Eddie Cicotte is pitching today, the Reds certainty have their work cut out for them. Ivy Wingo leads-off the bottom of the 3rd by working Knuckles for a walk (BB).

Harry "Slim" Sallee then steps into the batter's box. In a sure bunt situation, Reds manager Pat Moran lets Sallee swing away and he lifts a fly ball out to RF Hap Felsch (F-9), who puts the squeeze on the ball for the first out.

It is now back to the top of the order for the Reds, with one on and one out. Morrie Rath grounds a sure double play ball to SS Swede Risberg, but 2B Eddie Collins only manages to get the lead runner Wingo (FC 6-4). Another potential DP not turned.

Now there are two outs, with Rath on at 1st base. Cicotte gets Jake Daubert to tap back to the mound (1-3) ending the inning. Eddie has not given up an earned run in twelve straight innings.

Cicotte's Pitching Line

	INN	H	R	ER	BB	K	HBP	WP	E
	1	0	0	0	1	0	0	0	0
Total	3	1	0	0	1	1	0	0	1

Bottom 4th inning

Chicago still holds a slender 2-0 lead against Slim Sallee and the Reds, as Cincinnati comes to bat in the home half of the 4th. Heinie Groh starts off the inning with a two hopper to a busy 2B Eddie Collins (4-3), for the first out.

Copycat Edd Roush does the same, 2B Collins to 1B Gandil (4-3), for out number two.

Cicotte now has everything going his way, as Pat Duncan chops the ball to 3B Buck Weaver (5-3), ending an easy 4th frame.

Cicotte's Pitching Line

	INN	H	R	ER	BB	K	HBP	WP	E
	1	0	0	0	0	0	0	0	0
Total	4	1	0	0	1	1	0	0	1

Bottom 5th inning

The Chicago White Sox took a 4-0 lead in the top of the 5th inning, with two more runs off Slim Sallee. The Reds have a steep uphill climb, with the way Eddie Cicotte is pitching this afternoon. Larry Kopf leads-off the bottom of the 5th with a lazy fly out to LF Joe Jackson (F-7).

Next up for the Reds, Greasy Neale belts a one out single to left field (1B), the Reds first hit since Larry Kopf's single in the 2nd inning.

Ivy Wingo follows with his second walk of the game (BB), moving Neale to 2nd base with one out. This is Cincinnati's first real threat of the game off Eddie Cicotte.

Hard hitting pitcher, left-handed Dutch Ruether, who went 3-3 with two triples in game one, comes up to the plate to pinch hit for pitcher Ray Fisher (14-5 2.17), who came into the game relieving Slim Sallee, during the Sox two run 5th inning. But Ruether fouls out to 3B Buck Weaver (FO-5) for out number two and a huge out for Cicotte.

With two out it is back to the top of order, as Morrie Rath smacks a grounder to 3B Buck Weaver (5-3), ending the threat. This inning really showed what Eddie's determination was today.

Bottom 8th inning

Eddie Cicotte walks out to the mound with the look of a tiger, and with Chicago still holding a 4-1 lead he is starting to growl. Heinie Groh leads-off the bottom of the 8th inning with a routine fly ball to LF Joe Jackson (F-7), for the 1st out.

Edd Roush follows Groh with a ground ball to 2B Eddie Collins, who gobbles it up on the run while flipping the ball to 1B Chick Gandil (4-3), for out number two (Collins's sixth assist of the game).

Finishing off an easy one, two, three inning, Pat Duncan swats a worm burner to SS Swede Risberg (6-3).

Cicotte's Pitching Line

	INN	H	R	ER	BB	K	HBP	WP	E
	1	0	0	0	0	0	0	0	0
Total	8	5	1	1	3	4	0	0	1

Bottom 9th inning

Eddie Cicotte would not be denied today. The huge rally Cincinnati was looking for would never materialize. Starting off the final frame, Larry Kopf fouls out to 2B Eddie Collins down the 1st base line (FO-4), for the first out.

Next batter Greasy Neale, fly's out to Joe Jackson in left field (F-7), for the 2nd easy out.

Prolonging the obvious, Ivy Wingo reaches base for the 4th straight time with a single (1B) to right- field (3 walks, 1B).

The few Cincinnati faithful who remain are able to get a little excited when pinch-hitter Sherry Magee, batting for Dolph Luque, singles (1B) to right field, sending Wingo to 2nd base. Reds utility man Jimmy Smith then enters the game to run for Magee.

Desperately needing a three-run homer, Morrie Rath (who had hit only one home run all season in 563 at bats including the World Series) fly's out to CF Happy Felsch in right center field (F-8), to end the game. Kid Gleason had moved Felsch back to center field in the late innings (when I'm not sure). Eddie must have felt vindicated, but he had made his bed in the 4th inning of game one. In less than a year, he would have to sleep in it. With the 4-1 victory, the Sox will live another day and only trail the Reds by a single game, four to three.

Cicotte's Pitching Line

	INN	H	R	ER	BB	K	HBP	WP	E
	1	2	0	0	0	0	0	0	0
Total	9	7	1	1	3	4	0	0	1

WP- Cicotte (1-2) LP- Sallee (1-1)

Game Seven Summary

Meet the real Eddie Cicotte.

A lot of people have asked "Why did Cicotte pitch to win in game seven?" Well I believe Eddie also tried to win game four. You the reader have the option of agreeing with me or not. In both games he pitched like the man who won 29 games in the regular season. With any support at all Cicotte would have won two games in the 1919 World Series. Along with Dickie Kerr's two wins, and Kerr scheduled to pitch in game nine, baseball might have seen its greatest comeback at least until the Boston Red Sox won four straight from the New York Yankees in the 2004 American League Championship Series after trailing three games to nothing. So why did Eddie pitch his best in games four and seven? I think Eddie said, "The heck with it." When no more money came in after the first $10,000, I believe he tried to screw over the gamblers who were screwing over the ball players. There is not a person still living who knows firsthand the answer to that question.

In any event, Eddie Cicotte gave his team a chance to win in two of his three games. He pitched masterfully in game seven. Cincinnati left nine base runners on base. In Eddies last eighteen innings pitched he only gave up one earned run. The bottom line is that Cincinnati could not hit Eddie Cicotte. The only runs the Reds got off Cicotte in three games, Eddie spoon fed to them (with the exception of Groh's non home run). Cincinnati had the same chance of beating Cicotte in an up and up contest as Charlie Brown had of kicking that football with Lucy holding it. But Eddie did throw game one. He did receive a $10,000 pay off. He did deserve the fate that would come like a steamroller. On September 26, 1920, Eddie Cicotte would throw his last pitch in an 8-1 victory against the Detroit Tigers (the team Eddie started his career with in 1905). It is very ironic that Eddie's victory in game seven of the 1919 World Series would be his 30th win of the year. The exact number he needed to get his alleged $10,000 dollar bonus from owner Charles Comiskey, the bonus he was denied two years earlier (1917) that might have started this whole mess.

Chapter 2

Claude Preston Williams

Three games to infamy.

Claude Preston Williams was born on March 9, 1893 in Aurora, Missouri. Lefty was just twenty years old when he made his Major League debut with the Detroit Tigers in 1913. Williams appeared in five games going 1-1 with a 4.97 ERA. Lefty only got into one game for the Tigers in 1914 before being released. Williams didn't pitch in the Big Leagues in 1915, instead being sent back to the Minors playing for the Salt Lake City Bees where he won 33 games. Lefty was signed by the Chicago White Sox for the 1916 season, and at the age of twenty-three, Lefty pitched in 43 games for the White Sox going 13-7 with a 2.89 ERA. That season Lefty showed flashes of things to come. In the World Championship season of 1917, the Chicago White Sox left-hander established himself as a top left-handed pitcher in the American League. Williams went 17 -8 to go along with a 2.97 ERA. At just twenty-three years of age, Lefty's future seemed to reach the stratosphere. Following a war shortened 1918 season which saw Lefty's record at 6-4 2.73, Williams kicked it into full gear for 1919. At 23-11 2.64, Lefty was a big part in getting Chicago back to the World Series. No one could understand how such a fantastic left handed pitcher could lose three games in the 1919 World Series (a record tied in 1981 by New York Yankee pitcher George Frazier), particularly against a predominantly left handed hitting line-up. But Lefty also had a big secret, which would explain his poor performance in the Series. In 1920 Lefty's 22-14 record with a 3.91 ERA season would end suddenly on September 27, when he and seven other White Sox players were suspended by club owner Charles Comiskey, after news broke of the indictments by the Cook County Grand Jury, for their involvement in the alleged fixing of the 1919 World Series. Williams' last start would be a 6-1 victory against Cleveland on September 25, 1920, and Lefty never pitched again in a big league uniform when the indictments were handed down. His eventual banishment came by way of Commissioner Landis on August 3, 1921. Williams was paid a measly $3,000 salary for 1919, compared to his promised $10,000 pay off, and it must have seemed like a fortune to Lefty, although Williams only received $5,000 of the promised money.

There is absolutely no doubt that Lefty pitched to lose games two and five of the World Series. His performance in the fourth inning of game two and the sixth inning of game five leaves no room for doubt. In game eight any thoughts he might have had to throw his best were squashed by a death threat against his wife by a Mafioso type the night before. Lefty lasted only five batters, his wife lived but his career passed away. Eliot Asinof wrote in his fantastic book *Eight Men Out*, that this incident took place, but years later confessed that he made the story up. I believe this threat did happen, because Lefty wasted no time in blowing the game, unlike his other two starts where Williams waited until the middle innings to hand over the ballgames. Plus if Lefty did win game eight, Dickie Kerr was going again in the ninth and final ballgame, something gambling big shot Arnold Rothstein could not let happen. Perhaps in creating something for dramatic effects, Mr. Asinof was right on the money, or perhaps Lefty just didn't much feel like pitching that day. In any event, Lefty's wife in her golden years did say that the threat was real.

After his banishment, starting in 1921 Lefty pitched in the outlaw leagues for a couple of seasons. He finally left baseball for good and moved to California and opened a landscaping business. Claude "Lefty" Williams died on November 4, 1959 in Laguna Beach, California at the age of sixty-six. With a lifetime record of 82-48 3.13 ERA for a .631 winning percentage and only twenty-six years old, Lefty threw away a great chance of someday being enshrined in Cooperstown, home of baseball's Hall of Fame. Here are Lefty's three starts in the 1919 World Series, as seen through my eyes.

Game Two

Cincinnati, OH

October 2nd, 1919 Redland Field

Bottom 1st inning

29,698 paying customers turned out today to Redland Field for game two of the 1919 World Series. Chicago's Lefty Williams (23-11 2.64), will face Reds left hander Harry "Slim" Sallee (21-7 2.05), with Cincinnati holding a one game to zero lead after a thorough 9-1 thrashing of the Sox and Eddie Cicotte in game one. With Chicago failing to score in the top of the 1st, leading-off for the Reds in the bottom of the inning, Morrie Rath taps back to the mound P Williams to 1B Gandil (1-3), for the 1st out of the inning.

Next batter Jake Daubert raps a bounding ball to SS Swede Risberg (6-3), for the 2nd out.

Heinie Groh then drives the ball on a line to RF Shano Collins, who makes a wonderful catch (L-9) to rob Groh of extra bases, ending the inning for Lefty with the score tied 0-0.

William's Pitching Line

INN	H	R	ER	BB	K	HBP	WP	E
1	0	0	0	0	0	0	0	0

Bottom 2nd inning

With the score still tied 0-0 going into the home half of the second inning, Lefty Williams, known for his pin point control, starts the inning by walking Edd Roush (BB).

On a hit and run play, Pat Duncan lines a ball right at 2B Eddie Collins. Collins snags the ball in the air and throws to 1B Chick Gandil (DP L-4-3), easily doubling off Roush for a twin killing.

With two down, Larry Kopf lifts Lefty's offering for a can of corn fly ball to CF Happy Felsch (F-8), to end the second frame.

things off for the Reds in the bottom of the inning, by popping-out to C Ray Schalk (FO-2) in foul territory down the 3rd baseline.

Up next for Cincinnati, Slim Sallee lofts a fly-ball out to RF Shano Collins (F-9), making out number two.

Morrie Rath comes up with two down and smacks a hard liner right at 3B Buck Weaver (L-5) ending the inning. This was Lefty's first easy inning since the 3rd frame.

William's Pitching Line

	INN	H	R	ER	BB	K	HBP	WP	E
	1	0	0	0	0	0	0	0	0
Total	7	4	4	4	5	1	0	0	1

Bottom of the 8th

Slim Sallee held the Sox scoreless in the top of the 8th inning, the score still favoring the Reds 4-2. Jake Daubert starts things off with a bounding ball to SS Risberg, who gobbles it up and threw to 1B Gandil (6-3).

With one down Heinie Groh takes his turn at bat. Williams issues Heinie a free pass (BB), Lefty's sixth walk of the game.

In one of the finest plays of the Series, Edd Roush hits a Texas leaguer into short centerfield. CF Happy Felsch races in to make a shoestring catch, firing the ball to 1B Chick Gandil for an inning ending double play (DP F-8-3), to force out Groh. Chicago would not score in the 9th, ending the ballgame. It would have very interesting to see what Williams would have done if the Sox had gotten any closer before Lefty was removed for a pinch-hitter in the top of the 9th. But the Sox did not score anymore runs and lost 4-2, and now trail the Reds 2 games to 0.

William's Pitching Line

	INN	H	R	ER	BB	K	HBP	WP	E
	1	0	0	0	1	0	0	0	0
Total	8	4	4	4	6	1	0	0	1

WP- Sallee (1-0)   LP Williams (0-1)

Game Two Summary

A Fourth inning gift.

By just looking at the box score, there is no way anyone would have thought Lefty Williams was trying to give this game away. Unlike Eddie Cicotte's terrible 4th inning in game one, when even the ball girl was begging for a chance to hit, Lefty's terrible 4th inning was due in part by his wildness. So much so the sportswriter I. E. Sanborn described Lefty's control as "criminal." By the way, what was the deal with the 4th inning? In two games the Reds have scored seven runs, and in the eight games played in the Series they would score ten, their biggest total of any inning. Williams only gave up four hits in the game, but three of them helped produce the four runs that made the difference. But six walks were just terrible for a man who had only walked 58 batters in 297 innings pitched. Ray Schalk was so mad at Lefty after the game, that he tried to get at Williams throat in the runway leading to the clubhouse and he had to be pried off Lefty by teammates. Schalk complained at the time that Williams kept crossing him up, throwing fastballs instead of his nasty curveball when he called for the hook. Schalk later denied any of this happened, but I believe Charles Comiskey told him to say this when the case went to trial.

Even though Chicago out hit Cincinnati ten to four and Sallee issued one walk, the White Sox only scored when the Reds committed two errors on the same play. So what looked like a decent pitching job, except for the walks, Lefty did his more than part in throwing game two. And the hitters, especially

Chick Gandil and Swede Risberg, also helped bag the game with no clutch hitting. Joe Jackson who went three for four, struck out looking in his only chance with a runner on base in the 6th inning, after Buck Weaver hit a one out double. Very curious indeed.

So now the Southsiders head back home to Chicago down two games to none, with Dickie Kerr going in game three. The gamblers must have been jumping for joy with all the money they made in the first two games. But a lot of people were about to go bust in game three.

Game Five

October 6th, 1919 Chicago, ILL

Comiskey Park

Top 1st inning

Nobody in their right mind could have believed Chicago would be down three games to one after four games of the 1919 World Series, nobody but Cincinnati. After a day off on account of rain, the teams get ready for the last game at Comiskey Park before the Series shifts back to Cincinnati. For game five, the Reds will send to the mound their fifth straight different starting pitcher in right-hander Hod Eller (20-9 2.40). The White Sox send back to the hill game two loser Lefty Williams. Lefty, whose control problems (six walks) led to his downfall in his first start of the Series, begins the ballgame by walking Reds lead-off man Morrie Rath (BB). Much to the dismay of the 34,379 already disappointed Sox rooters, the largest crowd of the Series.

With Rath on 1st base, Jake Daubert drops down a sacrifice bunt which C Ray Schalk pounces on and fires to 1B Chick Gandil (SAC 2-3), moving Morrie to 2nd base.

With one gone, Heinie Groh drives a ball to centerfield, which CF Happy Felsch hauls in (F-8), for the 2nd out.

Now with two down and Rath still on 2nd base, Edd Roush grounds to 1B Chick Gandil, who backhands the ball and flips to P Lefty Williams (3-1) stranding Rath (Chick has always been a great fielder).

William's Pitching Line

INN	H	R	ER	BB	K	HBP	WP	E
1	0	0	0	1	0	0	0	0

Top 2nd inning

Tied 0-0 after one inning, Lefty gets into a groove by striking-out Pat Duncan (K) leading-off the 2nd Inning.

Next batter Larry Kopf cracks a high pop-up behind home plate that C Ray Schalk gets under (FO-2), for out number two.

This brings up Greasy Neale who becomes Lefty's 2nd strike-out victim of the inning (K), doubling his game two strikeout total. Williams has now set down six hitters in a row after his lead-off walk to Morrie Rath.

William's Pitching Line

	INN	H	R	ER	BB	K	HBP	WP	E
	1	0	0	0	0	2	0	0	0
Total	2	0	0	0	1	2	0	0	0

Top 3rd inning

After Jimmy Ring's three-hit shut-out of the Sox in game four, Chicago was having no better luck with Hod Eller. With the score 0-0, Williams goes to work in the 3rd inning. Bill Rariden, leading off for the Reds, swings late on a

Top 6th inning

Ray Schalk could not believe it, and neither could anyone else watching. How could Williams lose it so quickly? Locked in a classic 0-0 pitcher's duel, Lefty Williams takes his one-hitter into the 6th inning. Hod Eller opens up the Reds half of the 6th by lining a double (2B) up the left centerfield alley. Happy Felsch cuts the ball off and makes a terrible throw to SS Swede Risberg (E-8), letting Eller trot into 3rd base. With the Reds not scoring any runs either, Felsch must have felt now was the time to chip in.

Cincinnati's lead-off hitter Morrie Rath follows with a solid RBI single (1B) to right field, to put the Reds out in front 1-0.

Jake Daubert sacrifices Rath to 2nd base with a bunt down the 3rd base line, which 3B Buck Weaver fields and throws to 1B Chick Gandil (SAC 5-3) for the 1st out.

With one out and Rath on at 2nd base, Williams control problems return and he walks Heinie Groh (BB). In hindsight right here Manager Kid Gleason should have sent Lefty to the showers and then shipped him off to Siberia. How could he though, the way Lefty is pitching.

He didn't and Edd Roush hits Lefty's nothing on it pitch to deep centerfield for a two run triple (3B). On the play, an incredibly pissed-off C Ray Schalk was tossed out of the game by umpire Charles Rigler (NL), for arguing the call on Groh at the plate, following a throw from Swede Risberg. With three runs in Gleason again chose not to remove Williams. Schalk was probably fuming not only with Lefty's pitches but also at Happy Felsch who should have caught Roush long drive, but dropped the ball while running in with it. This makes no sense to me, if Felsch caught the ball and was running in with it, why wasn't Roush out? With men on base, why was Happy running in with it? Why wasn't Felsch charged with an error? That's exactly how it was reported in the Chicago Tribune (Oct. 6th 1919). Byrd Lynn comes into the game to replace Schalk behind the plate. I wonder what Ray Schalk said to Kid Gleason before he went to the clubhouse? He had to of told him about Williams' pitches mysteriously flattening out, and not throwing what he was calling. What did Gleason say back to Ray, if he does it again I'm going to pull him?

After all that, Pat Duncan hits a one out fly ball to shallow left field. Tagging up on the play, Roush tore for home plate challenging the famous Jackson arm. The throw was up the 1st base line though and Lynn, who had time to make the catch and get back to the plate, drops the ball allowing Roush to score (SF-7). Remember game two, bottom of the sixth inning when Joe had a chance to also nail Roush trying to score from 2nd base? That time Jackson chooses not to throw home. Think about it, here are two runs Joe could have prevented.

The seventh man to bat in the inning is Larry Kopf. Kopf flies out to CF Hapless, I mean Happy Felsch (F-8) to finally end the crazy 6th inning. Take a good look at Lefty's pitching lines; he will not come close to giving up another hit the rest of his stay in this ballgame.

William's Pitching Line

	INN	H	R	ER	BB	K	HBP	WP	E	PB
	1	3	4	4	1	0	0	0	0	0
Total	6	4	4	4	1	2	0	0	0	1

Top 7th inning

Here's another funny thing, after getting his butt handed to him in the 6th inning, Lefty returns to his near perfect form in the 7th. With the Reds still leading 4-0, Greasy Neale leads-off the 7th, grounding out to 2B Eddie Collins (4-3).

Bill Rariden next flies out to Sox RF Nemo Leibold (F-9), for the second quick out.

Hod Eller, whose leadoff double started off the Reds big 6th inning was no match for the real Lefty Williams in the 7th, Williams strikes Eller out (K), to end the frame.

William's Pitching Line

	INN	H	R	ER	BB	K	HBP	WP	E	PB
	1	0	0	0	0	1	0	0	0	0
Total	7	4	4	4	1	3	0	0	0	1

Top 8th inning

Chicago was on their way to their second straight three-hit shutout loss. The White Sox had not scored in twenty consecutive innings and after today would run it to twenty-two. Morrie Rath leads-off the Reds 8th by lining the ball right at LF Joe Jackson (L-7).

With one out Jake Daubert pops-out to CF Hap Felsch (F-8).

Batting with two down, Lefty makes quick work of Heinie Groh, who also fly's out to CF Felsch (F-8) to end the inning. Chicago would not score a run again today and lose 4-0. They now trail four games to one.

William's Pitching Line

	INN	H	R	ER	BB	K	HBP	WP	E	PB
	1	0	0	0	0	0	0	0	0	0
Total	8	4	4	4	1	3	0	0	0	1

Top of the 9th

Erskine Mayer (1-3 8.25) is now pitching for Chicago in the top of the 9th, after Lefty was lifted for a pinch-hitter in the bottom of the 8th inning.

Mayer gives up one unearned run to finish off Cincinnati's scoring. Cincinnati wins game five, 5-0 to take a huge four games to one lead in the Series. White Sox fielding plays of note with Erskine Mayer pitching- Eddie Collins booted Edd Roush's grounder (E-4), leading off the 9th. Roush scored when Swede Risberg, with runners on 2nd and 3rd base and one out, choose to throw to 1st base (6-3), instead of trying to keep the fifth run from scoring.

Mayer's Pitching Line

INN	H	R	ER	BB	K	HBP	WP	E	PB
1	0	1	0	1	0	0	0	1	0

WP – Eller (1-0) LP – Williams (0-2)

Game Five Summary

Sixth inning gift

If anyone had any doubts remaining about Lefty Williams being involved in the throwing of the 1919 World Series, all they have to do is look at the 6th inning of game five. The Cincinnati Reds could not have hit Lefty on this day if Williams was on the up-and-up. Not getting their first hit until SS Larry Kopf lead-off single in the 5th, and then not getting a man on base in the 7th or 8th innings. So what in the hell happened in the 6th inning. Catcher Ray Schalk would later say, and then deny, that Lefty Williams continuously crossed him up, throwing curves that didn't break much, and fast balls that couldn't break a pane of glass. Balls that were painting the corners in the first five innings were coming straight down Broad Street in the 6th. Hod Eller's lead-off double, followed by Happy Felsch's horrible throw back to the infield, allowed Eller to move to 3rd base. Morrie Rath then singled off a pitch with not much on it, to score the only run Eller would need today. With Rath on 2nd base after a sacrifice by Jake Daubert, and a walk to Heinie Groh, Edd Roush then crushed a Williams pitch to deep centerfield scoring Rath and Groh on a ball that Happy Felsch should have caught. Happy had almost as bad an inning as Lefty Williams did. After Ray Schalk was tossed from the ballgame, replacement catcher Byrd Lynn dropped Joe Jackson's poor throw from short left field. It was certainly a team effort in throwing away game five.

As mad as Ray Schalk must have been at Lefty Williams, he completely lost his mind on umpire Rigler when he called Heinie Groh safe on a close play at the plate. Schalk poked Rigler in the chest with his glove and after a few choice words was given the heave-ho from the ball game. To show that there is no way this inning was not a gift to the gamblers, Lefty Williams then sets down the next six batters in a row. With the exception of the 6th inning, Lefty Williams in the other seven innings he pitched gave up a grand total of one hit (Larry Kopf in the 5th), one walk, and no runs. But his grade for the 6th inning was a big F. Trying to keep his team from going down four games to one, manager Kid Gleason's judgment has to come into question here too. How anyone can watch a man pitching like Cy Young and Christy Mathewson combined for five innings, then pitch like a back up bullpen catcher in the 6th and not make a pitching change before things got too out of hand, just doesn't make any sense to me (or anyone else?), especially after watching Williams do the exact same thing in game two. Even if Lefty would have shut the Reds down in the fateful 6th inning, the White Sox were not going to score off of Hod Eller on this day anyway. They only made three hits themselves in game five, two by Buck Weaver and the other by Ray Schalk, who took an early shower. For a team that didn't strike out much, 358 times in 140 games or 4675 at-bats, for a percentage of .08% of the time or 1 every 13.06 times at bat, they struck out 9 times in 9 innings on the day against the Reds Eller, or 1 every 3.33 times at bat. So with Lefty Williams unexplainable 6th inning, added with the White Sox featherweight hitting, the combination of the two were not going to allow the White Sox to win game five. But then again, this game should have been 0-0 until the relievers took over, and who knows what would have happened then.

Game Eight

Chicago, Ill - October 9th, 1919

Comiskey Park

Top 1st inning

After winning the last two games, Chicago was making an increditable comeback. In front of 32,930 finally excited Comiskey Park fans, the Sox send games two and five loser Lefty Williams out to face game five winner Hod Eller (20-9 2.40). But in only 1/3 of an inning, Chicago's fans would sit in total shock. What they saw was a man intent on ending this Series in the 1st inning. Why Kid Gleason sent Williams out to pitch in the first place is a total mystery. If he didn't realize Lefty was on the take by now, he had no business running this ball club (maybe this is the reason after Gleason's stint with the White Sox was over, he never managed in the Big Leagues again). Leading-off for the Reds in the top if the 1st, Morrie Rath pops-up to SS Swede Risberg (F-6) for the only out Lefty will get today. Even Major League hitter's pop-up batting practice pitches every now and then.

With one gone, Jake Daubert singles up the middle (1B), to start the stampede.

With one down and Daubert on 1st, Heinie Groh singles to right field (1B). Right here, if Gleason had any sense at all, he would have removed Williams and beat his butt all the way back to the dugout, but he didn't.

Edd Roush next takes Lefty's meatball and doubles (2B), just over 1B Chick Gandil's head into right field (could Chick have jumped a little higher?), scoring Daubert and sending Groh to 3rd base for a 1-0 Cincinnati lead. Even now with the Sox down, Gleason chose to keep Williams on the hill. What was he waiting for, Lefty to get his act together?

Pat Duncan next comes to the plate with Groh on 3rd base and Roush on at 2nd and one out. The last batter Lefty would face, smashes another double (2B) over 3B Buck Weaver's head (Wilt Chamberlain couldn't have gotten this one), for two more runs bringing the score to 3-0. After five batters

Game Eight Summary

I don't feel much like playing today.

It was a must win game for the Chicago White Sox, down four games to three, just like it was a must win the last two ball games. After clawing their way back into the Series by winning the last two games, why Sox Manager Kid Gleason sent Lefty Williams out to pitch game eight is beyond me. Gleason had to have known that Williams was in on the biggest scam in sports history by now. If he didn't he was a complete and total moron. With all the rumors before the Series started, and then seeing a totally different pitcher throw against Cincinnati than he had seen pitch all season, what the hell was Kid thinking. If Gleason had any guts at all Lefty should have been removed and then dropped from the Chicago roster during the 6th inning of game five. Kid Gleason did not do this and Lefty Williams took all of five batters to lose the game and the Series to the Cincinnati Reds in game eight. As well as Lefty threw in game five with the exception of the 6th inning, maybe that convinced Manager Gleason to go with Williams again in this must win game. He was going with a three man rotation on only two days rest in between starts. So with the rain out before game five on October 5^{th,} the pitchers, whose arms had to have felt like lead pipes, had an extra days rest.

Legend has it that the mob or some other bad people had gotten to Lefty the night before game eight, and told Lefty that either the White Sox lost or his wife was going to die. Lefty heroically saved his wife's life, but he committed career suicide. Meanwhile, rumors flying around the ballpark that morning said it was going to be the biggest 1st inning anyone has ever seen. And though it wasn't the biggest inning ever, it was big enough to doom the Sox, two singles and two hard hit doubles accounted for Williams' day. Lead-off hitter Morrie Rath must have felt like a little leaguer for popping-up Lefty's pitch to start the game. Bill James pitching line wasn't much better than Williams, but at least he was trying (and he could have pitched scoreless ball if the Sox fielded better). Roy Wilkinson pitched the last four innings, giving up two unearned runs (so he and James proved they could get out Cincinnati batters, Kid!). The White Sox had their biggest inning of the World Series with a five run 8th, but it was too little and way too late.

So the Cincinnati Reds were Champions of the World, a 10 to 5 winner in game eight, to take the Series five games to three. Lefty Williams and Eddie Cicotte accounted for all five of Chicago's losses. For his efforts, Williams was paid only $5,000 of the 10,000 dollars he was promised and almost got his wife killed. Lefty only pitched like crap in 2 1/3 innings of the 16 1/3 he pitched in the Series, but that was enough to lose three times. In the other 14 innings his pitching line would read;

INN	H	R	ER	BB	K	ERA
14	**2**	**1**	**1**	**4**	**4**	**0.64**

Compared to his thrown innings:

GM	INN	H	R	ER	BB	K	ERA
2	**1**	**2**	**3**	**3**	**3**	**0**	**27.00**
5	**1**	**4**	**4**	**4**	**1**	**0**	**36.00**
8	**1/3**	**4**	**4**	**4**	**0**	**0**	**109.09**
Totals	**2 1/3**	**10**	**11**	**11**	**4**	**0**	**42.49**

Lefty was almost un-hittable in the innings he tried in. No doubt between Williams, Cicotte and Little Dickie Kerr, the Cincinnati Reds was no match for the White Sox pitching. Lefty, if he were given another chance, should have gone up to Gleason before game eight and said sorry Kid, I don't feel much like playing today, and maybe Kid would have started someone else. I doubt it though.

Chapter Three

Richard Henry Kerr

That's Mr. Busher to you!

Richard Henry Kerr was born July 3rd, 1893 in St. Louis, Missouri. Nicknamed Little Dickie because of his 5'7, 155lbs frame, Dickie had another dubious nickname given to him by teammates- "Busher", no doubt because of his years in the Minor Leagues. Kerr finally broke into the Major Leagues when he made the White Sox roster at age twenty-five in the spring of 1919. Knowing he had made the pitching staff of a quality team must have been exciting for Dickie, but come October, he never would have guessed the role he would play in the most historic World Series ever played.

Dickie Kerr had a fine rookie campaign in 1919, the left-hander going 13-7 with a 2.88 ERA. In two hundred and twelve innings pitched, Kerr only walked sixty-four batters and in seventeen starts would complete ten of them with one shut-out. Good numbers, but no indication of his two complete game victories, one a three-hit shutout, of the Cincinnati Reds in the World Series that year. Dickie also didn't know that half the guys playing behind him were trying to lose. This confirmed what guts this young lad possessed in his performance. If the Series would have gone the full nine games, Kerr was penciled in to pitch the final contest. It would have been very interesting to see what would have happened in this ballgame.

Dickie Kerr blossomed in 1920, winning 21 games to 9 losses with a 3.37 ERA. Dickie had an equally impressive 19-17 record with a 4.72 ERA (under 5.00 wasn't that bad in the beginning of the live ball era) in 1921, with a White Sox team decimated by the bouncing of five full time starters and their top two pitchers from baseball, for their involvement in the 1919 Series fixing. When Charles Comiskey cut Dickie's 1922 salary by $500, Kerr asked for his release and quit. Commissioner Kennesaw Mountain Landis then placed Dickie on the permanent ineligible list. Dickie pitched in outlaw ball from 1922 to 1925 when Judge Landis reinstated Kerr with the White Sox for the 1925 season. Dickie would only appear in twelve games going 0-1, a sore arm sidelining him for good.

After retiring, Dickie worked in the cotton business for 10 years in Texas and Arkansas. Then Kerr managed teams in the minor leagues, until he became a fulltime scout for the St. Louis Cardinals. In 1940, while managing the Daytona Beach Islanders, legend had it one of Dickie's pitcher's came up with a sore arm. Since the pitcher showed a little bit of hitting ability, Kerr suggested that the young man try a switch to the outfield, the sore armed ball player was none other than the great Stan Musial (and the start of a friendship that lasted until Kerr's death, though Musial denies it happened this way in his auto-biography). Dickie Kerr died of cancer in Houston Texas May 4th, 1963 at the age of 69.

Game Three

Chicago, Ill October 3rd, 1919

Comiskey Park

Top 1st inning

After two unbelievable wins for Cincinnati, the Series shifts to Chicago for game three. As 29,126 fans turns out to Comiskey Park to witness Chicago's rookie left-hander Dickie Kerr (13-7 .288) versus Cincinnati's big right-hander Ray Fisher (14-5 2.17) do battle. Morrie Rath leads-off the game against the young White Sox hurler, grounding out to SS Swede Risberg (6-3).

With one down, Jake Daubert hits a high arching fly ball to CF Happy Felsch (F-8) for out number two.

Kerr then finishes off a perfect 1st inning like a seasoned veteran, striking-out Heinie Groh (K).

Kerr's Pitching Line

INN	H	R	ER	BB	K	HBP	WP	E
1	0	0	0	0	1	0	0	0

Top 2nd inning

Tied 0-0 after Ray Fisher's perfect 1st inning, Dickie takes to the mound to start the 2nd inning. Edd Roush chops a routine grounder to SS Swede Risberg, tossing to 1B Chick Gandil (6-3).

Pat Duncan greets Dickie with the Reds first hit of the game, a clean single (1B), to right centerfield.

With Duncan on at 1st base and one out, Duncan brakes for 2nd base on a hit and run play. Larry Kopf hits a ground ball to SS Swede Risberg with Swede's only play to 1st base (6-3), for out number two.

Now with Duncan on 2nd and two down, Dickie entices Greasy Neale to bounce out to 2B Eddie Collins (4-3), putting an end to the mini threat.

Kerr's Pitching Line

	INN	H	R	ER	BB	K	HBP	WP	E
	1	1	0	0	0	0	0	0	0
Total	2	1	0	0	0	1	0	0	0

Top 3rd inning

The White Sox took a 2-0 lead with a pair of runs in the bottom of the 2nd inning, thanks to a Chick Gandil single, so some of the pressure was off of the nervous young pitcher. Leading-off for the Reds in the top of the 3rd, Bill

Rariden chops a ground ball to 3B Buck Weaver, who throws over to 1B Chick Gandil (5-3).

With one out, next batter pitcher Ray Fisher hits a swinging bunt that Kerr fields, but his throw to Gandil is too late and Fisher is credited with a single (1B).

With Fisher on 1st base and one out, Reds lead-off man Morrie Rath digs in. Dickie is up to the challenge, and gets Rath to pop-up to SS Risberg (F-6), for the second out of the inning.

Jake Daubert next hits a ground ball up the middle that 2B Eddie Collins scoops up and flips to the Swede (FC 4-6), forcing Fisher out at 2nd base, ending another scoreless inning for Dickie Kerr.

Kerr's Pitching Line

	INN	H	R	ER	BB	K	HBP	WP	E
	1	1	0	0	0	0	0	0	0
Total	3	2	0	0	0	1	0	0	0

Top 4th inning

Chicago still holds a 2-0 lead after three innings, with Kerr pitching in complete control. Leading-off the top of the 4th, Heinie Groh waits out Dickie for a walk (BB).

Even with Groh on the move, SS Risberg choose not to try for the force out at 2nd on Edd Roush's grounder (even though he may have had a play Groh), instead throwing to 1B Gandil (6-3), for the first out of the 4th.

With Groh on 2nd base and one out, Pat Duncan hits a screaming line drive at SS Risberg. Swede grabs the ball in the air and catches Groh napping on the job for a welcomed double play (DP L-6-4), flipping to 2B Eddie Collins to end another potential threat.

Kerr's Pitching Line

	INN	H	R	ER	BB	K	HBP	WP	E
	1	0	0	0	0	1	0	0	0
Total	7	3	0	0	1	2	0	0	0

Top 8th inning

Dickie Kerr is now in a groove. Since Larry Kopf's single starting off the 5th inning, Dickie has set down nine straight Cincinnati batters. Ray Fisher was pitching fine also, but still trails 3-0. Greasy Neale leads-off for the Reds in the top of the 8th, but Dickie strikes Greasy out (K).

With one away Bill Rariden is up next for the Reds, making out number two when he grounds out to 2B Eddie Collins (4-3).

Trying to get something going, Cincinnati manager Pat Moran sends Sherry Magee in to pinch-hit for Ray Fisher. But Magee becomes Kerr's twelfth straight victim, by popping-out to RF Nemo Leibold (F-9), putting an end to the 8th inning. The Southside faithful could now taste the victory that had eluded them the first two games.

Kerr's Pitching Line

	INN	H	R	ER	BB	K	HBP	WP	E
	1	0	0	0	0	0	0	0	0
Total	8	3	0	0	1	3	0	0	0

Top 9th inning

Good thing Dickie Kerr was in top form today, because the White Sox weren't hitting much behind him (by design or not?). With just an infield single by Joe Jackson (5th inning) since the 4th inning, Chicago wouldn't get another base hit the rest of the game. So Chicago held a 3-0 lead going into the 9th, but Dickie would only need one of those runs today. Morrie Rath starts the Reds last chance at Kerr by grounding out to 2B Eddie Collins (4-3).

Dickie then strikes-out Jake Daubert (K), putting the second out into the history books.

Heinie Groh will become Dickie's fifteenth straight foe, grounding out to 3B Buck Weaver (5-3), ending today's ballgame 3-0, in favor of the Sox. Kerr has pitched a three-hit shut-out in front of the home crowd, and the White Sox now trail only two games to one.

Kerr's Pitching Line

	INN	H	R	ER	BB	K	HBP	WP	E
	1	0	0	0	0	1	0	0	0
Total	9	3	0	0	1	4	0	0	0

WP- Kerr (1-0) LP- Fisher (0-1)

Game Three Summary

A rookie no more.

It was a lot to ask of a rookie. With the White Sox losing while using their aces the first two games (Cicotte and Williams), Chicago needed a victory in the worst way. Nobody thought that much of Dickie Kerr, not the gamblers betting against him or his own crooked teammates, who thought Dickie was not good enough to beat Cincinnati. Manager Kid Gleason had other options, experience pitchers like Bill James, Roy Wilkenson and Erskine Mayer at the ready (although 1917 World Series hero future and Hall-of-Famer Red Faber, who won three games in that Series, was hurt with an ankle injury and was not available). Gleason instead chose a twenty-five year old rookie with a 13-8 record with a 2.89 ERA. From the very first inning Dickie started mowing the

Reds down. Giving up only a scratch single in the 2nd, an infield single in the 3rd and a lead-off single in the 5th, the Cincinnati Reds were completely at Dickie's mercy. Setting down the last fifteen Reds in a row, Dickie finished with a 3-0, three-hit shut-out victory making Kid Gleason look like a genius. Dickie Kerr's win got Chicago back into the Series, now down only two games to one.

Many gamblers went bust after this ball game, namely Sleepy Bill Burns and Billy Maharg. Although the one man who had the capital to survive a White Sox victory was New Yorker Arnold Rothstein. Rothstein wanted the Sox to win game three, to make the odds better for Chicago, even though he would be none too pleased when the Sox started winning some ballgames later in the Series, and as Lefty Williams would later find out, he was not playing games (I only mention the gamblers here to show maybe why Lefty Williams would have to be threatened before game eight).

Game Six

October 7th 1919 Cincinnati, Oh

Redland field

Bottom 1st inning

The Cincinnati Reds are now out in front of the Chicago White Sox with an overwhelming four games to one lead, and need only one more win to eliminate the Sox and win the World Championship of Baseball. Today's game will match Sox game three winner Dickie Kerr against opening game winner for the Reds, lefty Dutch Ruether (19-6 1.81). After Ruether held Chicago to a scratch single in the top of the 1st inning, Morrie Rath leads-off for the Reds. Rath pops-up to SS Swede Risberg (F-6).

With one out, Jake Daubert hits a come-backer to Kerr, who throws to 1B Chick Gandil (1-3), for out number two.

Heinie Groh drills Dickie's next offering to center-field, a ball Happy Felsch should have hauled in, but somehow he lets the ball drop in for a two out double (2B) (This ended Dickies string of seventeen straight batter, going back to game three). Sox manager Kid Gleason must be getting sick to his stomach with Chicago's shoddy fielding (if he's awake).

Swede Risberg of all people decides to do something very clever. With Groh on 2nd base and two out, Edd Roush hits a slow roller to the Swede. Not being able to get Roush at 1st base (1B), Risberg faked a throw to Chick Gandil and spins around to catch Groh creeping off 3rd, SS Risberg to 3B Buck Weaver (FC 6-5), to end the inning.

Kerr's Pitching Line

INN	H	R	ER	BB	K	HBP	WP	E
1	2	0	0	0	0	0	0	0

Bottom 2nd inning

Chicago failed to score in the top of the 2nd inning and with the score tied 0-0; Dickie Kerr goes back to work. I guess the Swede couldn't stand making a great play, because he boots Pat Duncan's routine grounder to start the bottom of the 2nd (E-5).

Next up for the Reds, Larry Kopf draws a walk (BB), and Dickie Kerr is in trouble again.

Now with runners on 1st and 2nd base and no outs, Greasy Neale steps into the batter's box. But Neale's sacrifice bunt attempt is not a good one. Dickie fields the ball quickly and throws to 3B Buck Weaver (FC 1-5), to cut down Duncan at 3rd base.

With Larry Kopf now on 2nd base and Greasy Neale on at 1st, Bill Rariden steps up to the plate for his turn at Dickie. Rariden sends a sure double play ball to 2B Eddie Collins, but again Chicago can't turn a double play to save their lives. SS Swede Risberg does get the force however (FC 4-6), but his relay is way too slow to get Rariden.

There are now two gone with Larry Kopf on 3rd base and Bill Rariden at 1st, hard hitting Reds pitcher Dutch Ruether (who had two triples and a single in game one) takes his turn at bat. Kerr gets out of the huge jam by getting Ruether to hit back to the box. Dickie makes the play, throwing to 1B Chuck Gandil (1-3), keeping Cincinnati off the scoreboard.

Kerr's Pitching Line

	INN	H	R	ER	BB	K	HBP	WP	E
	1	0	0	0	1	0	0	0	1
Total	2	2	0	0	1	0	0	0	1

Bottom 3rd inning

This game was shaping up to be another pitcher's duel, as Ruether held Chicago in check in the top of the 3rd inning, keeping the score at 0-0. Dickie's string of eleven straight scoreless innings is about to end though. The inning starts innocently enough when Morrie Rath grounds out to 2B Eddie Collins (4-3).

Jake Daubert rudely greets Kerr with a one out single (1B) to right field. Daubert's single is the Reds third hit off Kerr, matching their game three totals.

Dickie did have a chance to get out of the inning unscathed. As Heinie Groh was striking-out (K), for the 2nd out, Daubert steals 2nd base (SB). If catcher Ray Schalk had thrown out Jake, the 3rd inning would have been in the books with no runs scored.

With Daubert on 2nd base and two away, Dickie plunks Edd Roush (HBP) in the buttocks.

The Reds now have Daubert on 2nd base and Roush on at 1st with two down with Pat Duncan coming up to bat. Dickie has pitched in and out of trouble every inning so far, but his luck had to run out sometime. Sometime was right now, as Duncan splits the gap in right-center field for a two run double (2B), the first runs off Kerr in eleven and two thirds innings.

Cincinnati now leads 2-0 and the way Ruether had been handling the Sox, the crowd started smelling victory. Still with two out, Larry Kopf takes his turn at the plate. Kopf sends a soaring fly ball to deep center-field that Happy Felsch races back and gets under for the 3rd out of the inning (F-8).

Kerr's Pitching Line

	INN	H	R	ER	BB	K	HBP	WP	E
	1	2	2	2	0	1	1	0	0
Total	3	4	2	2	1	1	1	0	1

Bottom 4th inning

After having completely controlled Chicago in the Series opener and cruising through four scoreless innings in game six, Dutch Ruether looked poised to end the White Sox hopes of a history making comeback. Taking the mound down 2-0, Dickie immediately runs into trouble again. Greasy Neale greets Kerr with a lead-off triple (3B), into the right-field corner. In a win or go home contest, how manager Kid Gleason did not replace Dickie Kerr in the 4th is just mind boggling. Dickie has been in trouble every inning, and the bottom of the 4th was no exception, but the Chicago manager must have had all kinds of balls, one made of steel, the other crystal.

Bill Rariden follows Neale's triple with a shot right at 2B Eddie Collins, who fields the ball on one hop, looking Neale back to 3rd base, and fires to 1B Chick Gandil (4-3), for a big first out.

With one down now and Greasy still on 3rd base, Dickie should have given Dutch Ruether, (the way he was hitting), an intentional walk. He didn't, and Ruether strokes an RBI double (2B) to left field. Joe Jackson, the man whose glove is where "triples go to die," had no trouble letting doubles live in this Series. Of the ten doubles Cincinnati hit in the eight games, six went Joe's way.

With Ruether now on at 2nd base and one out, it was time for SS Swede Risberg to get into the act. Morrie Rath raps a ground ball right at Swede, and with Dutch on the move towards 3rd base, Risberg's throw to 3B Buck Weaver hits Ruether right in the back (E-6). The ball rolls all the way to the stands, allowing Ruether to score and Morrie to reach 2nd base (well done Swede). This was a good time for manager Kid Gleason to remove the gutsy little pitcher, but Kid must have been taking his afternoon nap. Chicago is now down 4-0, and there is no tomorrow if they lose this ballgame.

As Jake Daubert settles into the batter's box, Dickie must have still been shaken up, because Rath steals 3rd base (SB) without a throw. With one out, Daubert sends a fly ball to left field. Joe Jackson comes up big on this play (rare for this series), as he makes the catch (F-7) and rifles the ball to C Ray Schalk to nail Morrie Rath at home plate, for an inning ending double play (DP F-7-2). With two runs in, Cincinnati now leads 4-0.

Kerr's Pitching Line

	INN	H	R	ER	BB	K	HBP	WP	E
	1	2	2	1	0	0	0	0	1
Total	4	6	4	3	1	1	1	0	2

Bottom 5th inning

The Chicago White Sox comeback started with a single run in the top of the 5th inning, making the score 4-1 Cincinnati. Dickie goes back to work in the bottom half, facing Heinie Groh leading-off. Groh flies out to CF Happy Felsch (F-8) for the first out.

Next up for the Reds, Edd Roush sends a fly ball out RF Shano Collins's way (F-9), two down.

In what should have been a easy one, two, three inning, Pat Duncan makes it all the way to 3rd base after CF Happy Felsch, trying his famous basket catch (Willie Mays did it much better), drops the ball (E-8) for a three base error (if you wonder what Kid thought of that, Happy started in right-field in game seven, but Kid did nothing right then). This is also the third error of the game for the Sox.

Swede Risberg must have thought the Sox couldn't come back from a three run deficit, because he makes another big play behind Kerr. With Duncan on at 3rd base and two out, Larry Kopf bounces a ball to SS Risberg, who throws a strike to 1B Chick Gandil (6-3), ending the 5th inning.

Kerr's Pitching Line

	INN	H	R	ER	BB	K	HBP	WP	E
	1	0	0	0	0	0	0	0	1
Total	5	6	4	3	1	1	1	0	3

Bottom 6th inning

Chicago had their biggest inning so far in the Series, scoring three runs in the top of the 6th to tie the game 4-4. This really quieted the Hamilton County crowd, as Dickie went to the mound in the bottom half with a new confidence. Greasy Neale though, belts a smash back to the box that Kerr couldn't handle for a lead-off single (1B). This was the sixth inning in a row that Kerr is pitching in trouble and I'm starting to wonder if the Sox bullpen is on strike.

Next up for the Reds, Bill Rariden lifts a soft fly ball to right-field that RF Shano Collins takes care of (F-9).

With one out and Neal on at 1st base, right-hander Jimmy Ring (10-9 2.26), who replaced Dutch Ruether on the mound in the 6th, strikes-out (K), for the second out.

Back to the top of the order in Morrie Rath, Greasy Neale breaks for 2nd base on the first pitch. Greasy is out stealing (CS 2-6), C Schalk to SS Risberg to end the 6th frame. In six full innings pitched, Kerr has given up seven hits, one walk, one hit batsman, and his backup in the field has made three errors. That's a total of twelve base runners. How longer would Billy Martin or Earl Weaver have let Dickie continue on?

Kerr's Pitching Line

	INN	H	R	ER	BB	K	HBP	WP	E
	1	1	0	0	0	1	0	0	0
Total	6	7	4	3	1	2	1	0	3

Bottom 7th inning

Jimmy Ring held Chicago scoreless in the top half of the 7th inning, so the score is still tied 4-4, when Cincinnati comes to bat in the home half. Morrie Rath (who was at the plate when Greasy Neale was cut down to end the 6th), starts the inning off by hitting a bloop single (1B) into centerfield. Dickie's roller-coaster game marches on.

Jake Daubert sacrifices Rath to 2nd base, with a bunt Kerr fields and throws to 1B Chick Gandil (SAC 1-3).

This brings Heinie Groh into the batter's box with the go ahead run on 2nd base and one out. Groh works Dickie for a free pass (BB) and Kerr is in hot water again. A fresh arm in the game would have been a good idea, considering the gut wrenching performance Dickie has put in for the Chicago White Sox in this game. Kid Gleason must have known something that no one else did, because he leaves Kerr in the ballgame.

Swede Risberg finally decided to start playing some baseball. Edd Roush, batting with one out and Rath on 2nd base and Groh on at 1st , chops a bounding ball to Swede who flips to 2B Eddie Collins who relays to 1B Chick

Gandil completing a (DP 6-4-3) double play. That puts a sudden stop to the inning, keeping the score locked at 4-4.

Kerr's Pitching Line

	INN	H	R	ER	BB	K	HBP	WP	E
	1	1	0	0	1	0	0	0	0
Total	7	8	4	3	2	2	1	0	3

Bottom 8th inning

Jimmy Ring, with the help of Edd Roush, kept Chicago off the scoreboard in the top of the 8th inning. In a 4-4 game, the Reds take their turn at bat. Nothing will be easy for Dickie today. After Pat Duncan fouls-out to 1B Chick Gandil (FO-3) for the 1st out, things start looking better for the rookie.

Larry Kopf hits a ball that almost takes Kerr's head off, but Dickie somehow catches the ball (L-1), for the second quick out.

Dickie had not had a three up, three down inning all day. The 8th would be no different either, as the red hot Greasy Neale gets his third hit of the day, a two out single (1B) past 1B Chick Gandil into right field. In a 4-4 game Gandil (one of the best fielders in the game), could have come up with the ball but hey, what do you want from Chick?

With two down and Neale on 1st base, next batter Bill Rariden hits a hard bouncer that Dickie knocks down but has no play for another single (1B). I'm now thinking that Kid Gleason must have looked down to the bullpen, but no one saw his signal because they were all across the street having an afternoon beer. It's the only reason that I can think of that Gleason would leave Dickie in the ballgame after being in trouble every inning. Why, in the bottom of the 8th in a 4-4 tie, with your team only having three outs remaining if the Reds score, would Kid not put a fresh arm into the game? By the way relief pitchers in the late teens were not unheard of.

With runners on at 1st and 2nd base, it was Reds manager Pat Moran's turn to make an odd decision. The way the Reds pitchers were handling the White Sox batters, especially Dolph Luque (9-3 2.63), Moran lets pitcher Jimmy Ring hit for himself. Kerr gets Ring to bounce to SS Swede Risberg, flipping the ball to 2B Eddie Collins (FC 6-4), forcing Bill Rariden at 2nd base to end yet another Cincinnati threat.

Kerr's Pitching Line

	INN	H	R	ER	BB	K	HBP	WP	E
	1	2	0	0	0	0	0	0	0
Total	8	10	4	3	2	2	1	0	3

Bottom 9th inning

After Jimmy Ring shuts down the Sox in the top of the 9th inning, the game and the Series could be Cincinnati's with only one run in their ups. Lead-off man Morrie Rath makes the first out though, grounding to 3B Buck Weaver (5-3).

Jake Daubert, who has had great at- bats all day off Kerr, rips a stinging single (1B) up the middle, this puts the winning run on 1st base with one.

Following Daubert's one out single, Heinie Groh hits what should have been an inning ending double play. SS Swede Risberg gloves Groh's grounder and tosses the ball to 2B Eddie Collins (FC 6-4), forcing Daubert at 2nd base, but Risberg and Collins again fail to complete a twin killing.

Reds captain Edd Roush is now at the plate with two down and Heinie Groh on at 1st base. Before Roush has a chance to do any damage, Groh is out trying to steal 2nd base, C Ray Schalk to 2B Eddie Collins (CS 2-4), to end the inning and send the game into overtime. I hope this game doesn't go too much longer, because Dickie Kerr's arm might just fall off. In spite of seven Cincinnati base runners since the 5th inning, Kerr has not given up anymore runs.

Kerr's Pitching Line

	INN	H	R	ER	BB	K	HBP	WP	E
	1	1	0	0	0	0	0	0	0
Total	9	11	4	3	2	2	1	0	3

Bottom 10th inning

This was another game in which Chick Gandil made a huge game winning hit (See 2nd inning, game three), when Dickie Kerr was pitching. Gandil's single in the top of the 10th scored Buck Weaver to give the Sox a 5-4 lead going into the bottom of the 10th inning. Edd Roush who was up when Groh was caught stealing ending the 9th, leads-off, hitting a hard grounder to 2B Eddie Collins, who scoops up the ball and tosses to 1B Chick Gandil (4-3), to start the Reds last hope.

Next batter Pat Duncan hits a high pop-fly behind home plate which C Ray Schalk snatches (FO-2), for the second nail in the Reds coffin.

Larry Kopf ends the Reds day by sending a ground ball out 2B Eddie Collins way. Eddie gobbles it up and throws to (hero?) 1B Chick Gandil (4-3), to end the exciting game six 5-4 for Chicago. This schedules game seven for tomorrow at Redland Park, with the Reds still leading the World Series four games to two.

Kerr's Pitching Line

	INN	H	R	ER	BB	K	HBP	WP	E
	1	0	0	0	0	0	0	0	0
Total	10	11	4	3	2	2	1	0	3

WP- Kerr (2-0)   LP- Ring (1-1)

Game Six Summary

Guts of steel.

If you looked up guts in the dictionary, you would see a picture of White Sox pitcher Dickie Kerr. What an incredible pitching performance from a rookie hurler against the National League Champion Cincinnati Reds. The only easy inning Dickie had all day was the 10th inning, after pitching in and out of trouble the whole ballgame. The Reds had seventeen base runners; left eight of those runners stranded on base, and ran themselves out of four innings. In a do or die game, how Kid Gleason continued to stick by Dickie in this rollercoaster ball game, I just can't imagine. Did he just not trust anybody else? Remember, Gleason did not use a relief pitcher in any game in the Series until the outcome of those games were already decided. Manager Kid Gleason should have pulled Kerr in the 4th inning after Reds pitcher Dutch Ruether smashed a one out double to left field to score Greasy Neale and put the Reds up 3-0. Cincinnati scored their final run in the 4th inning on an error by SS Swede Risberg to take a 4-0 lead, with the inning finally ending on LF Joe Jackson's huge catch and throw double play, nailing Morrie Rath at home plate.

Gleason stuck with Kerr in spite of the seventeen Reds base runners. Dickie escaped trouble when Heinie Groh was picked off 3rd by a nice SS Swede Risberg play ending the 1st. Kerr also stranded two runners in the 2nd inning and another in the 3rd after two runs were already in. After two more runners scored in the 4th inning Dickie continued his struggle. In the 5th Pat Duncan was stranded on 3rd base, and Greasy Neale singled and was eventually caught stealing in the 6th. A rare (for the White Sox) infield double play in the 7th inning helped Dickie out of a huge jam, and the Reds left two more runners stranded in the 8th. Ray Schalk threw Heinie Groh out stealing to end the 9th inning. How in the World Kid Gleason stuck by Dickie Kerr with all the trouble he was in throughout this game was amazing. Like I said earlier, Kid must have had a crystal ball in the dugout. In a game the White Sox had to win, to let a rookie pitcher keep getting into jams, inning after inning and not send out a fresh arm is either pure genius or increditably stupid. Gleason came out looking like a genius (for once) because of Kerr's guts of steel performance.

Because of all the pitches Dickie threw in game six, that is why I think Gleason didn't go with Kerr in game eight (with Cicotte for game nine?) on two days rest (which was not unusual in those days, not so much today), instead of Lefty Williams who Gleason had to have known was not trying to win ball games for the White Sox (but who knows what Gleason was thinking). Even if he wanted to save Kerr for the ninth game, if there was one, he could have thrown the bullpen catcher in game eight and had a better chance of winning.

Today's story was Dickie Kerr though; ten innings of pure effort from a guy not even his teammates gave a chance to win one ballgame, let alone two. The man who knocked in the winning runs in both of Dickie's wins was none other than the fix ringleader Chick Gandil. As my pop would have said, "Who'd of thunk it."

Section Two

The White Sox Hitters

Chapter Four

Joe Jackson-LF

I'm afraid it's so Joe!

Joseph Jefferson Jackson was born July 16, 1889 in Pickens County, South Carolina. Joe acquired his nickname "Shoeless Joe", while playing for Greenville in 1908. While breaking in a new pair of baseball cleats, Joe developed a blister. Not being able to take the pain anymore, Jackson took his shoes off for his next at bat. Joe promptly hit a triple and someone from the stands yelled "You shoeless son of a gun you!" and the name stuck. Not being able to read or write, which was not uncommon for that area, Jackson was no less a genius on the baseball field. Signed by Connie Mack of the old Philadelphia A's in 1908, Joe appeared in five games hitting .130. No indication of what was about to burst upon the American League. Jackson only played in five games again in 1909 hitting .294 in seventeen plate appearances. In what turned out to be one of the worst trades in history, Mack sent Joe to Cleveland for outfielder Bris Lord halfway through the 1910 season. Mack really missed the boat on Joe, not playing him at all before the trade. The trade was a great thing too, because Jackson was ready to hang up the spikes and return to the mills of South Carolina. Joe played in twenty games for the Indians, hitting .387 in seventy-five at bats. Under today's rules, 1911 would have been Joe's rookie season, and what a season it was. Jackson hit .408 with two hundred and thirty-three hits, one hundred and twenty-six runs scored and eighty-three RBI's. From 1912 to 1914 Joe averaged .395, .373 and .338. Shoeless Joe slumped in 1915 and was traded August 21, to the Chicago White Sox for three players and $31,500 cash. Joe finished the year hitting .308. Jackson rebounded in 1916 with a .341 average, but fell off again hitting "only" .301 in the Sox Championship season of 1917. Because of World War I, Joe appeared in only seventeen games in 1918, instead choosing to work in the Navy shipyards like most of his teammates. In the fateful 1919 season, Joe was back on top of his game with a .351 average, and helped get Chicago back to the World Series. The Cincinnati Reds upset the White Sox, 5 games to 3 to shock the baseball world. With rumors of the series being fixed, nobody could have accused Joe Jackson. With the exception of Ivy Wingo, who hit .571 in only seven at bats, Joe led everyone in hitting with a .375 batting average. Jackson also recorded twelve base hits, a record he tied (Buck Herzog New York Giants 1912) and co-held until 1960 when Bobby Richardson of the Yankees smacked thirteen base hits. Joe also drove in six runs, scored five and hit the only home run (Heinie Groh would argue this), of the World Series. Something just wasn't right though with Jackson's over all play though. He left a lot of runners on base, and his play in the outfield, even though he didn't commit an error (thanks to some friendly scoring), left a lot to be desired. Joe's base running, especially in the crucial seventh game was befuddling.

In 1920 Joe was back in top form hitting .382, with two hundred and eighteen hits and topping the one hundred RBI mark for the first time in his career with one hundred and twenty-one. Jackson also scored one hundred and five runs, but as the season inched closer to the end the 1919 World Series came back to haunt him. Joe was suspended by owner Charles Comiskey on September 27, along with seven other teammates, for their part in the Series fix. It came as a complete shock that Joe took a $10,000 pay-off, although Jackson always said he played nothing but his best. I believe Joe lied. Jackson's fielding was covered in the pitcher's section, and there he had numerous plays in which in which he did his part to help throw ballgames. Now decide how great Jackson's hitting really was in the 1919 World Series.

Joe was banned for life on August 4, 1921 by Commissioner Landis and never played Major League baseball again, forced to retire with the third highest lifetime batting average at .356. Jackson, at the age of thirty-one might have had eight or nine more years left. What would have been a first ballot Hall of Fame career, instead Joe is left for people to argue whether he should be in there or not. After researching Jackson's World Series, to me it's a definite not! I'm afraid Joe took the money and then did what he could to help lose (as long as he didn't look bad, even though that didn't always work out). Going back to South Carolina, Joe owned a barbeque restaurant and later a liquor store (that Ty Cobb probably paid for). Joe continued to play baseball whenever and wherever he could. Joseph Jefferson Jackson died of complications of cirrhosis of the liver, December 9, 1951 in Greenville, South Carolina. Joe was an immortal baseball player, who committed an amoral act, that caused spontaneous combustion to a legendary baseball career.

Game One

RHP Eddie Cicotte (29-7 1.82) vs LHP Dutch Ruether (19-6 1.81)

At Cincinnati, Oh **October 1st, 1919** **Redland Field**

Attendance-30,511

2nd inning **Score: 1-0 Reds**

1st at-bat **0 on 0 out**

After the Cincinnati Reds took a 1-0 lead in the bottom of the 1st inning, the Chicago White Sox were looking to quiet the screaming fans with some hitting of their own. The great Joe Jackson, the left handed hitting machine for the American League champions, leads-off the top of the 2nd inning. Jackson, who hit .351 for the White Sox in 1919, hits a routine ground ball to the Cincinnati Reds' SS Larry Kopf. Kopf nervously fields the ball but throws wildly passed 1B Jake Daubert (E-6), as Jackson hustles all the way into 2nd base. Shoeless Joe moves to 3rd base on Happy Felsch's sacrifice bunt (SAC 1-3), and scores the Sox first run on Chick Gandil's bloop single (1B) into short leftfield to tie the score 1-1.

4th inning **Score: 1-1**

2nd at-bat **0 on 1 out**

With the game still tied 1-1, Jackson comes to the batter's box in the top of the 4th with one out. The Reds big Dutch again gets Joe to ground to Kopf at short stop. This time Larry has no problems and throws out Jackson (6-3) for out number two. The Sox didn't score and the game moves on to the Reds half of the 4th.

6th inning **Score: 6-1 Reds**

3rd at-bat **2 on 1 out**

The disastrous five run 4th inning off Eddie Cicotte has put Cincinnati up 6-1. The White Sox show signs of life at the top of the 6th inning. With

Eddie Collins on 2nd base and Buck Weaver on 1st via singles (1B) off Dutch Reuther with one out, Joe Jackson has a chance for a big hit and maybe a big rally for the Sox. But Joe pulls Reuther's pitch down the 1st baseline that 1B Jake Daubert takes unassisted (3-U), with Collins and Weaver moving up a base. Ruether pitch's out of the jam without giving up any runs.

9th inning **Score: 9-1 Reds**

4th at-bat **0 on 0 out**

While the Cincinnati crowd razzed and hoorayed the beaten White Sox, they still have one final at bat in the first game of the 1919 World Series. Joe Jackson leads-off the top of the 9th and turns on Reuther's pitch with a long drive to deep right field which Greasy Neale catches (F-9) near the wall for the first out of the inning. Chicago would not score in the 9th inning and lost 9-1, to go down one game to zero in the best five out of nine contests.

Game One Summary

A slow start

The Chicago White Sox took an opening day pounding at the hands of the Cincinnati Reds 9-1. Joe scored the Sox only run in the top of the 2nd inning, after a throwing error by SS Larry Kopf moved Jackson to 2nd base. After a sacrifice bunt by Happy Felsch moving Joe to 3rd, Jackson scored on Chick Gandil's bloop single. That was all of Chicago's offence this first game of the 1919 World Series. In the only at–bat Joe had any chance to do damage, in the top of the 6th with one out and men on 1st and 2nd base and the Reds up 6-1, Jackson grounds out to 1B Jake Daubert, moving the runners up a base, but they would not score.

Game One Box **Running Total**

		AB	R	H	RBI	AVE	
1st AB	E-5, R	1	1	0	0	.000	
2nd AB	6-3	2	1	0	0	.000	
3rd AB	3-U	3	1	0	0	.000	2 LOB (2) 1 RISP (1)
4th AB	F-9	4	1	0	0	.000	

Game Two

LHP Lefty Williams (23-11 2.64) vs LHP Slim Sallee (21-7 2.05)

At Cincinnati, O **October 2nd, 1919** **Redland Field**

Attendance-29,698

2nd inning **Score: 0-0**

1st at-bat **0 on 0 out**

Another day and it's another left-handed starting pitcher for the Cincinnati Reds. Not as many fans turn out at Redland Field today to witness the second game of the World Series. After a scoreless 1st inning, Joe leads-off the top of the 2nd with a screaming line drive to center-field for a stand up double (2B). Happy Felsch follows with a sacrifice bunt (SAC 1-3), moving Jackson up to 3rd base. With the infield playing in with only one out, Chick Gandil raps a ground ball straight at SS Larry Kopf, who holds Joe at 3rd and chucks out Gandil (6-3). Swede Risberg next pops-out weakly to RF Greasy Neale (F-9), to end the threat. In a 0-0 ballgame in only the 2nd inning, Joe probably should have tried for home on contact on Gandil's grounder; I bet Ty Cobb would have.

4th inning **Score: 0-0**

2nd at-bat **1 on 0 out**

Locked in a 0-0 battle going into the top of the 4th inning, Jackson steps into the left-hand side of the batter's box with Buck Weaver occupying 1st base after his lead-off single (1B). Joe promptly slaps Sallee's fast one into left field for a single (1B), moving Weaver to 2nd base. Happy Felsch again sacrifices both runners up a base (SAC 1-3), but again Gandil and Risberg could do nothing to help the Sox cause, and the score remains tied.

6th inning **Score: 3-0 Reds**

3rd at-bat **1 on 1 out**

The Reds have taken a 3-0 lead with three runs off Lefty Williams in the bottom of the 4th inning. Chicago, who has now seen serious scoring threats go down the drain in the 2nd and 4th innings, blows another chance in the 6th. With Buck Weaver on at 2nd base after a one out double (2B), Joe comes up to the plate already two for two, looking to get the Sox on the scoreboard and back into the ballgame. Jackson, who only struck out ten times in five hundred and sixteen at-bats during the regular season, decides not to take the bat off his shoulder and K's on three straight pitches making out number two (K). A pattern is now starting with Joe when he has runners in scoring position.

8th inning **Score: 4-2 Reds**

4th at-bat **0 on 2 out**

With the Sox trailing 4-2 going into the top of the 8th inning, Joe lifts a short fly ball that makes its way over 1B Jake Daubert's head for a two out single (1B), Jackson's third hit of the day. After Daubert fields the ball on one hop, he tries to throw behind Joe at 1st base and instead tosses the ball over Slim Sallee's head (E-3) who was covering 1st base, allowing Joe to reach 2nd base on the error. The Sox didn't score, nor would they in the 9th and lose game two 4-2. Chicago is now trailing Cincinnati two games to none, heading home to the Windy City with their tails between their legs.

Game Two Summary

3-4 but no scores.

Joe caught fire in the 2nd game; though it didn't help Chicago much as they lost 4-2. Jackson had three hits in four at-bats including a lead-off double in the top of the 2nd inning. In Joe's only at-bat with a runner in scoring position, Jackson struck out looking on three pitches. Joe did make it to 3rd base twice and to 2nd once but nobody could deliver Jackson to the plate.

Game Two Box		**Running Total**					
		AB	R	H	RBI	AVE	
1st AB	2B	5	1	1	0	.200	2B (1)
2nd AB	1B	6	1	2	0	.333	
3rd AB	K-Looking	7	1	2	0	.286	K (1),1 LOB (3)
4th AB	1B	8	1	3	0	.375	

Game Three

RHP Ray Fisher (14-5 2.17) vs RHP Dickie Kerr (13-8 2.89)

At Chicago, Ill **October 3rd, 1919** **Comiskey Park**

Attendance-29,126

2nd inning **Score: 0-0**

1st at-bat **0 on 0 out**

Now trailing two games to zip to the underdog Cincinnati Reds, the White Sox desperately needs a victory today in game three. After facing two straight lefties, the Sox finally get to see a right-hander from the Reds. Tied 0-0 going into the bottom of the 2nd inning, Joe helps the less than capacity crowd get excited by slapping a sharp single (1B) into left field. Jackson is hotter than a firecracker right now with four hits in his last five plate appearances. Joe moves on to 3rd base when P Ray Fisher throws wildly into center trying to force Jackson at 2nd on Happy Felsch's tapper (maybe a bunt attempt?) back to the mound (E-1), with Happy ending up on 2nd base. Chick Gandil delivers both runners with a two RBI single (1B) to right field giving Chicago its first lead off the Series, 2-0.

3rd inning **Score: 2-0 Sox**

2nd at-bat **2 on 0 out**

As hot as Joe is right now, what in the world was Kid Gleason thinking of, giving Jackson the bunt sign? Or did Joe bunt all on his own doing? Whatever the case may be, Joe had two runners on at 1st and 2nd base and nobody out, hotter than Yuma, Arizona in August, and makes a poor bunt attempt, popping the ball up to 1B Jake Daubert for the first out of the 3rd inning (F-3). Happy Felsch then grounded into a (DP 5-4-3) double play to end the threat, with the Sox still leading 2-0. This is another case of Jackson not doing anything with a runner in scoring position (and not the last time he would try to bunt with a chance to break a game open).

6th inning **Score: 3-0 Sox**

3rd at-bat **0 on 0 out**

Joe Jackson continues his hot streak, with no one on base of course, legging out a lead-off single (1B) to shortstop to start off the bottom of the 6th inning. Joe is now five for his last seven, his only two outs coming with runners in scoring position. Jackson has not driven in a run yet either with his five hits, even though he will lead the team in that category with six. Joe tries to steal 2nd base with Happy Felsch at the plate but is cut down by Reds catcher Bill Rariden (CS 2-6). This was a huge win by the White Sox 3-0, now only trailing the Reds, two games to one.

Game Three Summary

A bunt? Really?

This was a game rookie Dickie Kerr will never forget, throwing a three-hit shutout at the Cincinnati Reds and winning 3-0. Now down two games to one, Joe continued his sizzling hitting streak by banging out two hits in three at-bats. Joe also continued his not hitting with runners in scoring position with that bunting fiasco in the 3rd inning. At the time Chicago held a 2-0 lead, with the hottest hitter on the planet in Jackson up at the plate, and Joe had four hits in his last five at-bats at the time. I believe this to be a prime example of Jackson earning his pay-off money, easing off a little bit, while still looking very good. In the box score anyway.

Game Three Box		**Running Total**					
		AB	R	H	RBI	AVE	
1st AB	1B, Run	9	2	4	0	.444	
2nd AB	F-3	10	2	4	0	.400	2 LOB (5) 1 RISP (3)
3rd AB	1B, CS	11	2	5	0	.455	CS (1)

Game Four

RHP Jimmy Ring (10-9 2.26) vs RHP Eddie Cicotte (29-7 1.82)

At Chicago, Ill **October 4th, 1919** **Comiskey Park**

Attendance-34,363

2nd inning Score: 0-0

1st at-bat 0 on 0 out

Excited by their teams first victory in game three, almost 5,000 more fans packed Comiskey Park for the fourth game of the Series. After a scoreless 1st inning, Joe starts things off in the bottom half of the 2nd inning by swatting a fly ball to right center field that CF Edd Roush misjudges, allowing Jackson to glide into 2nd base with a double (2B); Joe is now six for his last eight. Happy Felsch again gets his bunt down (SAC 1-3) moving Joe to 3rd base with one out. Chick Gandil then follows with a weak swing, that produces a weak pop-up out in front of home plate, that 3B Heinie Groh gloves (F-5) for the second out. Back to back walks to Swede Risberg and Ray Schalk (BB) load the bases, but Eddie Cicotte grounds out to 2B Morrie Rath (4-3), as Ring pitches out of the inning with no runs scored.

3rd inning Score: 0-0

2nd at-bat 1 on 2 out

Joe's hitting vicious streak comes to an end, but his streak of not hitting with runners in scoring position continues. With Eddie Collins on 2nd base and two away, Jackson hits what should have been an inning ending ground out to 2B Morrie Rath, but Rath boots the ball (E-4). With runners on the corners and two out, Happy Felsch finally has to swing away (four Sac bunts) and chops a grounder that 3B Heinie Groh gobbles up (5-3), ending another White Sox scoring chance.

6th inning Score: 2-0 Reds

3rd at-bat 0 on 0 out

Letting scoring chances slip away time after time, the Sox trail 2-0 going into the bottom of the 6th inning. Joe leads-off the inning, hitting a bounding ball to SS Larry Kopf, who handles the play (6-3). Jimmy Ring is handing the Sox nothing but goose eggs today.

8th inning **Score: 2-0 Reds**

4th at-bat **0 on 0 out**

Still trailing 2-0 to the Reds and pitcher Jimmy Ring, who would end up throwing a nifty three-hit shut-out at the Sox, Joe leads-off an inning for the third time in four at-bats today. Striking out (K) for the second time in the Series, was Joe really try his best in the 8th inning this afternoon? For a man who puts the ball in play 98.3 % of the time (only ten K's in five hundred and sixteen official at-bats all year), two strike outs in four games seems excessive. Losing today has now put Chicago down three games to one.

Game Four Summary

Picking and choosing.

Joe kept his hot streak going with a lead-off double in the bottom of the 2nd inning, Jackson's sixth hit in his last eight at-bats. When me and my dad would sit down and talk hitting, he told me of seeing Jimmy Foxx play in Philadelphia while Foxx was with the Boston Red Sox. My father was just a young boy, but he remembered Foxx being in the midst of an incredible hitting streak, pounding out four hits that day. Pop said he had never seen anything like it. I imagine Joe Jackson was in this type of hitting zone. Unlike Foxx though, who drove in four or five runs that day, Jackson with his six hits through four games in the Series, had yet to drive in a single run. Was that just a coincidence, or did Joe let off little bit with runners on base? After Joe's double he started to cool off a little bit, reaching base only one more time on an error his next three trips to the plate.

Game Four Box **Running Total**

		AB	R	H	RBI	AVE	
1st AB	2B	12	2	6	0	.500	2B(2)
2nd AB	E-4	13	2	6	0	.462	1 LOB (6) 1 RISP (4)
3rd AB	6-3	14	2	6	0	.429	
4TH AB	K	15	2	6	0	.400	K(2)

Game Five

RHP Hod Eller (20-9 2.40) vs LHP Lefty Williams (23-11 2.64)

At Chicago, Ill **October 6th, 1919** **Comiskey Park**

Attendance-34,379

1st inning **Score: 0-0**

1st at-bat **2 on 1 out**

With four games in the books, Cincinnati holds a three to one lead in games and thinking about a sweep in the house of Comiskey. Lefty Williams held the Reds scoreless in the top half of the 1st inning, and the Sox have something going quickly in the home half. With one out and Nemo Leibold and Buck Weaver on at the corners, Joe has a chance to bust up Eller right here in 1st inning. All Jackson can muster though is a pop-up to 3B Heinie Groh (F-5), for the second out. Another chance with runners on base, another chance with a runner on 3rd base and less than two out; gone right down the crapper. Starting to get the picture? By the way, Felsch flies out (F-7) to end the inning.

4th inning **Score: 0-0**

2nd at-bat **0 on 1 out**

Hod Eller is on one hell of a roll, after striking out six straight White Sox batters in the 2nd and 3rd innings, Buck Weaver broke up the K string by tapping back to the box (1-3), to start off the 4th. Now Joe steps into the batter's box, and he also taps back to Eller (1-3) for out number two. Happy Felsch then strikes-out (K), to end the frame. It should be noted that Hod Eller has now sat down the last eleven White Sox batters in a row, the last nine all by himself, seven K's and two tappers back to the mound. The next time this would occur in a World Series game, was never.

7th inning **Score: 4-0 Reds**

3rd at-bat **0 on 0 out**

The White now trail 4-0, after Lefty Williams gave up four runs in the top of the 6th inning. Now playing catch up, the Sox needed runs in a hurry. Joe leads–off the bottom of the 7th hoping to get something, anything started, I think. But Mr. Hod Eller wasn't having any of that. Leading-off, Joe rolls out (4-3) to 2B Morrie Rath, making the first out of the inning. Felsch and Gandil could do no better, and Eller has another scoreless inning. The Sox have not scored a run now in twenty consecutive frames.

9th inning **Score: 5-0 Reds**

4th at-bat **1 on 2 out**

Two are out with Buck Weaver on 3rd base, after a booming triple (3B) to right-center field, making only the third hit off Eller today. Joe Jackson is now up with another opportunity to drive in a runner in scoring position. Joe, hitless in his last six at-bats, makes it seven straight by grounding out to end the game (4-3), to 2B Morrie Rath. The Reds had scored an un-earned run in the top of the 9th off Erskine Mayer (1-3 8.25) to make the score 5-0, and that's where it ended. The sweep of the three games in Chicago has now put Cincinnati up four games to one, heading back down to the Buckeye State.

Game Five Summary

Two words, Hod Eller

Joe was now as cold as the rest of his teammates. After being shut-out twice in a row, both times on only three hits, the White Sox were in dire straits. Down four games to one, it was quite embarrassing for a team as talented as the White Sox were. All Jackson would produce in this game was three more men left on base, including two more left in scoring position, and seven at-bats in a row now without a base hit. That was about to change.

Game Five Box **Running Total**

		AB	R	H	RBI	AVE	
1st AB	F-5	16	2	6	0	.375	2 LOB (8) 1RISP (5)
2nd AB	1-3	17	2	6	0	.353	
3rd AB	4-3	18	2	6	0	.333	
4TH AB	6-3	19	2	6	0	.316	1 LOB (9) 1 RISP (6)

Game Six

RHP Dickie Kerr (13-8 2.89) vs LHP Dutch Ruether (19-6 1.81)

At Cincinnati, Oh **October 7th, 1919** **Redland Field**

Attendance-32,006

1st inning **Score: 0-0**

1st at-bat **1 on 2 out**

After Dutch held Joe hitless in the opener, it was time for the shoeless one to show Ruether a thing or two. With Buck Weaver on 1st base and two down, Jackson decides now is not the time. He pops-up to 3B Heinie Groh (F-5), to end the top of 1st inning.

4th inning **Score: 2-0 Reds**

2nd at-bat **0 on 1 out**

Dutch Ruether continued the Sox hitting woes by throwing four more shut-out innings. Joe could do nothing with Ruether in game one, going 0 for four, he now makes it 0 for six with a pop-foul that C Bill Rariden circles under and gloves (FO-2) for the second out of the 4th. Chicago would not score in the inning, and now has not scored a run in twenty-six straight innings.

6th inning **Score: 4-1 Reds**

3rd at-bat **1 on 0out**

Joe finally decides now is the time, and he and the Sox finally get to Dutch Ruether. Trailing 4-1, Buck Weaver's bloop double (2B) starts the rally the Southsiders had been looking for the whole Series. Joe next drives in his first run in twenty-two at-bats of the World Series, with a sharp single (1B) to center-field. Happy Felsch also gets into the act; cracking a double (2B) to left-center field to plate Jackson, and two outs later Ray Schalk comes through in the clutch, by singling (1B) in Happy to tie the game up at 4-4. Now pay very close attention to Joe's next two at-bats, for they will boggle the mind.

8th inning **Score: 4-4**

4th at-bat **0 on 0 out**

Jackson leads-off the top of the 8th inning of a 4-4 ballgame by working reliever Jimmy Ring for his first walk of the Series (BB). After nine lackluster at-bats in a row, Joe now has had two straight quality trips to the plate. Next up, Happy Felsch fly's out (F-9) making out number one (with all of the sacrifice bunts Happy has laid down in this series, swinging away with Jackson on 1st and no outs of a tied game, in the 8th inning, doesn't make much sense). Chick Gandil also receives a free pass (BB) from Ring, moving Joe to 2nd base. Jackson is now the potential go ahead run at 2nd base with one out. Joe has his head shoved completely up his butt, when Swede Risberg's fly ball to CF Edd Roush was caught (F-8). Roush did make an incredible catch, but Joe took off for home and was easily doubled off 2nd base (DP F-8-4). If the ball would have dropped in Jackson could have crawled home, so what Joe was thinking of only he knows. The double play ends the inning still tied 4-4. Wait until Joe's next at-bat, it gets worse.

10th inning **Score: 4-4**

5th at-bat **1on 0out**

On now to extra inning, still tied 4-4 as the Sox come up to bat in the top of the 10th. Buck Weaver leads-off with a stinging double (2B) to left off of Jimmy Ring. With the go ahead run already in scoring position, Joe drags a bunt single (1B), between 3rd base and the pitcher moving Buck to 3rd. My question is this, why would Joe drop down a bunt knowing that Felsch, Gandil; and Risberg were coming up? If Joe was playing to win, which he always claimed, and knowing that three of the biggest conspirators were coming up to bat in order, why didn't he try to swing away and drive in Weaver himself? As it turned out Felsch did his part by striking out (K). It works out though, as Chick Gandil of all people, hits a soft liner that finds its way over 2B Morrie Rath's head into right-field (1B), scoring Weaver with the eventual winning run as Joe takes 2nd base. Then incredibly, Jackson manages to get himself doubled off 2nd base again. Swede Risberg next lines to SS Larry Kopf who flips the ball over to 2B Morrie Rath forcing Joe at 2nd base ending another inning with a double play (DP L 6-4). Are you kidding me? This is the at-bat that 100% made up my mind that Joe Jackson was as guilty as the other five (I was only 99% up to this play). I will only say five because I will never include Buck Weaver in with this group (also Fred McMullin, though taking $5,000, only had two plate appearances with one base hit, so he didn't have a chance to help throw any games).

Game Six Summary

Did that really happen?

Shoeless Joe Jackson's box score looked pretty good, 4-1-2-1. What it didn't mention was his horrific base running and a drag bunt single that boggles the mind. Joe's day started off 0 for two, running his hitless streak to ten at-bats, before he delivered his first clutch hit in twenty-two plate appearances, a much needed RBI single in the 6th inning. As you just read in the 8th and 10th innings, Joe did just about everything he could not to win this ball game. I say just about everything because I guess he could have struck out both times up, but that also would have saved him the embarrassment of getting doubled off 2nd base twice in three innings. What did Joe say to his team after the second time, especially in extra innings of a game they had to win to stay alive? What did he say to Dickie Kerr, a man who pitched his heart out for ten grueling innings (sorry, busher?)? What in the good name of Christ did manager Kid Gleason say to Joe? If something like this happened in a softball game, you would have wanted to kill the player, let alone in the 6th game of the World Series (a must win game at that!). All this doesn't include the bunt Jackson dropped down in the 8th inning with Weaver already on 2nd base and no outs. We're not talking about most of his teammates who were mired in slumps, and trying to get a man to 3rd base any way they could. We're talking about the great Joe Jackson, the third leading hitter in Major League history (.356), a man who would have hit .375 sleepwalking his way through this Series, yes he was that hot. You say .375 is an awesome average, well it is, but it is about half of what Joe probably should have hit if he had tried every at-bat in this Series. Joe was on fire in this World Series, and think about this, Babe Ruth in the 1928 World Series would bat .625, and Cincinnati Reds outfielder Billy Hatcher batted .750 in 1990. I believe Jackson could have matched or even done better in 1919. This game proved to me that Joe Jackson deserved his eventual fate.

Game Six Box		**Running Total**					
		AB	R	H	RBI	AVE	
1st AB	F-5	20	2	6	0	.300	1 LOB (10)
2nd AB	F-2	21	2	6	0	.286	
3rd AB	1B,RBI	22	3	7	1	.318	
4TH AB	BB	22	3	7	1	.318	BB(1)
5th AB	1B	23	3	8	1	.348	

Game Seven

RHP Eddie Cicotte (29-6 1.82) vs LHP Slim Sallee (21-7 2.05)

At Cincinnati, Oh **October 8th, 1919** **Redland Park**

Attendance-13,923

1st inning **Score: 0-0**

1st at-bat **1 on 2out**

After losing the ten inning thriller yesterday, the Reds still need only one more victory, holding four games to two lead. This game is huge for the Sox, and it is huge for Joe Jackson also. If he thought Chick Gandil and Swede Risberg wanted to kill him a year later, imagine what Kid Gleason and the few teammates who were trying to win, must have wanted to do to Joe after game six. Today Joe gets the Sox on the board in the 1st inning, with an RBI single

(1B) to left, to plate Shano Collins (who led off the game with a single (1B)). You just can't make this stuff up; Jackson gets caught between 1st and 2nd base on the throw home and only makes it back to 1st when 1B Jake Daubert drops the throw from C Ivy Wingo (E-3). If Joe had been out, it would have made three times in a row that he was picked off a base he had occupied. Kid Gleason just might have kicked Jackson right in the nuts (but I doubt it). Chicago would do no more scoring in the 1st.

3rd inning **Score: 1-0 Sox**

2nd at-bat **1on 2 out**

Leading the Reds 1-0, Joe gets another big two out RBI knock (1B), again driving home Shano Collins with another single to left-field. This extends the Sox lead to 2-0, and the way Cicotte is pitching today this might just be enough. Happy Felsch grounds to SS Larry Kopf, who forces Joe at 2nd base (FC 6-4), ending the 3rd inning.

5th inning **Score: 2-0 Sox**

3rd at-bat **2 on 1 out**

The Sox are still up 2-0 going into the top of the 5th inning, has Eddie Collins on 2nd base and Buck Weaver on at 1st with only one out, with the hot again Joe Jackson stepping up to the plate. Joe smacks a hard double play grounder right at 2B Morrie Rath, but Rath is not able to handle the ball and boots it (E-4) loading the bases. Happy Felsch next gets into the act by delivering a huge two RBI single to center-field (1B) putting Chicago up 4-0, Gandil and Risberg could do no more damage, ending the inning.

7th inning **Score: 4-1 Sox**

4th at-bat **0 on 1 out**

The Sox are holding onto a 4-1 lead going into the top of the 7th inning after the Reds scored a run off Cicotte in the bottom of the 6th. With one gone, Joe comes to the plate facing Reds relief specialist Dolph Luque (9-3 2.63), the big right-hander from Cuba. Luque gets Jackson to ground hard, again to 2B Morrie Rath. This time Morrie has no problems and throw Joe out (4-3) for the 2nd out. Chicago would not score again, but neither would the Reds and the Sox win 4-1. That's now two wins in a row for Chicago and also maybe a little vindication for Eddie Cicotte. The Series now shifts back to Chicago, with the Sox trailing only four games to three, and they are on a roll. Unfortunately this roll is going to be eaten by Lefty Williams.

Game Seven Summary

Making amends

This is a Series of streaks for Joe Jackson. Going hitless in game one, Joe then ripped off six hits in his next eight at-bats. Jackson then went ten at-bats without a base hit, and again got sizzling hot with four knocks in a row, including two big RBI singles in game seven. Joe could have had an even bigger game, when Morrie Rath booted his grounder with two men on base. A base hit there and Joe's game box would have been incredible. This victory in game seven, sets up the fateful eighth game of the 1919 World Series, and nothing would ever be the same again.

Game Seven Box		**Running Total**					
		AB	R	H	RBI	AVE	
1st AB	1B, RBI	24	3	9	2	.375	
2nd AB	1B, RBI	25	3	10	3	.400	
3rd AB	E-4	26	3	10	3	.385	2 LOB(12),1 RISP(7)
4TH AB	4-3	27	3	10	3	.370	

Game Eight

RHP Hod Eller (20-9 2.40) vs LHP Lefty Williams (23-11 2.64)

At Chicago, ILL **October 8th, 1919** **Comiskey Park**

Attendance-32,930

1st inning **Score: 4-0 Reds**

1st at-bat **2 on 1 out**

The infamous 1st inning of game eight, where the Reds had five runs almost given to them by Sox starting pitcher Lefty Williams (losing hurler of games two and five) in the top half. The runs may have been made up by the Sox in the bottom half of the 1st, if they could have produced a big hit. The White Sox had Reds starter Hod Eller, winning pitcher of game five, on the ropes, with Nemo Leibold on 3rd base and Eddie Collins on at2nd and only one out. Joe comes up again with runners in scoring position and less than two out, but Jackson can only manage a soft pop-up to SS Larry Kopf that he pockets (F-6) for the 2nd out. Happy Felsch then strikes-out (K), to end the 1st. There would be no making up the Reds four runs today.

3rd inning **Score: 5-0 Reds**

2nd at-bat **0 on 2 out**

Down 5-0 going into the bottom of the 3rd, Joe gives the shocked hometown fans something to cheer about, by cracking Eller's two out pitch deep into the right field bleachers (HR). This would be the only official home run of the Series (see Heinie Groh, 6th inning of game seven, in chapter one). Of course, it was a solo shot, and Chicago still trails 5-1. Happy Felsch again ended another inning with a grounder to SS Larry Kopf (6-3).

6th inning **Score: 9-1 Reds**

3rd at-bat **1 on 0 out**

What was going on in Chicago? With one run in the 5th; and three more in the 6th inning, the Reds have taken a 9-1 lead. Hod Eller has shown no signs of weakening, so the Sox were in really deep trouble. The White Sox did have four innings left in the game, and needed to get something started in a real big hurry. Buck Weaver did his part with a lead-off single (1B). Joe follows with a very deep drive to center-field off Eller, but CF Edd Roush catches up to the ball and hauls it in (F-8) for out number one. The Sox would not score in the 6th.

8th inning **Score: 10-1 Reds**

4th at-bat **2 on 1 out**

This ballgame is now a laugher. The Reds have scored again, with a run in the top of the 8th, to take a 10-1 lead, and now only needs to play out the strings to capture the flag. With the game all but over, Joe looks like he might get himself another home run in the bottom of the 8th , drilling Eller's fast ball all the way to the fence in right field for a two RBI double (2B), making the score 10-3. The Sox will score two more runs in the inning (the four run inning their best output of the Series), to move within five runs, 10-5.

9th inning **Score: 10-1 Reds**

5th at-bat **2 on 2 out**

The party is over for the Chicago White Sox. The Cincinnati Reds are Champions of the World of baseball, winning game eight 10-5, and taking the Series five games to three. The Sox have one more trip to the plate in the 9th, and have a small rally going, but Joe ends the game and the Series by grounding out to 2B Morrie Rath (4-3), with Eddie Murphy (not the comedian) on at 3rd base and Eddie Collins on at 2nd.

Game Eight Summary

A great Series?

The White Sox two games in a row run, was pretty much over in the first inning, when the Reds scored five runs off Lefty Williams in the top of the 1st , that pretty much sealed the fate of the Chicago White Sox (and eventually eight ballplayers). The 1919 World Series was over, with the Cincinnati Reds winning the championship 5 games to 3. Joe's two hits in the final game produced three runs, and Jackson hit the only Series home run that counted in the 3rd inning. Joe Jackson batted five times in the ballgame, and the only time he batted without a man on base, he hit the homer. He also had the two run double in the 6th; accounting for three of the Sox five runs in those two at-bats. So Joe drove in two of the seven runners he had on base in the game (he drove home himself once), meaning he left another five runners stranded on the bases, four in scoring position. Out of all of Joe's great stats in the Series, the one that most sticks out in my mind are the seventeen runners he left on base in the eight games, including the eleven he left in scoring position. As hot as Joe was in this World Series, it seems to me he sloughed off a little bit when he had the chance to do the most damage. Combined with his purely atrocious base running, added to his sub-par play in the field, and the case against Joe Jackson is closed. I find Joe guilty. Guilty of crimes against baseball. Punishable by spending the rest of his life, in the ordinary world.

Game Eight Box		**Running Total**					
		AB	R	H	RBI	AVE	
1st AB	F-6	28	3	10	3	.357	2 LOB(14), 2RISP(9)
2nd AB	HR,RBI	29	4	11	4	.379	HR(1)
3rd AB	F-8	30	4	11	4	.367	1 LOB(15)
4TH AB	2B, 2 RBI	31	5	12	6	.387	2B(3)
5th AB	4-3	32	5	12	6	.375	2 LOB(17),2RISP(11)

Chapter five

Oscar Emil Felsch

One of the boys.

Oscar Emil Felsch was born on August 22, 1891 in Milwaukee, Wisconsin. Nicknamed Happy by his father, it was said that Oscar was born with a smile on his face. Like Jethro Bodine of the *Beverly Hillbillies*, Happy only had a sixth grade education. Excelling in most things athletic, Happy was most happy on a baseball field. A fast runner with a shotgun for an arm, Felsch had a look-see with a Minor League team in Eau Claire, Wisconsin around 1911. In 1912 he made the Fond du Lac club, playing so well that he was moved up to the old Milwaukee Brewers of the American Association in 1913. As his hitting and fielding skills improved, Happy's contract was bought up by the Chicago White Sox and Felsch made his Major League debut on April 14, 1915 (fifty years to the day Abraham Lincoln was shot). Happy had a so-so rookie year with a .248 batting average in one hundred and twenty-one games, but showed some power at the plate with eighteen doubles, eleven triples and three home runs. In 1916, Felsch came into his own as a ball player, hitting an even .300 with seventy RBI's. For the World Champion White Sox in 1917, Happy had his finest year to date with a .308 average. That was good for fifth place in the American League, and he finished second to only Detroit's Bobby Veach's league leading one hundred and three RBI's, with one hundred and two. It should be noted that it was the first time a player from the Sox had ever gone over the one hundred RBI plateau. What a future the twenty-six year old Felsch had in front of him. It's no wonder why Happy was always smiling.

On account of World War I, Happy only played in fifty-three ballgames in 1918; instead taking a job with the Milwaukee Gas Company under the work or fight order from the U.S. Government (Secretary of War Newton Baker). With baseball only playing a one hundred and forty game schedule in 1919, because of the end of the war and the uncertainty of how baseball would fare, Happy played in one hundred and thirty-five games and hit a respectable .275

driving home eighty-six runs, plus his power numbers were on the rise again with thirty-two doubles and eleven triples to go along with his seven dingers. He along with Joe Jackson and company helped Chicago back into the World Series. This is the Series that would end the careers of eight players off the Sox roster, including one Happy Felsch, who looked to blossom fully in the live ball era of the 1920's. In 1920 Happy hit .338 to go along with fourteen homers and a career high one hundred and fifteen RBI's. Felsch also smacked forty doubles and fifteen three baggers for a total of sixty-nine long hits.

But it all came crashing down on September 27, 1920 when Happy and seven other teammates were first suspended by club owner Charles Comiskey after Cook County indictments were handed down for defrauding the public in the 1919 World Series. That led to a trial in 1921, in which all eight players were acquitted, though new commissioner Kenesaw Mountain Landis still banned for life the Chicago eight. What might have come from Happy Felsch in the following seasons, no one will ever know. Just coming into his own maturity at twenty-nine years old, Felsch was only going to get better and he was already very, very good. He was also not the brightest bulb in the chandelier, though his parents have to take the blame for that one. Like Joe Jackson their environments were not conducive for education, so his gullibility might be excused, because Happy always needed someone to follow, but Felsch's actions on the field for the throwing of these ball games during the 1919 World Series, cannot. I feel sorry for Happy, maybe not knowing any better than to just say no, for once just not being one of the boys, but I have no sympathy towards his eventual fate. We definitely reap what we sow.

Happy along with Swede Risberg and Joe Jackson sued the Chicago White Sox in 1924 for $1,120.00 for his 1920 salary, plus $100,000 in damages to his reputation and ability to earn a living. They dropped the damages claim as it was too hard to prove in court, but they did settle the back salary with Charles Comiskey. Felsch also played in outlaw leagues and other semi-pro games, but never appeared in Organized Baseball again. After his playing days were over Happy ran a tavern in Milwaukee for the rest of his working days. Happy claimed for the remaining years of his life that he didn't do anything to help throw these ballgames. That he would have he said, but the opportunity did not materialize. Well, Felsch had plenty of chances to chip in, and he took full advantage of them. They're sometimes hard to spot in the box scores, other times they were blatant, but when looked at close enough there they all are. Happy Felsch passed away from liver disease, no doubt from many years of hard drinking, five days before his seventy -third birthday, August 17, 1964 in his hometown of Milwaukee.

Game One

RHP Eddie Cicotte (29-7 1.82) vs LHP Dutch Ruether (19-6 1.81)

At Cincinnati, Oh **October 1st, 1919** **Redland Field**

Attendance-30,511

2nd inning **Score: 1-0 Reds**

1st at-bat **1 on 0 out**

Already finding themselves down 1-0 to Dutch Ruether and the Cincinnati Reds going into the top of the 2nd inning, the Chicago White Sox were looking to quite the large Redland Park crowd. Joe Jackson leads-off the inning reaching 2nd base via SS Larry Kopf's throwing error (E-6). Happy Felsch, a right-handed hitting batter with a .275 season average, next steps into the batter's box for the first time in the Series. Happy lays down a beautiful sacrifice bunt, moving Jackson to 3rd base (Sac 1-3). Chick Gandil brings Joe home with an RBI single (1B), tying the score 1-1.

4th inning **Score: 1-1**

2nd at-bat **0 on 2 out**

With the score still tied 1-1, the game moves to the top of the 4th inning, with Cicotte and Ruether pitching like the aces they are. With two out and the bases empty, Happy, batting for the 2nd time, ends the inning by bouncing out to SS Larry Kopf (6-3).

6th inning **Score: 6-1 Reds**

3rd at-bat **2 on 2 out**

The Sox ace Eddie Cicotte got beat with a full house in the bottom of the 4th, as Cincinnati put up five runs to knock Eddie out cold and go up 6-1. Ruether though kept the White Sox in check, pitching out of a jam in the top of the 6th. The Sox have runners on 2nd and 3rd base with two out, when Happy comes to the plate with a chance to get a really big hit. Big hits for Happy Felsch in this Series will be few and far between though. Happy fly's out to RF Greasy Neale (F-9) in short right-field, ending the inning.

9th inning **Score: 9-1 Reds**

4th at-bat **0 on 1 out**

Chicago was completely stifled by Dutch Ruether today and is losing 9-1, going into the top of the 9th. The Sox do have one more at-bat to at least get back some respectability, but that was not going to happen this afternoon. Happy comes to the plate for the 4th time today with the bases clear and one out, and Ruether gets Felsch to fly out to CF Edd Roush (F-8) for the second out. Ruether retires the side in order, to take the opener.

Game One Summary

The beginning of the end.

In today's 9-1 loss to Dutch Ruether and the Cincinnati Reds, Happy drew a 0 for three, with a sacrifice bunt. In his third at-bat in the 6th inning with two runners in scoring position and two out, Felsch hit a lazy fly ball to right-field. This started a pattern with runners on base that would shake a better man. Like most of his teammates, Happy will start the Series in a slump, and stay there for quite a while.

Game One Box **Running Total**

		AB	R	H	RBI	AVE	
1st AB	Sac 1-3	0	0	0	0	.000	Sac (1)
2nd AB	6-3	1	0	0	0	.000	
3rd AB	F-9	2	0	0	0	.000	2 LOB(2) 2 RISP(2)
4th AB	F-8	3	0	0	0	.000	

Game Two

LHP Lefty Williams (23-11 2.64) vs LHP Slim Sallee (21-7 2.05)

At Cincinnati, Oh **October 2nd, 1919** **Redland Field**

Attendance-29,698

1st inning **Score: 0-0**

2nd at-bat **1 on 0 out**

After taking a 9-1 beating by the Cincinnati Reds in the Series opener, Chicago is looking to bounce back in game two. Scoreless after one inning, Joe Jackson gets the ball rolling off Reds 6'3" left-hander Slim Sallee, in the top of the 2nd with a solid double (2B) to center-field. Happy follows Joe by laying down a sacrifice bunt, moving Jackson over to 3rd base (Sac 1-3). Sallee takes care of Chick Gandil and Swede Risberg to strand Joe at 3rd base however.

4th inning **Score: 0-0**

2nd at-bat **2 on 0 out**

Buck Weaver and Joe Jackson give Chicago a great start to the top of the 4th inning with lead-off singles (1B) off Slim Sallee. Happy then comes to the plate and drops down his second sacrifice bunt (SAC 1-3) of the ballgame (and 3rd of the young Series), moving both runners into scoring position. Sallee again retires Gandil and Risberg without a run being scored, keeping the game scoreless.

6th inning **Score: 3-0 Reds**

3rd at-bat **1 on 2 out**

The Sox find themselves down 3-0 going into the top of the 6th, after Lefty Williams couldn't find the strike zone in the 4th inning and the Reds scored three times. Missing out on two great scoring chances off Slim Sallee in the 2nd and 4th innings, Chicago has another good chance in the 6th. With Buck Weaver on 3rd base and two down, Happy has his first opportunity to swing away in three at-bats. Felsch plows into one and sails a long drive to center-field, but Reds CF Edd Roush makes a fantastic one-handed catch (F-8) to end the inning.

8th inning **Score: 4-2 Reds**

4th at-bat **1 on 2 out**

Cincinnati holds a 4-2 lead going to the top of the 8th inning; with the Reds Slim Sallee pitching himself in and out of trouble all day. Excluding the 4th inning, the Sox Lefty Williams isn't pitching too badly either. For the 2nd time in the ballgame, Happy has a chance to drive home a runner in scoring position with two out. And for the second time, Felsch fails to do so, grounding out to 3B Heinie Groh (5-3) after Groh knocks Happy's line shot down, then picks the ball up and fires over to 1B Jake Daubert. Sallee holds the Sox in the 9th and the Reds win game two, sweeping both games in Cincinnati. The Reds are now up two games to nothing, as the Series shifts to Windy City for the next three contests.

Game Two Summary

Getting the bunts down.

Today's game was much closer and a little more exciting, but the Reds still took a 4-2 victory from the Sox. Chicago had Slim Sallee on the ropes several times throughout the ballgame, but only scored two unearned runs on a two error play in the 7th inning. Happy had a decent day at the plate, although he had no hits. Felsch had two sacrifice bunts, a deep fly out and a line drive to 3rd that turned into a ground out. Happy also stranded two more runners in scoring position though, and has left someone on base in three of his five official at-bats so far in the Series.

Game Two Box **Running Total**

		AB	R	H	RBI	AVE	
1st AB	Sac 1-3	3	0	0	0	.000	Sac (2)
2nd AB	Sac 1-3	3	0	0	0	.000	Sac (3)
3rd AB	F-8	4	0	0	0	.000	1 LOB(3) 1 RISP(3)
4th AB	5-3	5	0	0	0	.000	1LOB(4) 1 RISP(4)

Game Three

RHP Ray Fisher (14-5 2.17) vs RHP Dickie Kerr (13-8 2.89)

At Chicago, ILL **October 3rd, 1919** **Comiskey Park**

Attendance-29,126

1st inning **Score: 0-0**

2nd at-bat **1 on 0 out**

Joe Jackson led-off the bottom of the 2nd inning off Reds starter Ray Fisher with a single (1B) to left-field. Happy Felsch next supposedly swings away and taps back to Fisher, who in turn throws the ball into center-field (E-1), trying to nail Joe at 2nd base, allowing Jackson to 3rd base and Felsch to reach 2nd. I say supposedly because every time Happy has come to bat so far in the Series, with a runner on base and less than two out, he has sacrificed (no sacrifice was given to Happy on this at-bat, though I really think it was). Chick Gandil drives both in with a two RBI single (1B) giving Chicago and Dickie Kerr the lead 2-0, the Sox first lead of the World Series. After losing the first two games in Cincinnati, for the first time the Sox faithful have something to cheer about.

3rd inning **Score: 2-0 Sox**

2nd at-bat **2on 1out**

The big inning that has eluded Chicago for the first two games, seems to be on the horizon in the bottom of the 3rd. Eddie Collins and Buck Weaver open the inning by reaching base with lead-off singles (1B). Shoeless Joe then tries to lay down a sacrifice bunt, even though he has four hits in his last five at-bats, and pops-up to 1B Jake Daubert (F-3). Explain that one. With one out, Happy comes to bat still searching for his first base hit, and now would be a great time to do it. Felsch instead pulls a two hopper right at 3B Heinie Groh, who starts a (DP 5-4-3) double play, ending the inning.

6th inning **Score: 3-0 Sox**

3rd at-bat **0 on 1out**

Happy steps up to bat in the bottom of the 6th inning with one out and the bases empty, and works Ray Fisher for a walk (BB). Reds catcher Bill Rariden, who threw out Joe Jackson trying to steal (CS 2-6) a batter earlier, also nabs Happy attempting some thievery (CS 2-4), this time with 2B Morrie Rath applying the tag. Fisher and reliever Dolph Luque (9-3 2.63), who pitched the

9th inning, held Chicago the rest of the way. But the Sox didn't need any more runs, because Dickie Kerr threw a three-hit shutout, and the Sox won their first ballgame 3-0. The Reds now lead only two games to one, and Chicago fans are convinced that Cincinnati won't win another. That confidence will last one day.

Game Three Summary

You can't bunt everytime.

It was a huge win for the Sox and rookie Dickie Kerr, who three-hit the Reds in a 3-0 shutout victory. Happy scored a run today, but his hitless streak reached eleven at-bats, but includes three sacrifice bunts and a walk. There was a play involving Happy's first at-bat in the bottom of the 2nd inning that just doesn't sit right with me, and I'll tell you why. With Joe Jackson on 1st base and no outs, Happy reaches 2nd base and Joe 3rd, when P Ray Fisher threw the ball into Center-field, trying to force Jackson at 2nd on a ball Felsch tapper back to the box. Simple enough but the thing is, Happy has sacrificed every time he was up so far in the Series, with a runner on base and no outs. In a 0-0 ballgame and Jackson on 1st, you would think Kid Gleason would have had Happy bunt again. Plus the fact that the ball was hit back to Fisher makes me believe this was a bunt, and should have been scored Sac E-1. Especially since Jackson was a very fast runner and forcing him at 2nd base on a bunt would be extremely difficult, but no sacrifice was recorded in the official box score. This is just my opinion and 90+ years later there is no way I can prove it. The Chicago Tribune of October 4, 1919, only mentions Reds manager Pat Moran talking about Ray Fisher throwing the ball into center-field on the play and no other specifics. Anyway, Chick Gandil singled both runners home and gave Kerr all the runs he would need today.

Game Three Box **Running Total**

		AB	R	H	RBI	AVE	
1st AB	E-1, Run	6	1	0	0	.000	1 LOB (5)
2nd AB	5-4-3 DP	7	1	0	0	.000	2 LOB(7) 1 RISP(5)
3rd AB	BB, CS	7	1	0	0	.000	BB(1) CS(1)

Game Four

RHP Jimmy Ring (10-9 2.26) vs RHP Eddie Cicotte (29-7 1.82)

At Chicago, ILL **October 4th, 1919** **Comiskey Park**

Attendance-34,363

2nd inning **Score: 0-0**

1st at-bat **1 on 0 out**

Looking to tie up the Series at two games apiece, the Chicago White Sox sends opening game losing pitcher Eddie Cicotte; back out to the mound to try and redeem himself. Cincinnati counters with right-hander Jimmy Ring, as 5,000 more newly excited Chicago land patrons, turn out to Comiskey Park today than yesterday. Joe Jackson started off the bottom of the 2nd inning of a 0-0 game with a gift double (2B), courtesy of CF Edd Roush, who lost sight of the ball in the high sun. Happy then moves Joe over to 3rd base, with his 4th sacrifice bunt of the Series (Sac 1-3). This makes a better case for yesterday's scoring on Happy's comebacker. Enough about that though, Gandil and Risberg again would leave Jackson stranded to end the inning.

3rd inning **Score: 0-0**

2nd at-bat **2 on 2 out**

The Sox have the Reds Jimmy Ring on the ropes again in the 3rd inning, with runners on the corners and two out. Ring pitches out of the jam though, as Happy cannot produce the big hit the Sox need by grounding out to 3B Heinie Groh (5-3). Getting a clutch hit in this Series for the White Sox was not a popular thing to do.

6th inning **Score: 2-0 Reds**

3rd at-bat **0 on 0 out**

Happy Felsch is still looking for his first base hit of the Series, and Chicago was looking for some runs going into the bottom of the 6th inning. Cincinnati has taken a 2-0 lead on two Eddie Cicotte errors in the top of the 5th. Happy, batting with one out in the home half of the 6th, will have no change in his fortunes. Felsch raps a high towering fly ball to deep left-field that LF Pat Duncan gloves (F-7), near the wall for the second out. After Chick Gandil singles (1B), Jimmy Ring then retires Swede Risberg, to end the inning.

8th inning **Score: 2-0 Reds**

4th at-bat **0 on 2 out**

The Sox are now in danger of going down three games to one, and the Reds Jimmy Ring, after getting himself out of trouble in the 2nd and 3rd innings, has settled into a groove. Still trailing 2-0 in the bottom of the 8th, the Sox hopefuls were praying for the rally that will not come today. Batting with two outs and the bases clear of any baseball players wearing white socks, Happy delivers his first hit of the World Series. Felsch's single (1B) to left-field was only the third hit on the day for Chicago. Ring would not give up anything but a Ray Schalk walk (BB) in the 9th, and the Reds have their 2-0 defeat of the White Sox.

Game Four Summary

A base hit for Happy.

Happy made his first hit of the 1919 World Series today, one of only three Reds pitcher Jimmy Ring would give up today. Had Chicago gotten one or two more in the 2nd or 3rd innings, the outcome of today's game may have been different. Happy also made his fourth sacrifice bunt in as many games helping to produce a run, and almost knocked one out of the park. But he did have a huge at-bat in the 3rd inning where a base hit might have changed today's outcome, when he stranded runners on the corners with two out.

Game Four Box		**Running Total**					
		AB	R	H	RBI	AVE	
1st AB	Sac 1-3	7	1	0	0	.000	Sac (4)
2nd AB	5-3	8	1	0	0	.000	2 LOB(9) 1 RISP(6)
3rd AB	F-7	9	1	0	0	.000	
4th AB	1B	10	1	1	0	.100	

Game Five

RHP Hod Eller (20-9 2.40) vs LHP Lefty Williams (23-11 2.64)

At Chicago, ILL **October 6th, 1919** **Comiskey Park**

Attendance-34,379

1st inning **Score: 0-0**

1st at-bat **2 on 2out**

Another huge crowd turns up for this afternoon's game, wanting the Sox to take two of the three contests from the Reds at Comiskey Park. After Lefty holds the Reds in the top of the 1st inning, the Sox look like they are going to get to Eller early in their home half. The Sox have runners on the corners and two out, but Happy doesn't much feel like hitting with runners on base in this Series. Eller entices Felsch to pop-up to LF Pat Duncan (F-7), ending what turns out to be Chicago's only chance today to score off Hod Eller.

4th inning **Score: 0-0**

2nd at-bat **0 on 2 out**

Hod Eller was untouchable from the 2nd through the 4th innings, striking out seven White Sox including six in a row. When he strikes-out Happy (K) to end the 4th, not only were the last three innings perfect, Eller had a hand in getting all nine outs by himself (this includes two comebackers to start the 4th). Lefty Williams is also pitching well in a fantastic 0-0 pitcher dual.

7th inning **Score: 4-0 Reds**

3rd at-bat **0 on 1out**

Lefty Williams has a problem with big innings in this Series, and in the 6th Cincinnati roughed him up for four runs, taking a 4-0 lead. The Chicago White Sox were not only looking at a four games to one deficit, but their two star pitchers has lost all four games. Happy bats in the bottom of the 7th with one out and nobody on base, and hits a high pop-up behind home plate that Reds catcher Bill Rariden circles under and makes the grab (FO-2) for the 2nd out. Except for Buck Weaver's triple (3B) in the 9th, Eller has no problems the rest of the way and three-hits the Sox, the second Reds pitcher to do so in as many days. The Reds also picked up another run in the 9th off reliever Erskine Mayer (1-3 8.25), making the final score 5-0 Cincinnati.

Game Five Summary

A bad slump.

Game five was a big game and a big loss for the White Sox. Shut-out on three hits for the second game in a row, this time by Hod Eller, the Sox are now in a four games to one hole after the 5-0 defeat. Happy did no worse than anybody else did today, with the exception of Buck Weaver who got two of the Sox three hits. Then again if your ambition is to lose, and this proved to be the case, the White Sox were exceeding their goals. So what got into the White Sox in the next two games? When they showed the baseball world what kind of team they really were, when they were really trying to win. Well, most of them anyway.

Game Five Box				**Running Total**			
		AB	R	H	RBI	AVE	
1st AB	F-7	11	1	1	0	.091	2 LOB(11) 1 RISP(7)
2nd AB	K	12	1	1	0	.083	
3rd AB	FO-2	13	1	1	0	.077	

Game Six

RHP Dickie Kerr (13-8 2.89) vs LHP Dutch Ruether (19-6 1.81)

At Cincinnati, Oh **October 7th, 1919** **Redland Field**

Attendance-32,006

2nd inning **Score: 0-0**

1st at-bat **0 on 0 out**

Prior to the start of the game, manager Gleason has made a change to the line-up. He didn't bench any regular players, but what he did was move Happy to right-field and inserted Shano Collins in center, not very pleased with Felsch's fielding problems I guess. Back to the game, Ruether and Kerr held up their ends of the bargain in the 1st inning, and Happy Felsch leads–off the top of the 2nd for Chicago. Happy lays into Reuther's pitch and drills a deep fly ball to right that RF Greasy Neale races back on and catches near the wall (F-9). Ruether then sets down the dynamic duo Gandil and Risberg to retire he side.

4th inning **Score: 2-0 Reds**

2nd at-bat **0 on 0 2 out**

The Reds take the early lead with two runs off Dickie Kerr in the bottom of the 3rd. Ruether gets two quick outs in the bottom of the 4th, before Happy smashes a single (1B) into center-field (his 2nd hit of the Series). Chick Gandil then grounds out to SS Larry Kopf (6-3) ending the inning.

6th inning **Score: 4-1 Reds**

3rd at-bat **1on 0 out**

The big inning Chicago had been waiting for finally arrives in the bottom of the 6th inning of game six. Buck Weaver started the rally with a bloop double (2B) to short left-field. Joe Jackson next gets the Sox within two runs with an RBI single (1B) to center. As Hall of Fame shortstop and Yankee broadcaster Phil Rizzuto would have said, "holy cow," after Happy Felsch makes his 2nd hit in a row, with an RBI double (2B) to left-center field, scoring Jackson from 1st base (one of the few times a Sox base runner would take an extra base) making the score 4-3 Cincinnati. That blow knocks Dutch Ruether out of the ball game, as Reds manager Pat Moran makes only his second pitching change of the Series, bringing in right-hander and game four winning pitcher Jimmy Ring (10-9 2.26). Still with no outs, Ring very quickly retires old unreliables Chick Gandil and Swede Risberg, with Risberg's ground out moving Happy over to 3rd base. Now with two down, Ray Schalk cracks his biggest hit of the Series by driving home Felsch with an RBI single (1B) into left-field tying up the score at 4-4. The score would remain tied until the dramatic 10th inning.

8th inning **Score: 4-4**

4th at-bat **1on 0 out**

Joe Jackson is on 1st base after a lead-off walk (BB) when Happy steps up to bat in a 4-4 ballgame. Felsch lifts a soft fly ball to RF Greasy Neale (F-9) for the 1st out. Ring will hold the Sox, as would Dickie Kerr in the 8th and 9th innings and the game moves into extra dips. A side note, Gleason has moved Felsch back to Center-field and Shano Collins to right, why has not been established.

6th inning **Score: 4-1 Reds**

3rd at-bat **1on 0 out**

During the 1919 regular season Happy Felsch put the ball into play 93% of the time, striking out only thirty-five times in five hundred and two official at-bats. In the biggest at-bat of his short career, Happy did what he got paid to do. No not to win games on his meager salary of $4,000 a year, but to lose them for the $5,000 he was paid for his part in the fix, he strikes-out (K). With Buck Weaver on 3rd base and Joe Jackson on at 1st, Happy walks up to bat with a chance to put Chicago on top in the do-or-die ballgame. Jimmy Ring was hardly a strikeout pitcher either, striking out only sixty-one batters in one hundred and five innings pitched. Now I know anybody can have a bad at-bat and strike out, but I also know when a guy tanks one. Like Happy did in this situation. Unbelievably, Chick Gandil wins another Dickie Kerr start, driving home Buck Weaver with the go ahead run with an RBI single (1B) to right -field. Dickie Kerr held Cincinnati in the bottom of the inning and the Sox win game six, 5-4. Tomorrow will come after all.

Game Six Summary

Breaking out, sort off.

As the Series shifted back to Cincinnati, Happy's fortunes shifted too. For the good, though not all of it, and it only took six games. Felsch's two hits helped the Sox win game six, that and an incredible pitching performance by

Dickie Kerr. Instead of benching Happy, manager Kid Gleason started Felsch out in right-field moving Shano Collins to center because of Happy's poor defense. Gleason in the late innings, I'm not sure when, moved Happy back to center-field for, get this- defensive purposes. Happy had a single in the 4th and then a big RBI double in the Sox three run 6th inning, Felsch's first RBI of the Series. In the 10th, when Happy had a chance to put the Sox in front for the first time in the ballgame, with runners on the corners and no outs, he struck out. If you didn't take the good with the bad from Happy in this Series, you would have got nothing at all from him.

Game Six Box		**Running Total**					
		AB	R	H	RBI	AVE	
1st AB	F-9	14	1	1	0	.071	
2nd AB	1B	15	1	2	0	.133	
3rd AB	2B, Run	16	2	3	1	.188	2B(1)
4th AB	F-9	17	2	3	1	.176	1 LOB(12)
5th AB	K	18	2	3	1	.167	2 LOB(14) 1 RISP(8)

Game Seven

RHP Eddie Cicotte (29-7 1.82) vs LHP Slim Sallee (21-7 2.05)

At Cincinnati, Oh **October 8th, 1919** **Redland Field**

Attendance-13,923

1st inning **Score: 1-0 Sox**

1st at-bat **1 on 0 out**

The White Sox victory in game six, thanks in large part to Dickie Kerr's courageous pitching stayed off elimination for a least one more game. The Sox jumped right out the gate with their first earned run off Sallee (he gave up just two unearned runs in game two), when Joe Jackson knocked in Shano Collins from 2nd base with a two out RBI single (1B) to left-field. It was Chicago's first run in the 1st inning in the Series. Happy follows with a perfect drag bunt down the 3rd base line; the base hit (1B) moves Joe to 2nd base. Chick Gandil, after his game winning hit yesterday, was in no mood for more heroics today, as he grounds to SS Larry Kopf, who flips the ball to 2B Morrie Rath forcing Happy at 2nd base (FC 6-4) to end the inning.

3rd inning **Score: 2-0 Sox**

2nd at-bat **1 on 2 out**

Two and a half innings into game seven the Sox behind Eddie Cicotte, take a 2-0 lead with another run in the top of the 3rd inning, when Joe Jackson singled (1B) in Shano Collins for the second time in two at-bats. Happy then forces Joe at 2nd base when his grounder is scooped up by SS Larry Kopf (FC 6-4), who in turn tosses to 2B Morrie Rath ending the 3rd. Cicotte now has a two run cushion and was pitching like his reputation depended on it.

5th inning **Score: 2-0 Sox**

3rd at-bat **3 on 1out**

As the game moves into the middle innings, Chicago is clinging to a 2-0 lead, when they finally get to Slim Sallee. Happy hops up to bat with the bases drunk (loaded) and one out and makes his biggest hit (probably the last big hit of his career) of the Series, with a two run single (1B) into center field scoring Eddie Collins and Buck Weaver making the score 4-0 Chicago. The base hit also KO's Slim Sallee from the game. The Reds bring in to relieve game three losing pitcher right-hander Ray Fisher (14-5 2.17), and Fisher retires (you guessed it) Chick Gandil and Swede Risberg with no further damage.

7th inning **Score: 4-1 Sox**

4th at-bat **0 on 2 out**

Eddie Cicotte and the Chicago White Sox would not be denied today. The Reds had scored a single run in the bottom of the 6th inning, but that was all Cicotte would bend. The Sox were holding onto a 4-1 lead going to the 7th inning, with the "Pride of Havana," righty Dolph Luque (9-3 2.63) now pitching for the Reds. It was a good thing too that the Sox held a lead, because they could not hit Luque with a snow shovel. With two out and the bases empty, Luque whiffs Happy (K) to end the Top of the 7th. Cicotte would not be touched upon again this afternoon, and Chicago wins by a score of 4-1. Sweeping the Reds in Cincinnati brings the Sox within a game, four to three, and also sends the Series back to Chicago and a prelim to Al Capone's St. Valentine's Day massacre.

Game Seven Summary

Above the Mendoza line.

Happy Felsch had two more hits today in Eddie Cicotte's 4-1 victory over the Cincinnati Reds. The Sox are now within a game at four games to three, as the Series moves back to Chicago for game eight and possibly a ninth and final game, and the miracle all of the Southland has been praying for. Happy batted well again today with a 1st inning single, and in the 5th with the Sox already up 2-0 made his biggest hit of the Series, a two run single that ended Reds starter Slim Sallee's day. Even Happy's second strikeout of the Series could not overshadow Felsch's huge game. Happy's four hits in the last two games has raised his batting average from a very poor .071, one-hundred and fifty-six points to just a crappy .227.

Game Seven Box		Running Total					
		AB	R	H	RBI	AVE	
1st AB	1B	19	2	4	1	.211	
2nd AB	FC 6-4	20	2	4	1	.200	1 LOB(15)
3rd AB	1B, 2 RBI	21	2	5	3	.238	
4th AB	K	22	2	5	3	.227	K(2)

Game Eight

RHP Hod Eller (20-9 2.40) vs LHP Lefty Williams (23-11 2.64)

At Chicago, ILL **October 9th, 1919** **Comiskey Park**

Attendance-32,939

1st inning **Score: 4-0 Reds**

1st at-bat **2 on 2 out**

Even though Lefty Williams single handedly gave Cincinnati a 4-0 lead in the top of the 1st inning, Chicago had a real chance to get back into the game in the bottom half. No one expected the Series to return to Chicago, but the Sox swiped both games in Cincinnati. The Sox already had their hands full, facing big Hod Eller of the Reds, who pitch a three-hit shutout in game four. But Sox starter Lefty Williams, losing pitcher in both games two and five, didn't much feel like pitching today. After the Reds received the 1st inning gift, courtesy of Williams, the Sox got going in a hurry in the home half. A lead-off single by Nemo Leibold and a happy birthday double (2B) off of LF Pat Duncan's glove by Eddie Collins, and the Sox had runners on 2nd and 3rd base with no outs. But that's when Hod Eller bared down and retired in succession Buck Weaver on a called looking strikeout (K), Joe Jackson on a weak pop-up to SS

Larry Kopf (F-6), and our Happy Felsch who strikes-out again (K), to end what could have been a big inning.

3rd inning **Score: 5-1 Reds**

2nd at-bat **0 on 2 out**

After pitching eleven scoreless innings against Chicago, Hod Eller finally gives up a run, but only one, when Joe Jackson hit the only official homer (HR) of the Series with two out and the bases empty in the bottom of the 2nd inning. Happy bounces out to end the frame to SS Larry Kopf (6-3).

6th inning **Score: 9-1 Reds**

3rd at-bat **1 on 1 out**

The Reds were taking no prisoners today. Scoring one run in the 5th inning and three more in the 6th, Cincinnati took a 9-1 lead and were only twelve outs from the World Championship, going into the bottom of the 6th. After Buck Weaver led-off with a single (1B) to right-field, Eller sets down the next three batters, with Happy making the second out, flying out to CF Edd Rosh (F-8).

7th inning **Score: 4-1 Sox**

4th at-bat **0 on 2 out**

The Chicago White Sox biggest inning of the entire 1919 World Series came too little too late. In the bottom of the 8th inning, the Sox would score four runs off Hod Eller, what they needed was a nine run inning. A nine run inning and a Chicago White Sox World Championship was pure fantasy, as far as the Cincinnati Reds were concerned. After Joe Jackson doubled (2B) in Eddie Collins and Buck Weaver, Happy Felsch hit a high pop-up to 1B Jake Daubert (F-3) for out number two. The Sox scored two more runs in the 8th, but Eller did finally pitch out of the inning and after that it was all pretty much all over but the crying. Hod Eller pitched a scoreless 9th, and the 1919 World Series was over.

Game Eight Summary

Boo!

The Chicago White Sox needed a miracle, but the only miracle today was that the Reds didn't score more runs in the 1st inning, thanks to Lefty Williams. The Reds wrapped up the World Series with a 10-5 victory, which was worse than the score indicated. The Reds were winning 10-1 behind Hod Eller, before the Sox scored four runs in the bottom of the 8th. Happy's hitting streak ended just when the Sox needed him the most. His biggest at-bat came right in the 1st inning. After the Reds took a 4-0 lead in the top of the 1st, the Sox were rallying in the bottom half with runners on 2nd and 3rd base. Happy again managed to strikeout in a big scoring situation, his third strikeout in the eight ballgames, this from a man who only struck out thirty-five times in the regular season. Happy also left a runner on base in the 6th inning and another on in scoring position in the 8th. The four runners he left on base in today's game, made an astonishing total of nineteen runners left on base in the eight World Series games, including eleven runners in scoring position. That's just pitiful. So in conclusion, when Happy claimed years later that he didn't get a chance to help throw any ballgames, that the situations just never arose, - he lied.

Game Eight Box **Running Total**

		AB	R	H	RBI	AVE	
							K(3), 2 LOB(17)
1st AB	K	23	2	5	3	.217	2 RISP(10)
2nd AB	6-3	24	2	5	3	.208	1 LOB(18)
3rd AB	F-8	25	2	5	3	.200	
4th AB	F-3	26	2	5	3	.192	1 LOB(19) 1 RISP(11)

Chapter Six

John Francis Collins

I can hit righty's Kid.

John Francis Collins was born December 4, 1885 in Charlestown, Massachusetts. John was given the unusual nickname Shano by teammates, the Shano coming from wordplay on the Gallic name Sean. Shano's journey to the Major Leagues is obscured by time, but he broke into the big time with the Chicago White Sox at the age of twenty-four. Shano's debut with the Sox was on April 21, 1910, and appearing in ninety-seven ballgames. His rookie season was not one to write home about, batting just .197 and making nineteen errors playing mostly in the outfield. Collins rebounded in 1911, with a fine sophomore year. Shano batted .262 and drove in forty-eight runs out of the lead-off spot, playing at the 1st base position. 1912 saw Shano moving back to right-field and becoming a full time regular for the first time. Playing in one hundred and fifty- three games, Shano hit a healthy .292 with eighty-one RBI's. He also scored seventy-five runs while belting out thirty-four doubles, and ten triples. Shano followed up in 1913 with a rather poor season, in which his hitting fell off to a .239 clip in one hundred and forty-eight games. Playing in every ballgame in 1914 (154), Shano batted a solid .274 with thirty-four doubles and thirty stolen bases. By the time the 1915 season rolled around, Shano was reaching his physical prime at twenty-nine years old. Standing 6' tall and weighing 185 lbs, Collins was a right- handed hitter and thrower. Shano was also a dependable outfielder with a strong throwing arm that wrung up a lot of base runners. In 1915 Shano batted a respectable .257, and he also drove in a career high eighty-five runs, good for fourth best in the American League. Collins also swiped a career high thirty-eight bases, and recorded thirteen assists from left-field. Shano only missed one game for manager Pants Rowland playing in one hundred and fifty-three. Shano's batting average plunged again in 1916, falling to .243, and then Collins dropped even further in the Sox Championship season of 1917, when he lost his starting job as his average fell to .234 in eighty-two games. In the World War I shortened 1918 season, Shano's average climbed back up to .274, and he became a regular again, with most of his teammates leaving the team to work in what the

Department of War deemed a productive job, which baseball was not considered.

With everyone back in 1919, Shano became a substitute again, and he filled in well with a .279 average. The Sox won the American League Pennant and were at first overwhelming favorites over the Cincinnati Reds in the World Series. Sox manager Kid Gleason decided to play Shano in right-field against the Reds left-handed pitchers and Nemo Leibold, who batted left-handed, against the right-handed throwers. This platoon never really worked out for the Sox, until Shano got red hot in game seven, knocking out three hits. Kid in his ultimate wisdom, sat Shano down for the must win eighth game. Shano batted .250 in the Series with a double, and the Reds won the World Championship five games to three. The 1919 World Series would eventually prove that some of the White Sox players dumped the Series for money. Shano Collins was not one of those players.

1920 was Shano's last season in Chicago, and it was a good year for Collins (though not for eight of his teammates). Shano was moved to 1st base when Chick Gandil ran off to California with his loot, and Shano batted a career high .303 playing in one hundred and thirty-three ball games. Before the start of the 1921 season, Shano along with Nemo Leibold, were traded to the Boston Red Sox in exchange for future Hall of Famer (1971) Harry Hooper. Boston was a great change for Shano, and he stepped right into the Red Sox starting line-up. Playing in one hundred and forty-one games in right-field, Collins batted at a .286 clip, with twenty-nine doubles, twelve triples to go along with four dingers. Shano batted .271 in 1922 at the age of thirty-six, then slipped to .231 in 1923 becoming a utility outfielder and pinch hitter. 1924 would be Shano's last full season in the Majors, playing in eighty-eight games and batting .292. In 1925 Shano appeared in only two games, he slapped his last base hit, then retired as an active player after sixteen years.

Shano then coached for a few years with the Red Sox, and then managed Minor League teams in Des Moines and Pittsfield. Shano became the field boss of the Reds Sox in 1931, taking over for Heinie Wagner. Shano could not turn Boston around and he himself was fired after only fifty-five games in 1932, being replaced by Marty McManus. Shano in his retirement could tell his grand children (one being Bob Gallagher, a Major League outfielder in the early

1970's), that he was a steady ball player back in the day, and that he also held the Major League record for most bases loaded triples with eight. John Francis "Shano" Collins died on September 10, 1955 in his New England home in Newton, Massachusetts, at the age of sixty-nine. Here are Shano's four 1919 World Series ballgames

Game One

RHP Eddie Cicotte (29-7 1.82) vs LHP Dutch Ruether (19-6 1.81)

At Cincinnati, Oh **October 1st, 1919** **Redland Field**

Attendance-30,511

1st inning **Score: 0-0**

1st at-bat **0 on 0 out**

Home plate umpire Charles Rigler yells play-ball, and the right-handed hitting John "Shano" Collins steps into the batter's box. After taking a few pitches, Shano lines a single (1B) up the middle and the Sox are in business. Next up for the Sox is Eddie Collins, but Collins puts down a sacrifice attempt that is right back to Ruether (FC 1-6) who turns and fires to SS Larry Kopf, to force Shano at 2nd base. Ruether then retires the Sox with no damage in the 1st inning.

3rd inning **Score: 1-1**

2nd at-bat **0 on 1out**

With the score tied at 1-1, the Sox come to bat in the top of the 3rd inning. Shano steps up to the plate to face Ruether for the second time with one out and the bases empty. Collins lifts a fly ball out to CF Edd Roush (F-8), for the second out. Chicago would not score as the game heads to the bottom half.

6th inning **Score: 6-1 Reds**

3rd at-bat **0 on 0out**

The Reds pounded Eddie Cicotte out of the ballgame, scoring five runs in the bottom of the 4th inning to take a 6-1 lead. Shano leads-off the top of the 6th inning with a high fly into left center-field that CF Edd Roush glides over to (F-8) and snags, making out number one. Ruether is now throwing nothing but goose eggs at the Sox, who are in deep trouble of dropping the opener.

8th inning **Score: 8-1 Reds**

4th at-bat **1 on 0 out**

The White Sox have the talent to come back against any team, but Dutch Ruether will have none of that today. Scoring two more runs off Roy Wilkenson (1-1 2.05) in the bottom of the 7th inning, the Reds have taken an 8-1 lead. Fred McMullin, pinch-hitting for Wilkenson, singles (1B) up the middle to start the top of the 8th. Shano next up hits a lazy pop fly to LF Pat Duncan (F-7), for the first out. Ruether then retired the Sox in order to finish the 8th. The Reds would score another run off reliever Grover Lowdermilk (3-1 2.54) in the bottom of the 8th, to take a 9-1 lead and Ruether took care of the rest. The Reds now hold a one game advantage in the Series.

Game One Summary

Started out well.

The Reds didn't think too much of Eddie Cicotte before the Series started, and thought less of him afterward. Cincinnati scored six earned runs off Cicotte in less than four innings today, and rolled to a 9-1 win over Chicago. Shano lined a single to open the Series for the Sox, but a poor bunt by Eddie Collins set the stage for things to come in the opener. Shano then flew out three straight times. This certainly was not Chicago's day, but they look to Lefty Williams tomorrow to even up the Series.

Game One Box **Running Total**

		AB	R	H	RBI	AVE	
1st AB	1B	1	0	1	0	1.000	
2nd AB	F-8	2	0	1	0	.500	
3rd AB	F-8	3	0	1	0	.333	
4th AB	F-7	4	0	1	0	.250	1 LOB(1)

Game Two

LHP Lefty Williams (23-11 2.64) vs LHP Slim Sallee (21-7 2.05)

At Cincinnati, Oh **October 1st, 1919** **Redland Field**

Attendance-29,698

1st inning **Score: 0-0**

1st at-bat **0 on 0 out**

Anyone who thought that the Chicago White Sox would sweep the Reds in five straight games were sadly mistaken. The Reds 9-1 spanking of Eddie Cicotte and the Sox, was a humiliating defeat. Today is a different game though. Shano comes up to bat to start game two and taps back to Sallee (1-3), for the first out. Sallee holds serve in the 1st.

3rd inning **Score: 0-0**

2nd at-bat **1 on 1out**

The Sox missed out on a great scoring opportunity in the 2nd inning off Sallee, but Slim pitched out of the jam and the score remains 0-0. With Lefty Williams on at 1st base after a one out single (1B), Shano takes his turn at Sallee. Collins pulls a liner into left-field that looked like it was going to drop in, but LF Pat Duncan came racing in to make a beautiful shoe-string catch (L-7), for the second out as Williams scoots back to 1st base (some of his teammates should have learned from Lefty's base running). Sallee will get out of the inning with no runs scored.

5th inning **Score: 3-0 Reds**

3rd at-bat **0 on 2out**

The fourth inning was a charm for the Reds, after scoring five off Eddie Cicotte yesterday, they came back and scored three today off Left Williams to take a 3-0 lead. With two down and the bases lonely, Shano drills the ball right at SS Larry Kopf (6-3), who makes the play flawlessly, ending the top of the 5th.

7th inning **Score: 4-2 Reds**

4th at-bat **0 on 0 out**

The Reds took a 4-0 lead with another run off Williams in the bottom of the 6th inning. The Sox cut the lead in half with two runs off Sallee in the top of the 7th, on Ray Schalk's mad dash around the bases (along with Swede Risberg) courtesy of two Cincinnati errors. Now with two out, Shano hits the ball right on the nose, but it is straight at CF Edd Roush (L-8) ending the inning. Sallee would have no more trouble with the Sox the rest of the way, and Cincinnati wins the game two 4-2.

Game Two Summary

A tough o-fer.

What was going on in Cincinnati? The Reds swept both games at home, beating the Sox best two pitchers in the process. Losing today's game 4-2, the Sox made ten base hits off Slim Sallee but could only score two runs on a two error play. The Series now shifts up to Chicago for the next three games, and the way the Sox are playing, the Series might not come back to Cincinnati. With the exception of his first at-bat, Shano hit the ball well today with nothing to show for it. Even though Collins is swinging the bat well, manager Kid Gleason will go with Nemo Leibold (a left-handed hitter), starting tomorrow against the Reds right-handed pitching. It will be a long time before the Sox get any production out of the lead-off spot.

Game Two Box **Running Total**

		AB	R	H	RBI	AVE	
1st AB	1-3	5	0	1	0	.200	
2nd AB	L-7	6	0	1	0	.167	1 LOB(2)
3rd AB	6-3	7	0	1	0	.142	
4th AB	F-8	8	0	1	0	.125	

Game Six

RHP Dickie Kerr (13-8 2.89) vs LHP Dutch Ruether (19-6 1.81)

At Cincinnati, Oh **October 7th, 1919** **Redland Field**

Attendance-32,006

1st inning **Score: 0-0**

1st at-bat **0 on 0 out**

The Reds took two of three in Chicago, so the Series returns to Cincinnati (for at least one game). With the lefty Ruether on the mound today, Shano gets another shot in right-field. So far Kid Gleason's platoon system is not working, through five games the lead-off hitter has produced one base hit, by Shano leading off the first game of the Series. Collins leads-off the top of the 1st inning by looping a ball into short center-field that looked like it might drop in, but out of nowhere 2B Morrie Rath races out to make a nifty catch (F-4), for the first out of the ballgame. Except for a Buck Weaver single (1B), Ruether gets out of the 1st inning with no other damage.

3rd inning **Score: 0-0**

2nd at-bat **1 on 1 out**

After two scoreless innings were in the books, Shano leads-off the top of the 3rd. With one out Ray Schalk is at on 2nd base, following his walk (BB) and a sacrifice bunt by Dickie Kerr (SAC 5-4). Collins has an opportunity to put the Sox out in front, but Ruether gets Shano to fly out to CF Edd Roush (F-8), for out number two. Ruether with the help of LF Pat Duncan, who made an incredible shoe-string catch (L-7) on Eddie Collins's liner, exited the 3rd with no runs.

5th inning **Score: 4-0 Reds**

3rd at-bat **3 on 0 out**

The Reds broke through with two runs against Dickie Kerr in the bottom of the 3rd inning, and two more in the 4th, to take a 4-0 lead into the top of the 5th. Not scoring a single run in the last twenty-six innings, the Sox now have the bases loaded and no outs. Shano lofts a fly ball to medium center-field, which should have been deep enough for Swede Risberg to at least try to score on. CF Edd Roush catches the ball (F-8) and fires home but Swede holds up at 3rd base. The Sox would only score one run in the 5th, on Eddie Collins sacrifice fly to the same spot (SF-8). This was Shano's last at-bat of the game because Kid Gleason pinch-hit Nemo Leibold for him in the top of the 7th inning. Chicago went on to tie up the ball game and send it to extra innings, where Chick Gandil knocked in the winning run with a RBI single (1B), which gave the Sox a 5-4 must win victory.

Game Six Summary

We need lead-off production.

The White Sox entered game six needing a victory to stay alive in the Series. Trailing the Reds four games to one, they needed Dickie Kerr to pitch like the Dickie Kerr of game three. The Sox didn't get another three-hit shut-out, what they got was a pitching performance that deserved a standing ovation (even from the Reds fans). The only easy inning Kerr had was the 10th inning, and the Sox came away with a 5-4 thriller, to stick around for at least one more game. Shano hit the ball alright today, getting robbed of a base hit leading off the ballgame. When Reds manager Pat Moran brought in righty Jimmy Ring (10-9 2.26) to relieve Dutch Ruether in the top of the 6th inning, Sox manager Kid Gleason pinch-hit Nemo Leibold for Shano when his spot came up to bat in the top of the 7th. Tomorrow in game seven the Sox go with Eddie Cicotte, who lost the opener and game four. Cicotte has a lot to prove, especially to himself.

Game Six Box		**Running Total**					
		AB	R	H	RBI	AVE	
1st AB	F-4	9	0	1	0	.111	
2nd AB	F-8	10	0	1	0	.100	1 LOB(3), 1 RISP(1)
3rd AB	F-8	11	0	1	0	.091	3 LOB(6), 2 RISP(3)

Game Seven

RHP Eddie Cicotte (29-7 1.82) vs LHP Slim Sallee (21-7 2.05)

At Cincinnati, Oh **October 8th, 1919** **Redland Field**

Attendance-13,923

1st inning **Score: 0-0**

1st at-bat **0 on 0 out**

The dramatic ten inning 5-4 victory in yesterday's game six by Chicago, kept life flowing through their veins in the Series (at least for one more day, anyway). Today would be the last time the Reds would play in front of the home town people, win or lose, because if the Sox win today the Series and the last two games (if necessary) are scheduled for Chicago. How did the Cincinnati home folks thank the Reds for a great season? Only about fourteen thousand showed up for today's seventh game. Those who did got to witness the real Eddie Cicotte. The Reds starting pitcher, big left-hander Slim Sallee (game two winning pitcher) was given the ball by manager Pat Moran, to try to give the Reds their first World Championship since 1882 (when the Reds were in the American Association and managed by Pop Snyder). With the lefty Sallee on the hill, Shano got the nod leading- off and playing center-field (Kid Gleason was so upset with Happy Felsch's play in the field yesterday, that to teach him a lesson, he moved Happy to right-field instead of benching him). Collins gets the Sox off to a great start by lining Sallee's offering into center-field for his first hit (1B) since his lead-off single in the Series opener. Shano moves to 2nd base on Eddie Collins's sacrifice bunt (SAC 1-3), and after Buck Weaver flies out to CF Edd Roush (F-8), scores the Sox first run by their lead-off hitter (it was also the Sox first and only run scored, in the 1st inning of the entire World Series), on Joe Jackson's clutch two out single (1B) to left. Sallee then retires Chick Gandil, to end the first frame.

3rd inning **Score: 1-0 Sox**

2nd at-bat **0 on 0out**

The Sox take their thin 1-0 lead into the top of the 3rd inning, with Shano leading-off again. Collins belts a shot right back up the middle that Sallee gets his glove on, but he can't throw out the speedy Shano, for an infield single (1B). Shano then moves up to 2nd base on Eddie Collins's infield single (1B) to deep shortstop, with Shano barely beating SS Larry Kopf's throw to 2B Morrie Rath at 2nd base. With the Collins boys (no relation) on at 1st and 2nd base, Buck Weaver lines into a double play that again boggles the mind. In such an important game, it is hard to believe what was going through Eddie Collins's head. Weaver lined a shot right at SS Larry Kopf, and while Shano froze on the line drive, Eddie must have been off to see the wizard, because Kopf doubles him off 1st base (WOW). After all that Joe Jackson (who had his own troubles on the base path's yesterday), comes up big again with his second clutch two out RBI single (1B), this time to left-center giving the Sox and Eddie Cicotte a 2-0 lead. Sallee then got Happy Felsch to force Jackson at 2nd base (FC 6-4), to end the 3rd.

5th inning **Score: 2-0 Sox**

3rd at-bat **0 on 0out**

After four innings of play, Eddie Cicotte and the REAL Chicago White Sox still clung to their 2-0 lead. For the third straight at-bat, Shano will lead-off an inning. This time though, Sallee retires Shano for the first time today, when he flies out (F-9) to RF Greasy Neale. The Sox went on in the 5th to score two more runs and chase Sallee out of the ballgame, on Happy Felsch's huge bases loaded two run single (1B). The Reds game three losing pitcher, right-hander Ray Fisher (14-5 2.17) who relieved Slim Sallee, then sets down Gandil and Risberg to put an end to the inning.

6th inning **Score: 4-0 Sox**

4th at-bat **0 on 2out**

Eddie Cicotte was showing the Reds today the kind of stuff he possessed, that allowed him to win twenty-nine games this season. With the right-handed Cuban pitcher Dolph Luque (9-3 2.62) now on in relief of Ray Fisher, Shano trots up to bat in the top of the 6th with two down and the bases empty. Take special notice of this at-bat by Shano Collins, because it is the only time in the Series that manager Kid Gleason didn't go with the righty-lefty platoon with Collins and Leibold. Shano drives a stinging double (2B) down the left-field line (his third hit of the game). Not only did the right-handed hitting Collins pull the ball off the right-handed pitching Cincinnati fireballer, it would be the only hit Dolph Luque would give up in two relief outings (five innings with no walks and six strikeouts). Luque then strikes-out Eddie Collins (K), to end the inning.

9th inning **Score: 4-1 Sox**

5th at-bat **0 on 1out**

The Reds scored one run off Eddie Cicotte In the bottom of the 6th inning, but that was all Cicotte would give up today. In what would be Shano's last at-bat in the Series, Collins puts good wood on Luque's fastball again, but he sends a fly ball out to CF Edd Roush (F-8) for the second out of the 9th. Luque would retire the Sox in order in the 9th but Cicotte, despite giving up two singles in the last of the 9th, would not give up any more runs to the Reds.

Game Seven Summary

Three hits and benched?

In the last two games the Sox finally played like the team that won the tough American League pennant. Eddie Cicotte finished off a two game

Chicago sweep in Cincinnati, with a Cicotte like 4-1 triumph, to send the Series back to Chicago for game eight. The Sox now trail the Reds by only a game, four to three. Shano Collins also showed the Reds what a Chicago lead-off man could do when he got on base. Three hits including a double, and two runs scored. Shano was also the only White Sox player who hit the right-handed throwing Dolph Luque hard (2B, F-8). What did Sox manager Kid Gleason do with this hot hitting lead-off man in another win or else game eight? He benched him for the hitless (0 for 13) left-handed hitting Nemo Leibold, against the Reds righty Hod Eller. It just amazes me how Kid Gleason didn't get run out of Chicago on a rail after this World Series. His managing in these eight ballgames was about on par with the players who were throwing the Series. You now can now understand why Gleason, after his stint with the White Sox ended after the 1923 season, never managed in the Big Leagues again.

Game Seven Box		**Running Total**					
		AB	R	H	RBI	AVE	
1st AB	1B, Run	12	1	2	0	.167	
2nd AB	1B, Run	13	2	3	0	.231	
3rd AB	F-9	14	2	3	0	.214	
4th AB	2B	15	2	4	0	.267	2B(1)
5th AB	F-8	16	2	4	0	.250	

Chapter Seven

Harry Loran Leibold

At least he was trying.

Harry Loran Leibold was born on February 17, 1892 in Butler, Indiana. Nicknamed Little Nemo, after the popular comic strip of the time, Nemo was a small stocky man at 5′ 6 ½″ and 157 lbs. At the tender age of twenty-one, the left-handed hitting, right-handed throwing Leibold made his Major League debut with the Cleveland Indians of the American League on April 12 (my son Kelly's birthday), 1913. Playing in eighty-four games, Nemo batted .256 in his rookie season. In 1914, Nemo improved his batting average a little bit to .264, while appearing in one hundred and fourteen ballgames for the Indians. Nemo had played in the first fifty-seven games with Cleveland in 1915, before the Indians placed him on waivers on July 7th, and when Charles Comiskey was looking for a back-up outfielder, he was picked up by the Chicago White Sox. Leibold played in thirty-six games for the Sox that season, and batted a combined .249. Nemo only played in forty-five games for the Sox in 1916, and batted .244 in his limited duty. In the White Sox World Championship season of 1917, Leibold's playing time increased to one hundred and twenty-five ballgames, though he batted a low .236. When he did get on base, one hundred and one hits to go along with his seventy-four walks, he did score fifty-nine runs, and stole twenty-seven bases. The War shortened 1918 season saw Nemo still only a .250 hitter, but he also drew a lot of walks with sixty-six, and for a low average scored fifty-seven runs.

Nemo enjoyed his best year to date in 1919, batting .300 for the first time with a .302, while appearing in one hundred and twenty-two games. Hitting out of the lead-off spot, Nemo scored eighty-one runs and stole seventeen bases, though he still didn't hit with much power (four career homers). Leibold was a decent outfielder and when he did get on base, he knew how to score runs. In the World Series against the Cincinnati Reds, manager Kid Gleason platooned Nemo with John "Shano" Collins in right-field, with Collins starting all the games played on the road and Leibold starting all the games played in Chicago. Nemo had a Series he would have liked to of forgotten, batting a dismal .056, with just one base hit in eighteen at-bats. He fit right in with most of his teammates, but not the crooked ones, because Nemo was not in with the fix conspirators, he just had a terrible Series. Like Eddie Collins, he picked the wrong time to play badly, and hitting lead-off, he hurt the Sox badly.

Playing in what would be his last season in Chicago in 1920, Nemo's slump continued hitting just .220, though he still managed to score sixty-one runs with his ninety-one base hits, in one hundred and eight games. After eight of his teammates were booted out of baseball, Comiskey was looking to shore up his outfield, and on March 4, 1921 Leibold along with Shano Collins, were traded to the Boston Red Sox for future Hall of Famer (1971) Harry Hooper. 1921 was also Nemo's finest season, with career highs in average .306, runs with eighty-eight, base hits with one hundred and forty-three and doubles with twenty-six. After this very good season, Nemo saw his playing time drop considerably in 1922, getting into just eighty-one games, and his average dropped to .256. 1923 was another good season for Leibold, batting .294, but he played most of the year with the Washington Senators. On May 26, he was placed on waivers by the Red Sox. Nemo was feisty little man, and sooner or later he would ware out his welcome. The 1924 season was another fantastic year for Little Nemo, batting .293 in a utility role. The Senators would win the World Series against the New York Giants four games to three, but Nemo only saw action in three games. He played a big part in Washington winning game seven though, pinch-hitting in the bottom of the 8th with the Senators trailing 3-1; Leibold hit a one out double down the third base line.

He went on to score as the Senators tied up a ballgame that they would win in ten innings. 1925 would be Nemo's last year in the Big Leagues, but he went out in style. Playing in just fifty-six games, he batted 274 and the Senators again won the American League pennant, although they lost the Series to the Pittsburgh Pirates four games to three. Nemo pinch hit three times in the Series with another double and a run scored, to go along with a walk.

Nemo retired from baseball after the 1925 World Series with a .266 lifetime average in thirteen seasons. Not a bad career for a little man from Indiana. In 1928, Nemo began a twenty-one year stint as field manager in the Minor Leagues. Working mostly for the Boston Red Sox organization, Nemo retired from baseball for good in 1948 (the same year Babe Ruth died). Nemo then scouted and coached a little bit for the remaining years of his life. Harry Loran "Little Nemo" Leibold died February 4, 1977 in Detroit, Michigan at the age of eighty-four, the last of the old White Sox to pass on. Here are Nemo's five games in the 1919 World Series.

Game Three

RHP Ray Fisher (14-5 2.17) vs RHP Dickie Kerr (13-8 2.89)

At Chicago, ILL **October 3rd, 1919** **Comiskey Park**

Attendance-29,126

1st inning **Score: 0-0**

1st at-bat **0 on 0 out**

The Chicago White Sox had the air knocked out of them in Cincinnati, losing the first two games of the 1919 World Series. Coming home to Comiskey Park, the Sox were looking for a fresh start, with a fresh lead-off man, Nemo Leibold playing right-field. The left-handed hitting Nemo takes his turn in the batter's box after the Reds fail to score in the top half of the 1st inning. Leibold pulls a routine fly ball out to RF Greasy Neale, who gloves the ball (F-9), for the first out. Fisher would also hold the rest of the Sox order at bay, to end the 1st inning.

2nd inning **Score: 2-0 Sox**

2nd at-bat **2 on 2 out**

The Sox have taken their first lead of the Series, 2-0 in the bottom of the 2nd, on Chick Gandil's 2 RBI single (1B). With two outs, Nemo has a chance to break the game open, with Ray Schalk on 2nd base and Dickie Kerr on at 1st. Nemo cannot deliver the big hit though, slapping a grounder to 3B Heinie Groh, who ends the 2nd inning (5-3).

5th inning **Score: 3-0 Sox**

3rd at-bat **0 on 0 out**

Chicago upped their lead to 3-0, with another run in the bottom of the 4th, and Dickie Kerr was throwing like a seasoned veteran. Nemo leads-off the bottom of the 5th inning, making the first out, bouncing to 1B Jake Daubert (3-U), who makes the play himself.

8th inning **Score: 3-0 Sox**

4th at-bat **0 on 0 out**

Dolph Luque (9-3 2.63) was now in the ballgame for the Reds, replacing Fisher who had been pinch-hit for in the top of the 8th inning. In what might have been the smallest battle in Word Series history, the right-handed Reds hurler, who stood 5' 7, was pitching to the 5' 6 ½" Leibold. Luque won the battle by striking Nemo out (K), but the Sox win the war, taking game three 3-0, behind Kerr's three-hit shut-out.

Game Three Summary

Little man, little production.

It was only game three, but it was also a big game for Chicago, trying to avoid going down three games to nothing. Dickie Kerr came up huge today, throwing a three-hit shut-out at the Reds. The 3-0 victory had put the Sox on the board, and moved them to within a game, two to one. Nemo didn't hit the ball too badly today, but he drew an 0 for four with a strikeout. In his biggest at-bat of the game, Leibold grounded out to 3B Heinie Groh with runners at 1st and 2nd base. Chicago looks to tie up the Series tomorrow, with ace Eddie Cicotte back on the mound.

Game Three Box **Running Total**

		AB	R	H	RBI	AVE	
1st AB	F-9	1	0	0	0	.000	
2nd AB	5-3	2	0	0	0	.000	2 LOB(2), 1 RISP(1)
3rd AB	3-U	3	0	0	0	.000	
4th AB	K	4	0	0	0	.000	K(1)

Game Four

RHP Jimmy Ring (10-9 2.26) vs RHP Eddie Cicotte (29-7 1.82)

At Chicago, ILL **October 4th, 1919** **Comiskey Park**

Attendance-34,363

1st inning **Score: 0-0**

1st at-bat **0 on 0 out**

The Chicago White Sox heading into game four are only one game down to the Reds, two games to one. Cicotte held the Reds in the top half of the 1st, and Nemo leads-off the bottom half of the inning. Leibold gets out in front of Rings offering and pops-up to 1B Jake Daubert (F-3), for the first out of the inning. Ring would breeze through the 1st, with no Sox reaching 1st base.

3rd inning **Score: 0-0**

2nd at-bat **0 on 0 out**

The Sox have had their opportunities with Jimmy Ring, but so far they haven't been able to push across any runs. Neither have the Reds though, as Eddie Cicotte is in top form today up to this point of the ballgame. Nemo is again leading-off an inning, but again Ring is a little better. Leibold hits a lazy fly ball out to RF Greasy Neale, who puts the squeeze on the ball (F-9), and sends Nemo back to the dugout. Ring will hold the Sox in the 3rd.

5th inning **Score: 2-0 Reds**

3rd at-bat **0 on 1 out**

The Reds scored two unearned runs off Cicotte to take a 2-0 lead in the top off the 5th inning, helped by two Eddie Cicotte errors (maybe one by Joe Jackson?). It is now time for Nemo to start showing some leadership out of the lead-off spot, but it will take a bad 3B Heinie Groh throw to get Leibold on base. With one out in the bottom of the 5th, Nemo slashes a ball the opposite way to Groh, who fields the ball cleanly but throws well over 1B Jake Daubert's head (E-5), allowing Nemo to waltz into 2nd base. Now it is Nemo's turn to get his name into the base running blunder book. Still with one out, Eddie Collins tops a bouncer to 3B Heinie Groh, Groh fields the ball with no problem but instead of throwing to 1st base, fires the ball to 2nd catching Nemo napping (FC 5-4), for the second out. Ring will then pitch out of the inning with no runs.

7th inning **Score: 2-0 Reds**

4th at-bat **1 on 1 out**

The Reds and Jimmy Ring take their 2-0 lead into the bottom of the 7th inning. With Ray Schalk on 1st base after getting hit by a pitch (HBP), Nemo struts up to bat with one out. All Leibold can manage though, is a lame duck fly ball out to CF Edd Roush (F-8), for the second out. Jimmy Ring escapes to the eighth inning with his shut-out still intact.

9th inning **Score: 2-0 Reds**

5th at-bat **1 on 2 out**

The Sox have had plenty of chances today, but could push no runs across against Jimmy Ring. Chicago has Ray Schalk on at 1st base after a walk (BB), and one out when Nemo comes to bat for the fifth time this afternoon. Nemo catches a good piece of the ball, but hits a line shot right at 3B Heinie Groh (L-5) ending the ballgame. Ring took care of Chicago on three hits today, winning 2-0. The loss has put the Sox into a deep abyss, down three games to one.

Game Four Summary

Can we rent a lead-off man?

Eddie Cicotte pitched well today (two unearned runs), but the Reds Jimmy Ring pitched better. Throwing a three-hit shut-out and winning 2-0, the Reds have taken control of the Series, up three games to one. Again going hitless, Nemo had run his streak to nine at-bats with a 0 for five, and even got himself picked off 2nd base by 3B Heinie Groh and killing a great chance to score off Jimmy Ring. It might just be time for Kid Gleason to give Shano Collins another chance at lead-off (he did have a base hit in the opener), but Kid isn't ready to make any changes to his grand scheme (whatever that is?).

Game Four Box **Running Total**

		AB	R	H	RBI	AVE	
1st AB	F-3	5	0	0	0	.000	
2nd AB	F-9	6	0	0	0	.000	
3rd AB	E-5	7	0	0	0	.000	
4th AB	F-8	8	0	0	0	.000	1 LOB(3)
5th AB	L-5	9	0	0	0	.000	1 LOB(4)

Game Five

RHP Hod Eller (20-9 2.40) vs LHP Lefty Williams (23-11 2.64)

At Chicago, ILL **October 6th, 1919** **Comiskey Park**

Attendance-34,379

1st inning **Score: 0-0**

1st at-bat **1 on 1 out**

What is wrong with the Chicago White Sox? After losing three of the first four games, and Eddie Cicotte taking the losses in two of those games, they just didn't look like the team that had won a tough American League pennant. After yesterday's rainout, today is a new game. A big crowd comes through the turnstiles this afternoon, to watch two twenty game winners do battle in an almost must win for Chicago. Lefty held the Reds in the top of the 1st, and Nemo leads-off for the Sox by working Eller for a free pass (BB). Eddie Collins next hits a slow roller to short (6-3), moving Leibold into scoring position at 2nd base. Buck Weaver laces a ball headed for center-field and an early Chicago lead, but Eller was able to reach up and get enough of the ball to keep Weaver to an infield single (1B) as Nemo takes 3rd. With runners on the corners and only one out, Eller is able to retire Joe Jackson on a pop-up to 3B Heinie Groh (F-5) and Happy Felsch (F-7), to end the inning without the Sox scoring.

3rd inning **Score: 0-0**

2nd at-bat **0 on 1 out**

If you like pitchers duels, then you liked today's ballgame. Williams and Eller both take early no-hitters into the 3rd inning, and Lefty set the Reds down in order in the visitors half. Nemo takes his turn at Eller looking to just get a piece of the ball, but Eller blows him away (K). Eddie Collins becomes Eller's sixth straight strikeout victim (K), ending the inning.

6th inning **Score: 4-0 Reds**

3rd at-bat **0 on 0 out**

Somebody had to eventually give, and it turned out to be Lefty Williams who was Santa Claus. Going into the top of the 6th with a one-hitter going, St. Lefty left an early Christmas gift in the Reds stocking, giving up four runs on three hits and a walk. Ray Schalk was so crazy mad at Williams that he completely blew his stack on home plate umpire Charles Rigler, and got himself thrown out of the ballgame after a close play at the plate. Nemo leads-off the bottom of the inning, trying to get something going against a man throwing like Sandy Koufax on a great day, but slaps a two hopper to 3B Heinie Groh (5-3), the first out of another perfect inning by Eller.

9th inning **Score: 5-0 Reds**

4th at-bat **0 on 0 out**

The Reds added insult to injury by scoring their fifth run in the top of the 9th inning, off Sox reliever Erskine Mayer (1-3 8.25), who had come into the game when Eddie Murphy had pinch-hit for Williams in the bottom of the 8th. Nemo starts off the Sox final chance against Eller with a ground-out to 2B Morrie Rath (4-3). With the exception of Buck Weaver's triple (3B), Eller retires the Sox in the 9th and wins 5-0, the second Reds pitcher to pitch a three-hit shut-out in as many days.

Game Five Summary

My kingdom for a base hit.

In a game where one run would probably decide it, Lefty Williams gave the Reds four runs in the top of the 6th inning. Gave is the only word you can use, because Williams had a one-hitter going into the 6th, gave the Reds four runs, then pitched a perfect 7th and 8th, before being pulled for a pinch-hitter. Who was he fooling, other than Kid Gleason? The 5-0 loss has given the Reds a four games to one lead, and all but ended the 1919 World Series. The

Championship now heads back to Cincinnati, where the next two games are scheduled, if they need more than one. Nemo is in a funk, going 0 for three today with a walk, and is now 0 for the World Series (0-12). Nobody with the exception of Buck Weaver (two of the three hits, Schalk had the other) could hit Hod Eller today, but the Reds couldn't hit Lefty Williams either, until Williams mysteriously took the 6th inning off.

Game Five Box **Running Total**

		AB	R	H	RBI	AVE	
1st AB	BB	9	0	0	0	.000	BB(1)
2nd AB	K	10	0	0	0	.000	K(2)
3rd AB	5-3	11	0	0	0	.000	
4th AB	4-3	12	0	0	0	.000	

Game Six

RHP Dickie Kerr (13-8 2.89) vs LHP Dutch Ruether (19-6 1.81)

At Cincinnati, Oh **October 7th, 1919** **Redland Field**

Attendance-32,006

7th inning **Score: 4-4**

1st at-bat **0 on 0 out**

Sticking with his platoon of Shano Collins starting in right-field against a left-handed pitcher, when the Sox chased starter Dutch Ruether in the top of the 6th inning to tie the game up at 4-4, the game four winning pitcher, right-handed Jimmy Ring (10-9 2.26) came in to relieve. Gleason pinch-hit the left-handed hitting Nemo for Collins (who was 0 for 3), to lead-off the top of the 7th. Leibold smacks the ball on the nose, but it is right at SS Larry Kopf (6-3), who handles the play with no difficulty. Ring would hold the Sox in the 7th.

9th inning **Score: 4-4**

2nd at-bat **0 on 2 out**

Dickie Kerr was still pitching in trouble every inning, but he hasn't given up a run since the 4th. Jimmy Ring on the other hand, except for a couple of walks, has thrown as well as he did in winning game four with a three-hit shut-out. With the score still tied at four, Nemo comes to bat with two out and the bases empty. Leibold works Ring for a free trot down to 1st base (BB), and immediately steals 2nd (SB). Eddie Collins can't deliver the potential go ahead blow though, and flies out to CF Edd Roush (F-8), to end the top of the 9th. The Sox will score a single run in the top of the 10th inning, then Dickie Kerr threw his only perfect inning of the ballgame, as the Sox win game six 5-4.

Game Six Summary

This isn't working.

The incredible pitching performance by Dickie Kerr has given the Sox a chance to play again tomorrow. Ten innings of hair pulling baseball, with the Sox coming out on top 5-4. Chick Gandil played the part of hero today with the game winning hit, a single in the top of the 10th. Nemo came into the game in the top of the 7th inning, pinch-hitting for Shano Collins with the right-handed throwing Jimmy Ring on in relief of starter Dutch Ruether. Leibold grounded out, but in the 9th he drew a walk and stole a base. The Sox have to do something with their lead-off hitter, through six games Leibold and Collins are a combined one for twenty-four (.042). Ray Schalk would be a good idea, he's fast afoot and he is hitting the ball well, but I don't think Kid Gleason has any light bulbs going off inside his head. The victory gives Chicago another game tomorrow, and they now trail the Reds four games to two, with Eddie Cicotte back on the hill for game seven.

Game Six Box		**Running Total**					
		AB	R	H	RBI	AVE	
1st AB	6-3	13	0	0	0	.000	
2nd AB	BB, SB	13	0	0	0	.000	BB(2), SB(1)

Game Eight

RHP Hod Eller (20-9 2.40) vs LHP Lefty Williams (23-11 2.64)

Chicago, ILL **October 9th, 1919** **Comiskey Park**

Attendance-32,939

1st inning **Score: 4-0 Reds**

1st at-bat **0 on 0 out**

Almost 33,000 people could have been called by the Cook County Grand Jury, to testify that indeed Lefty Williams threw the eighth game of the 1919 World Series. Giving up four runs while facing just five batters, Kid Gleason should have punched Lefty out right there on the pitcher's mound. But of course that would have taken a managerial decision, and we now know Kid didn't make many of those in this Series. With the right-handed Hod Eller pitching for the Reds today, Kid stuck with his platoon system. Starting Nemo in center-field with Happy Felsch moved over to right, because of Felsch's fielding problems, even though Shano Collins had three hits yesterday (maybe Gleason thought Collins had used up all his hits?). The Sox still had nine innings to make up four runs, but Hod Eller does not blow four run leads. For the moment Kid looked very smart, when Nemo picks up his first hit of the Series with a solid lead-off single (1B) into left-field. Eddie Collins follows with an official scorer's gift double (2B), off LF Pat Duncan's glove, moving Nemo to 3rd base. The fun ended quickly though, as Eller retired Weaver, Jackson and Felsch without giving up a run.

2nd inning **Score: 5-0 Reds**

2nd at-bat **2 on 2 out**

The Reds have increased their lead to 5-0, scoring a run off right-handed reliever Bill James (3-1 2.54), in the top of the 2nd inning. Nemo is hitting for the first time in this Series with a chance to get a really big hit. With Swede Risberg on at 2nd base and Ray Schalk on 1st, Leibold takes his spot in the batter's box with two out. Big Hod Eller isn't about to let Little Nemo beat him though, and strikes Leibold out (K), to end another scoring opportunity.

5th inning **Score: 6-1 Reds**

3rd at-bat **0 on 1 out**

Instead of pitching his entire staff until he found someone who could get the Reds out today, Kid Gleason stuck with Bill James. Even letting James hit in the bottom of the 2nd inning, when a big hit might have gotten the Sox back into the ballgame. Kid Gleason managed in this Series as well as his players played-terrible. Cincinnati now holds a 6-1 lead, with another run off James in the top of the 5th. Nemo now comes up to bat in the home half of the 5th, with the bases clear and one out. Eller gets Leibold to slap a grounder to SS Larry Kopf (6-3), for the second out of a perfect inning.

8th inning **Score: 10-1 Reds**

4th at-bat **0 on 0 out**

Scoring three runs in the top of the 6th inning off James and Roy Wilkenson (1-1 2.05), and another run off Wilkenson in the top of the 8th, Cincinnati has turned this game into a laugher (just like the Series opener). Hod Eller was taking the breeze out of the Windy City (one run in the last sixteen inns pitched), the Sox are down to their last six outs. Nemo leads-off the bottom of the 8th inning, and Leibold does something he rarely does, he drives a ball to deep right-field. The Reds speedy RF Greasy Neale runs the ball down at the fence (F-9), for the first out. The Sox then erupted for their biggest inning of the Series, scoring four runs off Eller (did Reds manager Pat Moran forget the Sox couldn't hit reliever Dolph Luque?), making the score 10-5 before Eller puts out the flames.

9th inning **Score: 10-5 Reds**

5th at-bat **1 on 0 out**

Sill with a breath of air in the Chicago White Sox lungs, they needed a miracle in the bottom of the 9th inning. Lead-off pinch-hitter Eddie Murphy started the inning by getting drilled (HBP) by a Hod Eller pitch. Next batter Leibold gets ahold of another Eller pitch and sends a deep fly ball over the head of CF Edd Roush. What looks like extra bases quickly turns into the first out, as Roush ala Willie Mays, makes an unbelievable catch (F-8) over his shoulder. When Joe Jackson grounded out (4-3), the last bit of air was push from the Sox lungs.

Game Eight Summary

Not what the doctor ordered.

The momentum from the last two games was lost in the first five batters, and Lefty Williams proved to America that he was definitely on the take (I hope it was worth it Lefty). Giving any pitcher a four run lead, especially in the 1st inning, is an uphill climb even for a team as talented as Chicago. Giving a four run lead to Hod Eller is suicide. Eller took the gift and never looked back, and the Cincinnati Reds won the game and the Series 10-5. In less than one year, the Reds five games to three World's Championship would be tarnished. Nemo made his first and only hit of the Series, with a lead-off single in the 1st inning. With the exception of his 2nd inning strikeout, when a base hit could have really helped the Sox, Nemo hit the ball well today. Leibold also hit two shots off Eller in his last two at-bats, but had nothing to show for it. Too bad for Little Nemo, he had a bad Series and even Swede Risberg (.080), out - hit him.

Game Eight Box				**Running Total**			
		AB	R	H	RBI	AVE	
1st AB	1B	14	0	1	0	.071	
2nd AB	K	15	0	1	0	.067	K(3) 1 LOB(6),1RISP(2)
3rd AB	6-3	16	0	1	0	.063	
4th AB	F-9	17	0	1	0	.059	
5th AB	F-8	18	0	1	0	.056	1LOB(7)

Chapter Eight

Raymond William Schalk

A cracker-jack ballplayer!

Raymond William Schalk was born on August 12, 1892, in the small Illinois town of Harvel. Which is located about a hundred miles northeast of St. Louis in the central part of the Land of Lincoln. Ray was born to German immigrants, and grew up living the small town life. Ray was also a gifted athlete from a very early age, and when he grew up Ray starred on the Litchfield High School basketball team. Schalk also worked during school as a printer's apprentice, and after high school moved to Brooklyn, New York in 1908 at the age of seventeen. Ray went to school there to become a Master of the linotype machine, and after two years returned home to take up his new career. Ray also excelled in a sport-baseball. Schalk started playing on the hometown semi-pro team, making a whooping $2 a game for extra money in 1910. Ray played so well that in 1911, he signed to play Class D ball for Taylorville in the Illinois/ Missouri league. Being paid $65 a month, Schalk batted .387 in forty-seven games. By the middle of the season, Ray's contract was bought by the Milwaukee Brewers of the American Association, and Ray played the remaining thirty-one ballgames there (this is the same team Happy Felsch got his start with in 1913). Ray was turning into one fine catcher, and it was here in the Minors that Schalk perfected his trade with the tools of ignorance. He was also mastering pitch selection and working the hitter, skills that would eventually lead him into the baseball Hall of Fame. Ray began the 1912 season back in Milwaukee and was having himself a very good year, batting .271 with excellent defense, after eighty games. Then in mid-season, the Chicago White Sox of the American League bought Ray's contract for $10,000 and on August 11, 1912, one day before his twentieth birthday, Ray made his Major league debut.

Ray appeared in only twenty-three games for the Sox, batting .286, but made a staggering total of fourteen errors in those games. In Ray's first full season of 1913, Schalk batted a so-so .244, but he showed the baseball world why he was a big leaguer, making only fifteen errors in one hundred and twenty-eight games. Ray was not built like any other catcher either, only 5'7" and weighing 165 lbs. He was also very fast, and tough as nails. Schalk started coming into his own in 1914, hitting at a .270 pace and swiping twenty-four bases to go along with his usual solid defense. The following 1915 season saw Ray bat at a .266 clip with a career high nine triples, but in 1916 his average slipped to .232 although he had another stellar season behind the plate, committing only ten errors in one hundred and twenty-nine ballgames. In the Chicago White Sox World Championship season of 1917, Ray's slump at the plate continued, hitting .226, but he did drive in fifty-one runs with his ninety-six base hits. Ray always was a clutch hitter, and his leadership was irreplaceable. During the brief 1918 campaign, cut short because of World War I, Ray played in one hundred and eight games, but his average sank to a career low .219. Schalk made incredible strides at the plate in the fateful 1919 season, hitting at a career high .282 pace, and nobody in either league could match his defensive skills. All this helped get the Sox back to the World Series against the National League Champion Cincinnati Reds.

Ray was one of the few Sox players who could claim that they played a square Series, and he was also one of the few on the team, who could claim that they had a good Series. Ray batted .304 with seven hits in his seven and a half games. Ray also cut down nine would be base stealers in sixteen attempts, and picked Heinie Groh off second base. Schalk also probably knew before anyone else that something was terribly wrong with Lefty Williams.

I'm sure Ray was as surprised as anybody when Cicotte was implicated in the fix, because even though Cicotte was shelled off the mound in the fourth inning of the opener, Eddie pitched beautifully in games four and seven (Cicotte only won one of those games though). So not even Schalk could have guessed Cicotte threw the opening game, probably thinking Eddie just got hit by a good team in game one. Williams on the other hand, Ray wanted to strangle. In fact he did try to strangle Lefty, after the second game in the runway leading up to the clubhouse, and had to be pried off by teammates.

The reason Ray was so upset at Williams was that Lefty kept crossing Schalk up, throwing pitches Ray didn't call for. Plus the fact that Williams couldn't throw a strike, and when he did it had nothing on it. Also Ray had a bird's eye view of most (but not all) of his teammates screwing up in the field.

All of Ray's frustrations came to a head in the fifth game, when in the sixth inning, Lefty started his crap again. Throwing like a madman for the first five innings, Williams just didn't much feel like pitching in the sixth. Lefty lost his near perfect form, and the game, giving up four runs. The third run that scored in the inning was a close play at the plate, with Heinie Groh scoring just ahead of Ray's tag. With all the anger built up inside Schalk, he exploded on home plate umpire Charles Rigler of the National League. Ray, after telling Rigler what he thought of Him, the National League, the weather and his Mother, then poked Rigler in the chest with his glove. Rigler could take all of that, but when Ray talked trash about the weather, Rigler gave Schalk an early shower from the ballgame (just kidding). I sure would have liked to of been in the clubhouse though, when Williams came in after the game. For a player like Ray Schalk, the 1919 World Series had to of bothered him for the rest of his life.

Ray had another fine year in 1920, even with the cloud of the previous World Series hanging over the club most of the season. Schalk batted .270 and even hit his first homer in three years, Ray also knocked in a career high sixty-one runs while scoring sixty-four. Ray caught one hundred and fifty-one of his team's one hundred and fifty-four games, and only made ten errors all season. In successive years, Ray batted .252 in 1921, and .281 in 1922. Then Ray went into a two year slump, hitting only .228 in 1923, and .196 in 1924. Ray could get away with the low batting averages, because he was so valuable behind the plate. Schalk rebounded to hit .274 in his last full season of 1925, but his biggest contribution to the team that year was discovering a pitching prospect from Baylor University- Ted Lyons (Hall of Fame inductee 1955, same year as Ray). Injuries held Ray to just eighty-two games in 1926, and Ray hit a respectable .265. In 1927 Ray became Manager of the White Sox after Eddie Collins was let go. The Sox finished fifth, going 70-83, and Ray played in sixteen games behind the dish. Ray only penciled his name into two ballgames in 1928, instead concentrating on running the team. Ray was fired after only seventy-four games (32-42), after a dispute with miserly owner Charles Comiskey over, you guessed it, money (Ray was replaced by Lena Blackburne). John McGraw of the New York Giants signed Ray to a 1929 contract, but Schalk only appeared in five games for the Giants and retired as an active player. Ray stayed on the rest of the season as a coach, and in 1930-31, was a coach for the Chicago Cubs. Then from 1932 to 1937 Ray was the field Manager for the

Buffalo Bisons of the International League. From 1938 thru 1939 Schalk was at the helm of the Indianapolis Indians in the American Association, then finished a twenty-nine year career in Professional Baseball just about where he started, managing the Milwaukee Brewers in 1940. After running a bowling alley during World War II, Ray became a full time scout for the Cubs, and from 1947 until his retirement in 1963, Ray was a baseball coach for the Purdue University Boilermakers.

Ray Schalk was inducted into the baseball Hall of Fame in Cooperstown, New York in 1955. Ray passed away on May 19, 1970 in Chicago at the age of seventy-seven, with many great memories of his years in baseball, though the World Series of 1919 was not one of them.

Game One

RHP Eddie Cicotte (29-7 1.82) vs LHP Dutch Ruether (19-6 1.81)

At Cincinnati, Oh **October 1st, 1919** **Redland Field**

Attendance-30,511

2nd inning **Score: 1-1**

1st at-bat **1 on 2out**

There is so much interest in the World Series this year that it was moved from seven to nine games. Everything seems perfect, except for all the rumors that the Series is fixed. Cincinnati scored a run in the bottom of the 1st inning to take a 1-0 lead off Eddie Cicotte. Chicago comes to bat in the top of the 2nd, looking to show their might. Chick Gandil tied the score at one apiece with a one out bloop single (1B) to left-field, plating Joe Jackson. Now with two gone and Swede Risberg on at 1st base following a walk (BB), Ray steps up to bat for the first time in the 1919 World Series. Schalk makes good contact but he sails a fly ball to straight away center-field, that Reds Captain Edd Roush hauls in (F-8), to end the visitors 2nd.

5th inning **Score: 6-1 Reds**

2nd at-bat **1 on 1out**

By the time Ray bats in the top of the 5th inning the Reds hold a 6-1 lead, sending Eddie Cicotte to the showers with a five run 4th. Looking for the big inning themselves, Ray comes to the plate with Chick Gandil on at 1st base and one out. Schalk pulls Ruether's pitch right at 3B Heinie Groh, who funnels the hot grounder and forces Gandil at 2nd base (FC 5-4), for out number two, Ray avoiding the double play by hustling down the base line and beating the relay throw. Sox relief pitcher Roy Wilkenson (1-1 2.05), batting next, then forces Ray out at 2nd (FC 4-U), ending the Sox 5th with no runs.

7th inning **Score: 6-1 Reds**

3rd at-bat **0 on 2out**

The Reds still hold a 6-1 lead going into the top of the 7th inning, with the Sox sill looking for the big inning that will not come today. Ray is batting for the 3rd time today with two down and the bases empty. Dutch Ruether will not really be challenged this afternoon, and sends Ray back to the dugout to put his gear back on, on another ground out to 3B Heinie Groh (5-3). The Reds score two runs in the bottom of the 7th, and one more in the 8th to take a 9-1 opening day win against the White Sox.

Game One Summary

A tough ballgame.

Not a good start for the Chicago White Sox or Eddie Cicotte, losing the opener 9-1. Ray, although putting good wood on the ball all three at-bats today, drew a 0 for three collar. Ray also left two runners stranded on base. Not a whole lot to sum up here today, as the Sox sucked on both offense and defense. Maybe there is something to these rumors.

Game One Box **Running Total**

		AB	R	H	RBI	AVE	
1st AB	F-8	1	0	0	0	.000	1 LOB(1)
2nd AB	FC 5-4	2	0	0	0	.000	1 LOB(2)
3rd AB	5-3	3	0	0	0	.000	

Game Two

LHP Lefty Williams (23-11 2.64) vs LHP Slim Sallee (21-7 2.05)

At Cincinnati, Oh **October 1st, 1919** **Redland Field**

Attendance-29,698

3rd inning **Score: 0-0**

1st at-bat **0 on 0 out**

Scoreless going into the top of the 3rd inning, Ray leads-off with a lazy floater out to CF Edd Roush, who makes the catch (F-8) for the 1st out. Sallee will hold serve in the 3rd.

5th inning **Score: 3-0 Reds**

2nd at-bat **0 on 0 out**

The Reds have taken a 3-0 lead, when Lefty Williams forgot where the strike zone was and walked three batters, to go along with two well placed hits, to score three runs in the bottom of the 4th inning. Ray leads-off the top of the 5th; probably still mad at Lefty for not throwing the pitches he was calling. Slim Sallee gets Ray to fly out to CF Edd Roush again, this time in short left-field (F-8). Sallee would set the Sox down in order again.

7th inning **Score: 4-0 Reds**

3rd at-bat **1 on 1out**

This was a very wild play to say the least. After the Reds scored another run off Lefty Williams in the bottom of the 6th inning, taking a 4-0 lead, Ray comes to bat with Swede Risberg on 1st base and one out. The fun begins as Ray cracks a single (1B) into right-field for his first hit of the Series. RF Greasy Neale fields the ball cleanly, but his throw sails over SS Larry Kopf's head (E-9), all the way to the left-field fence. Risberg scores on the error as Schalk flies around the bases, and while trying to score himself, 3B Heinie Groh's throw hits Ray in the back (E-5) allowing Schalk to score the Sox second run. Ray is not credited with an RBI, so my question is this. Why did Neale have to throw the ball so hard to 2nd base that it ended up all the way out by the left-field wall? My guess is that he had a play on Risberg, who was either jogging into 2nd or was waiting to see if Neale caught the ball. But the angle of the throw had to of come from near the right-field foul line, because a throw from normal right-field wouldn't have ended up were it did. So was Swede pulling a Chick Gandil (game three, bottom of 2nd inning), and not hustling? Was the play really on Schalk, who was trying for a double? If that were the case, Ray would have been given a double, but that wasn't the case either, as Ray was only given a single. My guess is Swede wasn't hustling.

9th inning **Score: 4-2**

4th at-bat **0 on 2out**

Time is running out on the Sox today as they come to bat in the top of the 9th inning, still trailing 4-2. With two out after Swede Risberg hits into a double play (DP 4-6-3); Ray belts another single (1B), this time to center-field. Pinch-hitting for Lefty Williams (and I'm sure he was trying to tie up the game), Fred McMullin grounds out (4-3) to end the ballgame. The Reds 4-2 victory has given Cincinnati a sweep of the first two Series games at home, and puts the Sox in a two game dilemma, especially with their best two pitchers taking the losses. As the Series shifts to Chicago for the next three games, the White Sox look to a rookie to change their fortunes.

Game Two Summary

Good game for a great player.

Close but no cigar. Losing the second game of the 1919 World Series 4-2, the Sox were on their way back home to Chicago with their tails between their legs. Making matters worse, both Cicotte and Williams took the losses. Ray had a productive day at the plate, going two for four and scoring on that goofy play in the 7th. Even though the Sox had ten hits off Sallee, they couldn't put any of those hits together today. So it's on to Comiskey Park, and a rookie pitcher by the name of Dickie Kerr.

Game Two Box		**Running Total**				
		AB	R	H	RBI	AVE
1st AB	F-8	4	0	0	0	.000
2nd AB	F-8	5	0	0	0	.000
3rd AB	1B, Run	6	1	1	0	.167
4th AB	1B	7	1	2	0	.286

Game Three

RHP Ray Fisher (14-5 2.17) vs RHP Dickie Kerr (13-8 2.89)

At Chicago, ILL **October 3rd, 1919** **Comiskey Park**

Attendance-29,126

2nd inning **Score: 2-0 Sox**

1st at-bat **2 on 0 out**

Down two games to nothing, Chicago needing a victory was an understatement. Scoreless heading into the home half of the 2nd inning, the Sox had pushed two runs across against Fisher, on a Chick Gandil two run single

(1B). Now with Gandil on at 2nd base following Swede Risberg's walk (BB) and nobody out, Ray drops down a sacrifice bunt attempt that should have gone for an infield single. Chick was running (if you can call it running) so slow that Fisher has time to field the ball and force Gandil out at 3rd base (FC 1-5). Sallee would then induce Dickie Kerr to hit another ball back to him, and force Risberg at 3rd (FC 1-5), for the second out, Ray moving to 2nd base. Slim then pitches out of the jam by retiring Nemo Leibold (5-3) without giving up any runs.

4th inning **Score: 2-0 Sox**

2nd at-bat **1 on 1 out**

With one out and the Sox still holding a slim 2-0 lead, Swede Risberg received a gift triple (3B) from RF Greasy Neale, when his base hit to right-field skipped over Neale's glove. Ray follows with a drag bunt down the 3rd base line (1B), scoring Swede with the third White Sox run (sound like a suicide squeeze?). Before Dickie Kerr can take a cut at the ball, Ray is thrown out trying to steal 2nd base (CS 2-4), and then Sallee takes care of Kerr on a ground out 6-3, ending the inning.

7th inning **Score: 3-0 Sox**

3rd at-bat **0 on 1 out**

Kerr was in total command today, as the Sox held the 3-0 advantage heading into the home half of the 7th inning. With one out, Ray comes to bat for the third time and grounds out to 3B Heinie Grog (5-3), for the second out. Sallee would give up no more runs this afternoon, but neither would Dickie Kerr. The 3-0 three-hit shut-out is just what the doctor ordered.

Game Three Summary

Nice game Cracker!

Dickie Kerr shined bright today, pitching a three-hit shut-out at the Cincinnati Reds. Winning 3-0, the Sox now trail the Reds by a game, two to one. Ray had one bunt hit in the ballgame, but it drove home the third and final run. Chick Gandil helped Schalk lose a base hit with his base running in the 2nd inning, and caused Ray to be credited with two runners left on base. Overall it was a huge day for Chicago.

Game Three Box **Running Total**

		AB	R	H	RBI	AVE	
1st AB	FC 1-5	8	1	2	0	.250	2 LOB(4), 1 RISP(1)
2nd AB	1B, RBI	9	1	3	1	.333	
3rd AB	5-3	10	1	3	1	.300	

Game Four

RHP Jimmy Ring (10-9 2.26) vs RHP Eddie Cicotte (29-7 1.82)

At Chicago, ILL **October 4th, 1919** **Comiskey Park**

Attendance-34,363

2nd inning **Score: 0-0**

1st at-bat **2 on 2 out**

After a scoreless inning and a half, the Sox have Ring in trouble in the bottom of the 3rd. With Joe Jackson on at 3rd base and Swede Risberg on at 2nd and one out, Ray waits out Ring for a walk (BB) to load the bases. Ring gets Eddie Cicotte to ground out (4-3) to end the inning, after Eddie had worked Jimmy to a full count.

4th inning **Score: 0-0**

2nd at-bat **0 on 2 out**

A barnburner was shaping up today, as Eddie Cicotte and Jimmy Ring are hooked up in old fashioned 0-0 pitchers dual. With two down, Ray ends the 4th after he pops-up to SS Larry Kopf (F-6).

7th inning **Score: 2-0 Reds**

3rd at-bat **0 on 0 out**

Cincinnati has taken a 2-0 lead after two Eddie Cicotte errors led to the two Reds runs in the top of the 5th inning. Playing catch up now, the Sox come to bat in the bottom of the 7th still trailing by the same 2-0 score. Leading-off, Ray is nailed by a Ring pitch (HBP), but that's as far as Schalk would go, as Ring sets the rest of the Sox down in order to maintain his lead.

9th inning **Score: 2-0 Reds**

4th at-bat **0 on 1 out**

There would be no comeback today for the Chicago White Sox today. With one out and the bases lonely, Ray finishes his day by drawing his second walk (BB) of the ballgame (Schalk's third time on base, including a HBP). Again no one could move Ray along, as Ring completed his three-hit shut-out. In losing game four 2-0, the Reds have taken a comfortable three games to one lead, and have beaten the Sox ace Eddie Cicotte twice.

Game Four Summary

Can someone move me along?

The Reds Jimmy Ring three-hit the Sox today, as the Reds took game four 2-0. Ray did almost everything he could do, drawing two walks and a hit by pitch, though nobody could move Schalk up even one base. The Sox had their chances, but Ring continually pitched out of trouble. The trouble is the

Sox are down three games to one, with tomorrow's starter Lefty Williams back on the hill.

Game Four Box		**Running Total**					
		AB	R	H	RBI	AVE	
1st AB	BB	10	1	3	1	.300	BB(1)
2nd AB	F-6	11	1	3	1	.273	
3rd AB	HBP	11	1	3	1	.273	HBP(1)
4th AB	BB	11	1	3	1	.273	BB(2)

Game Five

RHP Hod Eller (20-9 2.40) vs LHP Lefty Williams (23-11 2.64)

At Chicago, ILL **October 6th, 1919** **Comiskey Park**

Attendance-34,379

2nd inning **Score: 0-0**

1st at-bat **0 on 2 out**

The last game in Chicago before the Series heads back to Cincinnati; the Sox are faced with a huge challenge. Not only facing three games to one deficit, the big right-hander Hod Eller stands in the Sox way. Williams stymied the Reds in the first two innings, as the Sox come to bat in the bottom of the 2nd against Eller in a 0-0 battle. After Eller struck-out the first two batters, Ray bats for the first time today. Hod Eller is on fire though, and strikes Ray out looking (K) for a perfect 2nd inning (Eller would strike-out six batters in a row).

5th inning **Score: 0-0**

2nd at-bat **0 on 2 out**

With two out and the bases missing any White Sox, Ray belts only the second hit off Eller today, a clean single (1B) to left-field. That's all the Sox get off Eller in the 5th, as Lefty Williams strikes-out (Eller's eighth), to end the inning. The game's still scoreless until Williams imploded in the sixth, giving up four runs. Schalk would implode himself in the sixth also, his anger at losing a close play at the plate, his anger at Lefty Williams, his anger at the world in general. Plus the fact that Ray poked umpire Charles Rigler in the chest with his glove, gave Ray an early exit from the ballgame. Chicago went on without Ray, but lost 5-0 as Hod Eller was just too tough today. Pitching the Reds second consecutive three –hitter, the Sox have not scored a run in the last twenty-two innings. The loss in game five has all but sunk Chicago, with little hope of the Series returning to the Windy City.

Game Five Summary

Man, was he ever mad!

Another day, it was the same story as the Sox were three-hit again, this time by the Reds Hod Eller. Chicago lost 5-0 and is now looking a four to one game deficit right in the eye. Ray had only two at-bats today, ripping a two out single in the 5th inning. In the top of the 6th though, Ray was forced to take an early leave of absence after losing his mind on home plate umpire Charles Rigler on a close play at the plate. I think Ray was angrier at Lefty Williams and his pitching, plus the fact that he has figured out what's going on with most of his teammates. The Series is now returning to Cincinnati, with the next two games scheduled for Redland Park. The Reds said goodbye to Chicago, hoping not to return this year.

Game Five Box		Running Total					
		AB	R	H	RBI	AVE	
1st AB	K, Looking	12	1	3	1	.250	K(1)
2nd AB	1B	13	1	4	1	.308	

Game Six

RHP Dickie Kerr (13-8 2.89) vs LHP Dutch Ruether (19-6 1.81)

At Cincinnati, O **October 7th, 1919** **Redland Field**

Attendance-32,006

3rd inning **Score: 0-0**

1st at-bat **0 on 0 out**

The score is still tied 0-0 going into the top of the 3rd inning, as Ray leads-off the inning by drawing a free pass (BB) off Ruether. Dickie Kerr follows with a sacrifice bunt (SAC 5-4), 3B Heinie Groh to 2B Morrie Rath covering 1st base, moving Schalk up to 2nd base. Ruether pitchs out of the inning with the help of LF Pat Duncan, who makes an awesome catch (L-7) on Eddie Collins's sinking liner for the third out.

5th inning **Score: 4-0 Reds**

2nd at-bat **1 on 0 out**

Halfway through game six the Reds were up 4-0, with two runs in the bottom of the 3rd inning, and two more in the 4th. Dickie Kerr has been pitching in and out of jams throughout the ball game, and it's a wonder why manager Kid Gleason hasn't inserted in a new pitcher yet. Dutch Ruether, who only walked one batter in the first game, walks (BB) Swede Risberg to open the Sox half of the 5th inning. Ray then works Ruether for another freebie (BB), with

Risberg taking 2nd base (Ray's fourth walk in the last two ballgames). In a sure bunt situation, Dickie Kerr swings away and singles (1B) off 3B Heinie Groh's glove to load the bases (may have been what's called a slash, when you fake a bunt and swing away). Now it is back to the top of the order, and Shano Collins lofts a fly ball to center-field that looked deep enough for Swede to at least tag up and try for home. Reds captain CF Edd Roush makes the catch (F-8) and fires home, but Swede holds his bag at 3rd base. Now with one out, Eddie Collins hits a ball almost to the same spot. This time however, Risberg tags up after the catch (SF F-8-U) and scores the Sox first run of the game, making the score 4-1. Dickie Kerr then shows everybody that he really is a rookie, when he takes off for 2nd base without looking to see if Ray was tagging and going to 3rd. Both runners end up on 2nd base, as Roush's throw goes to 3rd baseman Heinie Groh trying to keep Schalk on 2nd. Groh runs over to 2nd base and tags out Kerr, since the bag belonged to Schalk and Dickie was uninvited, turning a simple sacrifice fly into an unusual double play (DP SF F-8-5), ending the 5th inning with only one run scored.

6th inning **Score: 4-3 Reds**

3rd at-bat **1 on 2 out**

The big inning Chicago has been waiting for Series finally arrives in the top of the 6th. It started innocently enough when Buck Weaver chips a bloop double (2B) to short left-field. Joe Jackson then lines an RBI single (1B) to center, plating Weaver, making the score 4-2. Next, Happy Felsch delivers a ringing double (2B) to left-center scoring Shoeless Joe all the way from 1st base, bringing the Sox to within a run 4-3. The rare clutch hit also knocks Ruether out of the ballgame, as Reds manager Pat Moran brings in game four winning pitcher, righty Jimmy Ring (10-9 2.26) in to relieve Dutch. Ring immediately retires Gandil and Risberg, and almost gets out of the inning without giving up anymore runs. Almost, because with two down, Ray smacks the biggest two out hit the Sox had made so far in the Series, an RBI single (1B) through the hole at shortstop, scoring Felsch with the tying run. Ray then steals 2nd base (SB), while Dickie Kerr was waiting for a pitch to hit. Ring gets Kerr to ground out (5-3), ending the long 5th inning.

9th inning **Score: 4-4**

4th at-bat **0 on 0 out**

Dickie Kerr was having an up and down game to say the least. In and out of trouble the whole ballgame, somehow Kid Gleason stuck with Kerr through thick and thin. Tied 4-4 going into the top of the 9th inning, Jimmy Ring strikes Ray out (K), leading-off for the Sox. Ring will get out of the inning without giving up any runs. The White scored the winning run in the top of the 10th, on a single (1B) by non-other than Chick Gandil, driving in Buck Weaver. Dickie Kerr then pitches a perfect bottom half (his only perfect inning of the game), and the Sox hang on for an exciting 5-4 ten inning victory.

Game Six Summary

Why am I not leading-off?

In the most thrilling ball game of the entire Series, Dickie Kerr's gut wrenching 10 innings 5-4 victory has given the Sox another chance to play baseball in 1919. The Reds will have to celebrate another day as their lead shrank to four games to two. Ray had himself another fine game, getting on base three more times, with two walks and driving in the tying run in the 6th inning. Ray also stole a base and played his usual stellar defense. With Dickie Kerr's Herculean effort, the Sox live to fight tomorrow.

Game Six Box **Running Total**

		AB	R	H	RBI	AVE	
1st AB	BB	13	1	4	1	.308	BB(3)
2nd AB	BB	13	1	4	1	.308	BB(4)
3rd AB	1B, RBI	14	1	5	2	.357	SB(1)
4th AB	K	15	1	5	2	333	K(2)

Game Seven

RHP Eddie Cicotte (29-7 1.82) vs LHP Slim Sallee (21-7 2.05)

At Cincinnati, Oh **October 8th, 1919** **Redland Field**

Attendance-13,923

2nd inning **Score: 1-0 Sox**

1st at-bat **0 on 1out**

The Sox have taken an early 1-0 lead, after scoring a run in the top of the 1st inning. Ray, batting for the first time today off Sallee with one out in the top of the 2nd inning, hits the only hard shot of the inning, lining out to RF Greasy Neale (L-9), for the second out. The ballgame moves on to the 3rd, with the Sox still holding the 1-0 advantage.

4th inning **Score: 2-0 Sox**

2nd at-bat **0 on 2out**

The Sox upped their lead to 2-0 with another run off Slim Sallee in the top of the 3rd inning. Eddie Cicotte looks unbeatable today, pitching like the man who won twenty-nine games this season. Chicago has two down as Ray comes to bat in the 4th, and he hits a well placed swinging bunt that goes for an infield single (1B), 3B Heinie Groh's way. Eddie Cicotte follows with a routine fly ball that CF Edd Rush puts away (F-8), to end the inning.

6th inning **Score: 4-0 Sox**

3rd at-bat **0 on 0 out**

The White Sox had knocked Slim Sallee out of the ballgame, after scoring two more runs in the top of the 5th inning to take a 4-0 lead. In this game, Cicotte probably only needed a run or two, not having given up an earned run in his last fourteen innings pitched (the two runs he gave up in the fourth game were unearned). The "Pride of Cuba" Dolph Luque (9-3 2.63), who came into the game to start the top of the 6th after replacing Ray Fisher (14-5 2.17), continues his domination of the Chicago White Sox. Ray leads-off the 6th against Luque, by hitting a high fly ball out to LF Pat Duncan (F-7). Luque will give up double (2B) to Shano Collins, but otherwise strikes out two, ending the inning.

8th inning **Score: 4-1 Sox**

4th at-bat **0 on 2out**

Cincinnati finally scored a run off Cicotte in the bottom of the 6th, but Eddie would give up no more runs today. Good thing too, because the Sox couldn't hit Dolph Luque anymore than the Reds could hit Eddie Cicotte. Leading 4-1 heading into the top of the 8th inning, Ray chugs up to the plate for the last time this afternoon, with two out and the bases empty. Luque ends the inning by getting Schalk to ground out (6-3) to SS Larry Kopf. Cicotte would hold Cincinnati the rest of the way, and the Sox sweep the two games at Redland Park. The 4-1 victory has moved the Sox within a single game, four to three, and sends the Series back to Chicago, something not even the Sox players would have thought possible.

Game Seven Summary

Another solid game.

The low (13,923) turnout at today's elimination game just doesn't make any sense, but maybe the Cincinnati town folk were just sick of this year's World Series. Even so, you might have thought that the fans would have come out to say thank you for a season well played. Oh well. The Sox stayed off elimination by beating Slim Salle and the Reds 4-1, with Eddie Cicotte pitching like the ace of the staff that he was. Ray had another good ballgame, picking up another base hit, and hitting the ball well when he made out. Schalk also put the bat on Dolph Luque's pitches, something a lot of his teammates must have envied. So the Series is going to return to Chicago, with the Sox on a two game roll. The Reds must have been starting to get nervous, but they should have feared not, because Kid Gleason was going to start Lefty Williams in game eight. Why, only he knows for sure?

Game Seven Box **Running Total**

		AB	R	H	RBI	AVE
1st AB	L-9	16	1	5	2	.313
2nd AB	1B	17	1	6	2	.353
3rd AB	F-7	18	1	6	2	.333
4th AB	6-3	19	1	6	2	316

Game Eight

RHP Hod Eller (20-9 2.40) vs LHP Lefty Williams (23-11 2.64)

At Chicago, ILL **October 9th, 1919** **Comiskey Park**

Attendance-32,939

2nd inning **Score: 5-0 Reds**

1st at-bat **1 on 1 out**

If it wasn't so sad, it would have laughable. In just five batters the game was pretty much over, even though the White Sox had nine at-bats to go. As a little less than 33,000 watched in total shock, or were busy throwing up, Lefty Williams left the mound in disgrace, his career basically over (in less than a year, it would be). The recipient of these four gift runs, was the winner of game five (a 5-0, three hitter) Hod Eller. The Reds picked up another run off reliever Bill James (3-1 2.54) in the top of the 2nd inning, to take a 5-0 lead. Swede Risberg drew a one out walk (BB) off Eller in the bottom of the 2nd inning, as the Sox tried to get back into the ballgame. Ray follows with a high pop foul behind home plate that Reds catcher Bill Rariden dropped for an error (E-2), on his reprieve; Ray belts a line single (1B) into left-field, moving Risberg to 2nd base. Instead of trying to take advantage of the mini-rally, Kid Gleason in his optimum wisdom lets Bill James bat for himself. James pops-up his sacrifice attempt (F-5), for the second out, and Eller pitches out of the jam by retiring Nemo Leibold on a strikeout (K).

4th inning **Score: 5-1 Reds**

2nd at-bat **0 on 2 out**

The Sox broke an eleven inning scoring drought against Hod Eller in the bottom of the 3rd inning, when Joe Jackson cracked the only home run that counted (Heinie Groh should have had one in the bottom of the 6th inning of game seven), making the score 5-1 Cincinnati. Ray Schalk, batting with two gone in the bottom of the 4th, ends an easy inning for Eller, grounding out to 3B Heinie Groh (5 3).

7th inning **Score: 9-1 Reds**

3rd at-bat **0 on 1 out**

By the time the bottom of the 7th inning rolled around, the Reds had chased Bill James out of the ballgame, with a run in the 5th and three more in the top of the 6th, taking a 9-1 lead. Eller was still setting the Sox down like he was giving a small child a time out, and the 7th inning was no different. In another one, two, three inning, Ray makes the second out by fouling again straight back of home plate. This time though, Bill Rariden holds on to the baseball (FO-2).

8th inning **Score: 10-5 Reds**

4th at-bat **1 on 2 out**

The Reds scored another run in the top of the eighth, off third Sox pitcher Roy Wilkenson (1-1 2.05), who came into the ballgame in the top of the 6th, to take a seemingly insurmountable lead 10-1. Needing only six more outs to claim their first World Championship of the modern era, the Reds Hod Eller took to the mound. Then Chicago explodes for their biggest inning of the 1919 World Series, pushing across four runs. It all started with one out, when Eddie Collins singled (1B) to center-field. Followed by back to back doubles (2B) by Buck Weaver and Joe Jackson, making the score 10-3 Cincinnati. The Sox scored another run with two out, when RF Greasy Neale lost Chick Gandil's fly ball in the sun, as it went for a RBI triple (3B). Reds captain CF Edd Roush gave the Sox their last run of the year, dropping Swede Risberg's fly (E-8) allowing Gandil to score the fifth and final run. Ray ends the inning, with his ground-out to 2B Morrie Rath (4-3). The score was a little more respectable 10-5, but the game was never close. Eller snuffed out another Sox rally in the bottom of the 9th, and the Reds were World Series Champions with the five games to three victory over the White Sox.

Game Eight Summary

A Series to be proud of!

Today Chicago ran out of gas, and Lefty Williams was behind the wheel. What more can you say about Williams, to hell with him, but I can speak loudly for Ray Schalk. He was something Chicago could be proud of with his gutsy play. He swung the bat as well as anyone in the Series, and if Chick Gandil would have been hustling in game three, Ray's batting average would have been .348. With the Reds winning game eight 10-5, behind Hod Eller, Cincinnati pulled off the stunning upset of one of the best baseball teams to ever come down the turnpike. Ray finished his World Series one for four, and for the Series he reached base 12 times (seven base hits, four walks and a hit by pitch). Plus Ray only left five runners on base, although there weren't many base runners on when Schalk was batting. As poor as the top two Sox hitters in the order batted (whoever played right-field leading-off, and Eddie Collins), Gleason should have moved Ray up to the top of the order. Kid didn't make any moves in the Series to give his team a better chance to win though, especially since most of the team didn't much feel like playing.

Game Eight Box **Running Total**

		AB	R	H	RBI	AVE	
1st AB	1B	20	1	7	2	.350	
2nd AB	5-3	21	1	7	2	.333	
3rd AB	FO-2	22	1	7	2	.318	
4th AB	4-3	23	1	7	2	304	1 LOB(5)

Chapter Nine

Charles Arnold Gandil

Take the money and run.

Charles Arnold Gandil was born January 18, 1888 in St. Paul, Minnesota. Best known by his nickname Chick, the Gandil's moved to the Los Angeles, California area when Chick was only four years old, then up the coast to Oakland. At the young age of seventeen in 1905, Chick dropped out of high school and ran away from home, never to return. Showing up in Amarillo, Texas, Chick lived the life of a hobo riding the rails and playing semi-pro baseball to make his living among doing other odd jobs, including working at a copper mine. In 1906, Chick was earning $15 a game pitching in Mexico, decent money in those days. He was also making good money as a prize fighter, $150 a fight. Yes, Chick Gandil was as tough as they came, and lived his life accordingly. When Chick turned twenty in 1908, he began his professional baseball career, first playing in Shreveport, Louisiana then back to California in 1909 to play for Sacramento. Purchased by the Chicago White Sox owner Charles Comiskey after the season, Chick made his Major League debut on opening day, April 14, 1910.

Chick Gandil's first season for the Sox was not a good one, hitting only .193 in seventy-seven games, although he did play a good 1st base. It was said that Chick's hands were so hard that he didn't need a glove. Of course he did, and he used it well, as shown by his .992 lifetime fielding percentage. After the 1910 campaign, Gandil was released by the White Sox, and played the 1911 season back in the Minors with Montreal. Chick had a fine year with Montreal and was picked up by the Washington Senators for the 1912 season and would spend the next five years in D. C. It was here that Chick had his first fateful introduction to local bookmaker and gambler Joseph "Sport" Sullivan, who would play a huge part in the scandal of 1919. Chick's first two years in Washington were very good ones, hitting in succession .305 in 1912 and .a career high of .318 in 1913. Gandil followed those seasons with a sub-par .259 in 1914, but picked the pace back up in 1915 with a .291 average. Never hitting with much power, Chick hit well enough and was extremely handy around the bag at 1st base. So much so that Chick was sold for the sum of $7,500 by the Senators, to the Cleveland Indians on February 15, 1916. Chick only played the 1916 season for the Indians batting .259, but played his usual good defense.

Charles Comiskey must have thought he was getting a great deal on Chick, purchasing him back to the White Sox for the bargain price of $3,500 on February 25, 1917. Some bargain it turned out to be, probably the worst money Commie ever spent. But Chick did play well in Chicago this time around, batting .273 in the Sox World Championship season of 1917, and .271 in the World War 1 shortened stanza of 1918. Chick had his best all-round year, and his last, in the unforgettable 1919 season. Batting a crisp .290, Chick made only three errors in one thousand, one hundred and seventy-nine chances at 1st base, for an amazing .997 percentage. Still living the rough life, an example of Chick's disposition was an incident that took place that August, when Chick was suspended for only five games, for punching out the home plate umpire over a disputed strike call. But that was the kind of hairpin Chick was.

The 1919 World Series would be the last organized ballgames Chick ever played. Taking $35,000 of the $80,000 collected for the players cut of the fix money, Chick held out for more money on his 1920 salary, and left for California with his small fortune. After the scandal of the World Series broke, Chick along with seven other teammates were officially suspended by Sox owner Charles Comiskey on September 27, 1920, and was banned for life by new baseball Commissioner, Kenesaw Mountain Landis the following year on August 3, 1921. An interesting footnote, Gandil was hired to run an Outlaw League team in Douglas, Arizona in 1927 that happened to be managed by one Buck Weaver. To show what a great pal he was, and to also show how much he had mellowed over the years, Chick had Buck kicked out of the league (for some unknown reason). Supposedly Chick was still mad at Buck because Weaver had failed to help Chick out in the investigation of a pay-off to the Detroit Tiger players for throwing a four game series to the White Sox in the 1917 pennant chase, and also because Buck refused to lay down against the Cincinnati Reds in the 1919 World Series. Nothing came out of the investigation by Judge Landis, partly because Gandil and Swede Risberg were declared liars, but Chick sure knew how to pay back an old friend.

That was now twice Chick helped Buck out of baseball. After playing several more seasons of semi-pro ball along the California coast, Chick retired from ball for good to become a plumber in Oakland. When Chick retired in 1954, he spent the last years of his life in Calistoga in the Napa Valley. Chick died on December 13, 1970 in a convalescent home, after a long battle with heart disease at the age of eighty-two. His wife Laurel, who followed Chick thru sixty-two years of ups and downs, also followed Chick to the hereafter, just three months later. What you are about to read on the surface, would look like a so-so World Series. The numbers are not that bad compared to the rest of the White Sox. Chick batted .233, and out of the three games the Sox won, Gandil had two game winning hits (both of Dickie Kerr's starts). He also averaged a hit a game and only made one error in the field. Chick Gandil also did as much as anyone else, in the throwing of this Series.

Game One

RHP Eddie Cicotte (29-7 1.82) vs LHP Dutch Ruether (19-6 1.81)

At Cincinnati, Oh **October 1st, 1919** **Redland Field**

Attendance-30,511

1st inning **Score: 1-0 Reds**

2nd at-bat **1 on 1out**

The opening day of the World Series and everyone in Cincinnati was in a joyous mood, especially anyone with a bet on the Reds. The Reds took a 1-0 lead in the bottom of the 1st off Cicotte, as the Sox come to bat in the top of the 2nd inning. Chick's first at-bat in the Series is a productive one, tying the score with an RBI bloop single (1B) to left, plating Joe Jackson from 3rd base with one out. It wasn't all peaches for Chick, as he is tossed out trying to steal 2nd base (CS 2-4), by Reds catcher Ivy Wingo for the 2nd out. Ruther retires Swede Risberg to end the inning all square at one apiece.

5th inning **Score: 6-1 Reds**

2nd at-bat **0 on 0 out**

The Reds have taken a 6-1 lead after pounding Eddie Cicotte into submission and out of the ballgame with a five run 4th inning, all of the Reds scoring coming with two out. The Sox tried to regroup in their half of the 5th, with Gandil leading-off. Chick gets the ball rolling with another single (1B), this time to center-field. After Swede Risberg flies out to CF Edd Roush (F-8) for the first out, Ray Schalk forces Chick at 2nd base (FC 5-4), for out number two. Ruether would not bend for any runs in the frame.

7th inning **Score: 6-1 Reds**

3rd at-bat **0 on 0 out**

Leading-off the top of the 7th inning with the Sox still trailing the Reds 6-1, Chick flies out to RF Greasy Neale (F-9). Dutch Ruether was now on cruise control and sets the Sox down in order.

9th inning **Score: 9-1 Reds**

4th at-bat **0 on 2out**

Putting the final touches on a well pitched 9-1 victory, Ruether entices Chick to ground out to 2B Morrie Rath (4-3), ending this afternoon's contest. The win has staked the Reds to a one game to nothing lead in the best five out of nine World Series. What's really puzzling is not that the Reds beat Eddie Cicotte, but how quickly Eddie lost his stuff in the 4th inning.

Game One Summary

Losing while looking good.

Not a bad start for a bad guy. Chick had two hits today in the Series opener and drove in the Sox only run in a 9-1 smack down. Chick's RBI single off Reds starter and winning pitcher Dutch Ruether, momentarily tied the score at 1-1. A five run Reds inning off ace Eddie Cicotte in the bottom of the 4th, spelled doom for Chicago today. Chick also had a nice single up the middle, but Ruether kept him and the Sox at bay the rest of the way.

Game One Box		Running Total					
		AB	R	H	RBI	AVE	
1st AB	1B, RBI, CS	1	0	1	1	1.000	CS(1)
2nd AB	1B	2	0	2	1	1.000	
3rd AB	F-9	3	0	2	1	.667	
4th AB	4-3	4	0	2	1	.500	

Game Two

LHP Lefty Williams (23-11 2.64) vs LHP Slim Sallee (21-7 2.05)

At Cincinnati, Oh **October 1st, 1919** **Redland Field**

Attendance-29,698

2nd inning **Score: 0-0**

1st at-bat **1 on 1out**

After a scoreless 1st inning, the Sox have something cooking in the top of the 2nd. With Joe Jackson on at 3rd base and one out, Chick raps a grounder to SS Larry Kopf, who checked Jackson back to 3rd and tosses out Gandil (6-3). Jackson would not score as Sallee slipped out of the inning unscathed.

4th inning **Score: 0-0**

2nd at-bat **2 on 1out**

With the score still tied 0-0 heading into the top of the 4th inning, the Sox have Sallee in trouble again. Buck Weaver and Joe Jackson open the inning with singles (1B) and Happy Felsch advances both runners with a sacrifice bunt (SAC 1-3). With the infield playing in close, Chick grounds to 1B Jake Daubert, who makes a nice play, throwing out Buck at the plate (FC 3-2) with Jackson taking 3rd. Gandil will steal 2nd base (SB), but Sallee retires Swede Risberg to pull another Houdini act and escape danger.

7th inning **Score: 4-2 Reds**

3rd at-bat **0 on 0out**

There was something about the bottom of the 4th inning in games one and two. For the second day in a row, the Reds put together a big inning to take control of a ballgame. Today Lefty Williams lost sight of the strike zone and walked three batters, leading directly to three runs. The Reds scored another run in the home half of the 6th to take a 4-0 lead. Chick leads-off the top of the 6th and once again hits a grounder to 1B Jake Daubert, who flips the ball to Slim Sallee covering (3-1) the bag. The Sox would score two runs in the inning, on two base hits and a two error play, making the score 4-2.

9th inning **Score: 4-2 Reds**

4th at-bat **0 on 0 out**

The score was still 4-2 Reds going into the Sox last chance in the top of the 9th inning. Chick again leads-off an inning with a single (1B) over 2B Morrie Rath's head into right-field. The big inning Chicago was looking for was short lived, as Swede Risberg immediately hits into a (DP 4-6-3) double play. After a Ray Schalk single (1B), Swede's buddy Fred McMullin grounds out (4-3) ending the game (I'm sure Fred was looking for a big hit). The Sox 4-2 loss completed a two game sweep in Cincinnati, with Chicago's two aces taking the losses. Chicago now trails two games to zero heading home to Comiskey Park.

Game Two Summary

The Sox couldn't do much with Slim Sallee today, scoring only two unearned runs on a crazy play in the 7th inning. The 4-2 loss has made game three in Chicago very important, with rookie Dickie Kerr scheduled to start. Chick had another base hit today leading-off the 9th to no avail. In his two most important at-bats in the ballgame, Chick left three runners in scoring position without hitting the ball very hard. In retrospect you could say Gandil planned it that way, but so far his stats look pretty good.

Game Two Box		**Running Total**					
		AB	R	H	RBI	AVE	
1st AB	6-3	5	0	2	1	.400	1 LOB(1), 1 RISP(1)
2nd AB	FC 3-2, SB	6	0	2	1	.333	2 LOB(3), 2 RISP(3)
3rd AB	3-1	7	0	2	1	.286	
4th AB	1B	8	0	3	1	.375	

Game Three

RHP Ray Fisher (14-5 2.17) vs RHP Dickie Kerr (13-8 2.89)

At Chicago, ILL **October 3rd, 1919** **Comiskey Park**

Attendance-29,126

2nd inning **Score: 0-0**

1st at-bat **2 on 0 out**

Sweet home Chicago, it was a sight for sore eyes. Comiskey Park was also the sight of a lot of empty seats. Game three was not a do or die situation, but it was close. In a 0-0 game going into the bottom of the 2nd inning, the Sox had a little rally started, with Joe Jackson on at 3rd base and Happy Felsch at 2nd with no outs. Ironically Chick gives the Sox their first lead of the Series with a line shot two RBI single (1B) into right-field. Next batter Swede Risberg draws a walk (BB) to bring Ray Schalk to the plate, still with nobody out. Schalk lays down a nice bunt that looked like a sure base hit but Gandil, who is not in too big of a hurry to get to 3rd base, is forced out by Fisher (FC 1-5) for the first out of the inning. Fisher then retires Kerr and Leibold without any more runs, but the Sox still had the lead 2-0, though it could have been a bigger inning.

4th inning **Score: 2-0 Sox**

2nd at-bat **0 on 0 out**

Dickie Kerr was throwing like Cicotte and Williams should have in games one and two, and held a 2-0 lead going into the bottom of the 4th. Leading-off, Chick pulls a grounder to 3B Heinie Groh, who has no problems sending Gandil back to the dugout (5-3). A Swede Risberg triple (3B) and a Ray Schalk RBI bunt single (1B), give the Sox a 3-0 lead, and then Dickie Kerr took over the ballgame.

6th inning **Score: 3-0 Sox**

3rd at-bat **0 on 2 out**

With Dickie Kerr in total control of the Cincinnati Reds, the Sox sill held a 3-0 lead heading to the bottom of the 6th inning. With two down Chick strikes-out (K), ending the inning (it was Ray Fisher's only strikeout of the game). Dickie Kerr didn't need any more help today as he finished with a three-hitter. The 3-0 victory helped the Sox out in more ways than the obvious reason, which was winning, but would also help in ticket sales tomorrow.

Game Three Summary

Chick the hero!

A rookie did what the aces couldn't (or wouldn't), and that was taking a ballgame from the Reds. Dickie Kerr pitched a three-hit shutout in winning 3-0, giving the Sox their first victory in three games. Chick had the biggest hit of the game, a two run single in the 2nd inning that proved to be the winning runs. Chick pretty much took the rest of the day off, but the Sox and Kerr didn't need any more runs today. Chick did take away a base hit from Ray Schalk in the 2nd inning, when he took his sweet time trotting to 3rd, after Schalk had dropped a perfect drag bunt (Chick might drive home a couple of runs, but he'd be damned if he scored one). With the next two games still to be played in Chicago, the Sox were looking for their own home sweep and to take control of a Series many thought would be over in five games, in the White Sox favor.

Game Three Box **Running Total**

		AB	R	H	RBI	AVE	
1st AB	1B, RBI	9	0	4	3	.444	
2nd AB	5-3	10	0	4	3	.400	
3rd AB	K	11	0	4	3	.364	K(1)

Game Four

RHP Jimmy Ring (10-9 2.26) vs RHP Eddie Cicotte (29-7 1.82)

At Chicago, ILL **October 4th, 1919** **Comiskey Park**

Attendance-34,363

2nd inning **Score: 0-0**

1st at-bat **1 on 1 out**

Now that the home fans were excited again, they were out in full today on the Southside. The Sox had a chance to get to Ring early with Joe Jackson on at 3rd base with one out, as Chick came up to the plate with an opportunity to give the Sox the early lead, just like yesterday. Yesterday's moment was over though, and Chick probably wasn't looking for any heroics today. He hits a very weak pop-up out in front of the plate that 3B Heinie Groh takes charge of (F-5), making it two out. Ring then walked Risberg (BB) and Schalk (BB), but retires Eddie Cicotte on a ground out (4-3) with the count full.

4th inning **Score: 0-0**

2nd at-bat **0 on 0 out**

Still tied 0-0 in the bottom of the 4th inning, the Sox is looking for a fast start. Chick instead fouls-out to 1B Jake Daubert (FO-3) leading-off the inning. Ring would retire the Sox in order as the game moves to the 5th inning and some fielding problems.

6th inning **Score: 2-0 Reds**

3rd at-bat **0 on 2 out**

The Reds took a 2-0 lead in the top of the 5th with the help of two Eddie Cicotte errors. Now with two down in the bottom of the 6th, Chick delivers a base hit up the middle off Ring (1B). Gandil has now had a base hit in all four ballgames, the only Sox player to have done so. Ring retired Swede Risberg on a fly out to RF Greasy Neale (F-9) ending the inning.

8th inning **Score: 2-0 Reds**

4th at-bat **1 on 2 out**

The Sox were running out of time in game four, and trailing 2-0 to Jimmy Ring. Chicago has Happy Felsch on at 1st base with two away, as Chick came to bat for the fourth time today. Gandil did not look too energized at the plate though, striking-out (K) to end the 8th inning.

Game Four Summary

No heroics today.

A tight, well pitched ballgame came down to two Eddie Cicotte errors (one was Joe Jackson's?), which led to both Cincinnati runs and ruined Cicotte's otherwise well pitched ballgame today. Jimmy Ring ended up throwing a 2-0 three-hit shutout, giving the Reds a comfortable three games to one advantage. The White Sox backs were slowly creeping up against the wall, though they were not quite there yet. Chick had another base hit today, giving him a hit in every World Series game so far. He also did what he could to keep the Sox run total down, which today was nil. Chick had a great chance to get the Sox on the board early, with Joe Jackson on at 3rd base and only one out. All Chick had to do was put the ball in play, other than in the air to the infield and the Sox score, but Gandil popped up in front of the plate and the White Sox did not score. Chicago should have won this game, failing to score off of Jimmy Ring though they had plenty of chances. Besides the three hits, Ring also walked three and hit two batters, plus the Sox had two base runners via errors. No clutch hitting though. This loss was a big turning point in the Series.

Game Four Box		**Running Total**					
		AB	R	H	RBI	AVE	
1st AB	F-5	12	0	4	3	.333	1 LOB(4), 1 RISP(4)
2nd AB	FO-3	13	0	4	3	.308	
3rd AB	1B	14	0	5	3	.357	
4th AB	K	15	0	5	3	.333	K(2), 1 LOB(5)

Game Five

RHP Hod Eller (20-9 2.40) vs LHP Lefty Williams (23-11 2.64)

At Chicago, ILL **October 6th, 1919** **Comiskey Park**

Attendance-34,379

2nd inning **Score: 0-0**

1st at-bat **0 on 0 out**

Talk about a must win game, this is definitely one for the Sox. It's a great match-up today between two twenty game winners in front of another big crowd, no doubt many believing it will be the last time the home folks get to see their beloved White Sox in action this year. Chick leads-off the bottom of the 2nd inning in a 0-0 ballgame and is a strike-out victim (K). Gandil was the first of six consecutive strikeouts by Eller.

5th inning **Score: 0-0**

2nd at-bat **0 on 0 out**

What more could any baseball fan ask for? Lefty Williams and Hod Eller both had one-hitters going, in one of the best pitchers duals in World Series history. Chick leads-off an inning for the second time in as many at-bats, grounding out to 2B Morrie Rath (4-3). Eller would give up a base hit to Ray Schalk (1B), but that was all Eller would bend in the 5th.

7th inning **Score: 4-0 Reds**

3rd at-bat **0 on 2 out**

Question, how can Lefty Williams be throwing one of the best games in the history of the World Series, then become no better than a high school JV pitcher for an inning, then becomes Christy Mathewson, CY Young and Babe

Ruth (yes, the Babe was one of the greatest World Series pitchers) all rolled into one again? Don't know the answer? He gets paid a lot of money to throw the ballgame. Chick batted for the last time today with two out and the bases empty. All Gandil can do with Eller, is lift a lazy fly ball to CF Edd Roush out in straight away center- field (F-8), ending the bottom of the 7th. Eller finished off the Sox, giving up only one more hit, and the Reds now hold a seemingly insurmountable lead of four games to one.

Game Five Summary

One more to go!

The Sox backs are now totally against the wall. So we learned two things in game five, one was that Hod Eller was one fine pitcher. The other? So was Lefty Williams, except in the 6th inning. Chick had no worse a game than anybody else today, other than Buck Weaver who had two of the Sox three hits (Ray Schalk had the other before taking an early shower). This was also the third straight game that a pitcher has thrown a three-hit shutout, the others by Jimmy Ring of the Reds and Dickie Kerr of the White Sox. This Series is about to get interesting.

Game Five Box **Running Total**

		AB	R	H	RBI	AVE	
1st AB	K	16	0	5	3	.313	K(3)
2nd AB	4-3	17	0	5	3	.294	
3rd AB	F-8	18	0	5	3	.278	

Game Six

RHP Dickie Kerr (13-8 2.89) vs LHP Dutch Ruether (19-6 1.81)

At Cincinnati, Oh **October 7th, 1919** **Redland Field**

Attendance-32,006

2nd inning **Score: 0-0**

1st at-bat **0 on 1 out**

The Sox couldn't be in any worse shape, other than being swept in five games. They have lost four of the first five games, and their two best pitchers have lost all four games. They only have six hits in the previous two games, and haven't scored in twenty-two straight innings. A large Redland Park crowd showed up today to witness the first Reds World Championship in the modern era (last was 1882). After a scoreless 1st inning, Chick struts up to bat with the bases clear and one out. Ruether gets Gandil to bounce out to SS Larry Kopf (6-3) for out number two. Ruether also sets down Swede Risberg for an easy 2nd inning.

4th inning **Score: 2-0 Reds**

2nd at-bat **1 on 2 out**

The Reds scored two runs off Dickie Kerr in the bottom of the 3rd inning to take a 2-0 lead. Going into the top of the 4th, the Sox have not scored in the last twenty-five innings and this frame would be no different. With Happy Felsch on at 1st base and two out, Chick raps a bounding ball to SS Larry Kopf, who makes the long throw over to 1B Jake Daubert (6-3), making it twenty-six innings without a run.

6th inning **Score: 4-1 Reds**

3rd at-bat **1 on 0 out**

The Reds have taken a 4-0 lead with two more runs off Kerr in the bottom of the 4th , and were just half a game away from eliminating the Sox from this competition. There was some good news; the Sox ended their twenty-six inning scoreless streak, with a single run off Ruether in the 5th inning, but still trail 4-1 heading into the top of the 6th. This inning would change a lot of the Sox misfortune though, as they put together their biggest inning of the six games played so far, when the Southsiders finally start hitting Dutch Ruether. It all starts with a bloop double by Buck Weaver (2B) leading-off the 6th and then it snowballed. Joe Jackson next ripped an RBI single (1B) scoring Weaver making the score 4-2, followed by Happy Felsch's RBI double (2B) to plate Jackson. The big hit by Felsch not only made the tally 4-3, but also chased Ruether from the hill, bringing game four winning pitcher, righty Jimmy Ring (10-9 2.26) into the ballgame. Chick checks into the batter's box, still with nobody out, and maybe trying, maybe not, pops-up to 1B Jake Daubert (F-3) for the first out of the inning. Ray Schalk will tie up the score four all with an RBI single (1B) to left before Ring can put out the flames.

8th inning **Score: 4-4**

4th at-bat **1 on 1 out**

Dickie Kerr was still struggleling but has not given up anymore runs, as the game moves into the top of the 8th inning. With Joe Jackson on 1st with one out, Chick waits out Ring for a free pass (BB). This puts runners on 1st and 2nd base, and with only one out, a great chance to take the lead. It seems Joe Jackson wanted no part of that as he pulled the first of his disappearing acts. Swede Risberg, batting next drills a ball that was heading for a base hit until Reds CF Edd Roush came rushing over to make a shoestring catch (F-8), but Jackson never turned his head to look and was heading around 3rd base when Roush caught the ball. Roush turned it into an inning ending double play (DP F-8-4).

10th inning **Score: 4-4**

5th at-bat **2 on 1 out**

The way Chick Gandil kept winning World Series games for Dickie Kerr; you would never have guessed Chick hated Kerr's guts. As the game moved on into extra innings, the Sox had Jimmy Ring on the ropes. The Sox have Buck Weaver and Joe Jackson on the corners with one out, when Chick delivers the Sox biggest hit (1B) of the Series. Trying to get a base hit or not, only Chick knows for sure, Gandil sends a soft liner just barely over the head of 2B Morrie Rath into right-field giving the Sox a 5-4 lead. Then with Swede Risberg at the plate, Joe Jackson made sure the Sox wouldn't get too big a lead when Risberg's liner was caught by SS Larry Kopf (L-6), and for the second time in just three innings, Joe was doubled off 2nd base (DP L-6-4) ending another inning. Dickie Kerr then pitches his only one, two, three inning of the day, and the Sox live to fight another day.

Game Six Summary

Hero revisited!

The Sox were on life support coming into game six and their condition is still critical, but it's not time to pull the plug quite yet. Thanks to Dickie Kerr and one Chick Gandil. Kerr pitched ten rollercoaster innings and showed the Reds exactly what he was made of-steel. Gandil chipped in with his second game winning hit (both of Kerr's wins), and kept the Sox from an earth shattering defeat. Chick didn't hit the ball that well today, even his big knock wasn't hit that hard, but I'd rather be lucky than good any day. Before his game winner Chick hadn't hit a ball out of the infield all day. It was a huge clutch hit none-the-less. The Sox now go for their own sweep tomorrow in Cincinnati, trying to get the Series back to Chicagoland.

Game Six Box **Running Total**

		AB	R	H	RBI	AVE	
1st AB	6-3	19	0	5	3	.263	
2nd AB	6-3	20	0	5	3	.250	1 LOB(6)
3rd AB	F-3	21	0	5	3	.238	1 LOB(7), 1RISP(5)
4th AB	BB	21	0	5	3	.238	BB(1)
5th AB	1B, RBI	22	0	6	4	.273	

Game Seven

RHP Eddie Cicotte (29-7 1.82) vs LHP Slim Sallee (21-7 2.05)

At Cincinnati, Oh **October 8th, 1919** **Redland Field**

Attendance-13,923

1st inning **Score: 1-0 Sox**

1st at-bat **2 on 2out**

After watching the thrilling up and down ten inning game six yesterday, what could be better than seeing two pitchers with a combined fifty wins between them. Don't ask too many Cincinnati fans, as only about 14,000 bothered to show up. Even if the Reds win the World Series today, or in Chicago, or lose the last three games and the Series, this afternoon's game will be the final time the Reds will play at home this year. Maybe there was a beer fest down on the banks of the Ohio River, but not a lot of fan appreciation for a great season (win or lose). The people who did not show up missed Eddie Cicotte at his best. Chick must have felt terrible about his game winning hit yesterday, because with the exception of a sun lost triple in game eight, he would do nothing at the plate the rest of the Series. Joe Jackson's RBI single (1B) has given the Sox an early 1-0 lead. Chick's first at-bat saw Jackson on at 2nd base and Happy Felsch at 1st with two gone. Gandil hits a bunny hopper to SS Larry Kopf who flips the ball to 2B Morrie Rath, forcing Happy at 2nd base (FC 6-4), to end the top of the 1st inning.

4th inning **Score: 2-0 Sox**

2nd at-bat **0 on 0 out**

The Sox scored another run in the top of the 3rd inning to take a 2-0 lead into the 4th, and the way Eddie Cicotte was throwing, two runs was going to be plenty. Chick leads-off the inning by hitting Sallee's offering to medium right-field, which RF Greasy Neale takes care of (F-9) for the 1st out. Sallee gives up a two out single (1B) to Ray Schalk but leaves the inning unscarred.

5th inning **Score: 4-0 Sox**

3rd at-bat **2 on 1out**

The Sox upped the ante to 4-0 with two runs on Happy Felsch's single (1B). With Joe Jackson on 2nd base and Happy on at 1st and one out, Gandil is hitting against new Reds pitcher right-hander Ray Fisher (14-9 2.17). Fisher (who lost game three) gets Chick to hit a comebacker, which he momentarily bobbles but recovers in time to nab Gandil at 1st base (1-3) as both base runners move up a bag. Neither runner would score though as the game moves on into the sixth inning.

8th inning **Score: 4-1 Sox**

4th at-bat **0 on 0 out**

The Reds did score a run off Cicotte in the bottom of the 6th inning, making the score 4-1. That's all the scoring Eddie would yield today. Chick starts off the top of the 8th with a pop-up to SS Larry Kopf (F-6) off the third pitcher for the Reds today, Cuban right-hander Dolph Luque (9-3 2.63). Luque would strikeout five in his four inning of work, but the Sox didn't need to score off of him, it was a good thing too, because the White Sox couldn't hit Luque.

The 4-1 victory behind Eddie Cicotte's professionally pitched ballgame has given the Sox a two game sweep in Cincinnati. This victory will send the Series back to Chicago, with the Sox now trailing only by a game, four to three.

Game Seven Summary

Take the afternoon off!

The Sox are still on life support, and their condition has been upgraded to critical but stable, meaning they are holding their own. Eddie Cicotte pitched today like the superstar he is, and the Sox finally scored some runs for him. The 4-1 decision has moved the Series back to Chicago, something no one thought was possible, as the Reds lead has shrunk to four games to three. Chick did a whole lot of nothing today, going 0 for four, and he also left four men on base including two in scoring position. Chick's once stellar batting average has also slipped to a Series low .231.

Game Seven Box		**Running Total**					
		AB	R	H	RBI	AVE	
1st AB	FC 6-4	23	0	6	4	.261	2 LOB(9), 1 RISP(6)
2nd AB	F-9	24	0	6	4	.250	
3rd AB	1-3	25	0	6	4	.240	2 LOB(11), 2 RISP(7)
4th AB	F-6	26	0	6	4	.231	

Game Eight

RHP Hod Eller (20-9 2.40) vs LHP Lefty Williams (23-11 2.64)

At Chicago, ILL October 9th, 1919 Comiskey Park

Attendance-32,939

2nd inning Score: 5-0 Reds

1st at-bat 0 on 0 out

I would have loved to of heard what Kid Gleason really said, if anything, to Lefty Williams as he was removing him from the ballgame. As you know by now, Williams lasted just five batters and was replaced by Right-hander Bill James (3-1 2.54). The four runs the Reds scored was just the beginning of the grave being dug, the first shovel full "thrown" by Lefty. The hottest pitcher on the planet, Hod Eller of the Reds, was the recipient of this early Christmas gift, and he had no intention of returning it to customer service. In what would turn out to be Chick Gandil's last Major League baseball game, Chick steps up to bat for the first time in the bottom of the 2nd inning with the Sox trailing 5-0. After the Reds scored another run off James, courtesy of Chick being slow on a grounder to him by Heinie Groh (1B), then Joe Jackson let Edd Roush's long fly glance off his glove (another charitable scoring decision) for a RBI double (2B). I didn't include fielding plays in this section of the book (there in- depth in the pitchers section), but these two plays signify how some of the Sox were just not going to let their team have a chance to get back into this game, and the Sox did have their opportunities. Getting back to Gandil's at-bat, leading-off the 2nd inning, Chick slashes a soft liner to 1B Jake Daubert (L-3) for the first out. Eller has now pitched eleven scoreless innings against the White Sox.

4th inning **Score: 5-1 Reds**

2nd at-bat **0 on 0 out**

The Sox finally scored off of Hod Eller when Joe Jackson slugged a long homer (HR) to right-field in the bottom of the 3rd, making the score 5-1. Chick leads-off the 4th by lifting the ball into right-center field that Reds captain CF Edd Roush glides over to, making the catch (F-8). Eller breezed through the inning without a base runner.

6th inning **Score: 9-1 Reds**

3rd at-bat **1 on 2 out**

By the bottom of the 6th inning rolled around, the grave that Lefty Williams started to dig in the 1st was now ready for a body. The Reds have taken a commanding 9-1 lead after scoring one run in the 5th, and three more tallies in the top of the 6th. Imagine the conversation in the Sox dugout, if anybody was talking to anyone else. Batting for the third time today Chick steps up to bat with Buck Weaver on 1st base and two out. Gandil can manage nothing more than a tired fly ball out to RF Greasy Neale (F-9), who catches the pill ending the 6th inning.

8th inning **Score: 10-3 Reds**

4th at-bat **1 on 2 out**

With half a body in that grave, the Sox started showing little signs of life. With one out Eddie Collins singled (1B), followed by a Buck Weaver Double (2B). Joe Jackson then almost hits his second home run of game, short hopping the wall for a two run double (2B) making the score 10-3. In his final big league at-bat, Chick pokes what should have been an easy out, but RF Greasy Neale loses the ball in the sun as the ball rolls all the way to the wall, for a run scoring triple (3B) plating Jackson. Next batter Swede Risberg also hits what should have been an out, but Reds CF Edd Roush drops the ball (E-8), for an error. In thirty-one at-bats (with one walk), Chick scores his first (and only) run of the Series, making the score 10-5. After the little uprising in the 9th inning, Hod Eller finishes off the Sox, putting their whole team in the grave and covering them up with dirt. The Reds are champions of baseball defeating the White Sox in eight games, five games to three.

Game Eight Summary

California here I come!

The Chicago White Sox went brain dead today, and were taken off life support. The person pulling the plug today was Lefty Williams. Losing the eighth and final game 10-5, the ball game was virtually over after only five batters. Chick was really no help either this afternoon, his only contribution being gift triple and RBI in the five run 8th inning when RF Greasy Neale lost his fairly deep pop-fly in the sun. He also scored his only run in the eight games on a bonus gift when next batter Swede Risberg lofted a pop-fly out to CF Edd Roush, who dropped the easy play for an error. The Reds won the World Series, but we all know better, the White Sox gave them the trophy. Chick's Series numbers were better than most of his teammates, with seven hits and five RBI's to go along with his two game winning RBI's. He only batted for a .233 average (better than the teams .224), though it could have been much worse with better fielding on the Reds part. Chick would never appear in another big league game, taking his $35,000 pirates loot and leaving Chicago for the sunshine of California.

Game Eight Box **Running Total**

		AB	R	H	RBI	AVE	
1st AB	L-3	27	0	6	4	.222	1 LOB(12)
2nd AB	F-8	28	0	6	4	.214	
3rd AB	F-9	29	0	6	4	.207	
4th AB	3B, Run, RBI	30	1	7	5	.233	

Chapter Ten

Edward Trowbridge Collins Sr.

Sure picked a bad time!

Edward Trowbridge Collins was born May 2nd, 1887 in Millerton New York. At 5'9 175 lbs. Eddie was a stocky 2nd baseman who played Major League baseball for twenty-five years! Collins was inducted into the baseball Hall of Fame in 1939. Eddie was a rare breed for baseball players in that era; he attended Columbia University in New York City. Starring in baseball and quarterbacking the football teams, Eddie was truly a prize athlete. A late September call-up in 1906 for Connie Mack's Philadelphia A's, Eddie hit .235 in six games. While still attending Columbia, Eddie got another cup of coffee in the bigs in 1907, and then joined the A's for good in 1908 batting .273. Eddie began an eight year stretch of hitting over .300 in 1909 with a .346 average. Starting in 1910, Eddie helped Philadelphia win three of the next four World Championships, only missing out in 1912. Along with Stuffy McInnis, Jack Berry and Frank "Home Run" Baker, Collins helped form the famed $100,000 infield. Needing money in the worst way, Connie Mack started selling off his best players in 1914. Eddie, who also won the Chalmers Trophy for being the American League Most Valuable Player that season with a .344 average and leading the league in runs scored with one hundred and twenty-two, was sold in December to the Chicago White Sox for $50,000. Collins would spend the next twelve years in Chicago hitting over .300 in ten those seasons. Eddie became player manager for the Sox beginning in 1924 until he was released in 1926. From 1927 until he retired as a player in 1930, Collins rejoined Mack's Philadelphia A's, being mostly used as a pinch hitter.

In 1919 after two off years hitting below .300, Eddie helped Chicago back to the World Series batting .319 and leading the AL in stolen bases with thirty-three. The leading hitter for the White Sox in the 1917 World Series with a .409 average, when the Sox defeated John McGraw's New York Giants four games to two, to help win the World Championship, 1919 was a Series Eddie

Collins would rather forget. Plainly speaking, Collins sucked. Even with a scorching five for nine in games seven and eight, Eddie would only bat .226 for the eight World Series games. The first six games Eddie was in a two for twenty-two slump [.091], and only scored two runs for the Series hitting in the number two slot with one RBI. Although Eddie only made two errors in fifty-four chances in the field, there were a lot of balls scored base hits that could have been scored otherwise. Also, there were nine double play chances that Eddie had a hand in not turning. Toss in Eddie's base running and Collins had a World Series where he probably would have liked to have stayed home with a good book and sat by the fire, because this was definitely the wrong time to have a bad World Series.

Let me make one thing perfectly clear, there is no way Eddie Collins had anything to do with the fix. For one thing, nobody in the fix clique liked Collins. When they did have to talk to Eddie it was condescending, calling him college boy and the like. Eddie Collins was a well to do who was born with a silver spoon in his mouth, opposite the dead end kids. There is one more thing though, if in fact the sportswriters were looking for players who might be involved in the throwing of ball games, Eddie's would have been the first name I would have circled. Right off the get go in the top of the first inning of game one, Shano Collins led-off with a single to centerfield. Eddie batting 2nd, then dropped down a very poor bunt right back to Reds starting pitcher Dutch Ruether who forced Shano at 2nd base. On the very next pitch, Eddie was thrown out trying to steal 2nd base. Not a very good start to the World Series for Eddie, especially when you're looking for culprits. In the Series Eddie was also doubled off base twice! Once when runners were on 1st and 2nd base, and Collins was the man on 1st base! Now before people's eyes start popping out of their heads and want to chop off mine, I'm not accusing Eddie Collins of anything other than having a very poor World Series. It was sort of like being in the wrong place at the wrong time.

After Eddie's playing days, he coached for Philadelphia for two more years until 1932, then taking a job with the Boston Red Sox as general manager in 1933. Eddie was inducted into the baseball Hall-of-Fame in 1939. Collins remained with the Red Sox in the front office, until his death on March 25,

1951, of heart disease at the age of sixty-three. We're about to take a look at Eddie's eight games in the 1919 World series, you won't like what you read.

Game One

RHP Eddie Cicotte (29-7 1.82) vs LHP Dutch Ruether (19-6 1.81)

At Cincinnati, Oh | **October 1st, 1919** | **Redland Field**

Attendance-30,511

1st inning | **Score: 0-0**

1st at-bat | **1 on 0 out**

The city of Cincinnati welcomes the Chicago White Sox to game one of the 1919 World Series. In a preview of coming attractions, Eddie Collins really set the stage for a unforgettable White Sox World Series. With Shano Collins on 1st base after a Series opening single, future Hall of Famer Eddie tries to bunt Shano to 2nd base. Collins bunt is terrible though, hard and right back to Dutch Ruether who has plenty of time to force Shano at 2nd base (FC 1-6). On the very next pitch from Ruether, Collins is thrown out trying to steal 2nd by Reds C Ivy Wingo (CS 2-6) for out number two, the Sox will not score in the 1st. This is not the start Chicago was looking for.

3rd inning | **Score: 1-1**

2nd at-bat | **0 on 2 out**

The game is shaping up to be a really good one, tied 1-1 going into the top of the 3rd. Dutch Ruether gets two outs very quickly bringing Eddie up to the plate. The left-handed hitting Collins slices Ruther's pitch right at SS Larry Kopf, grounding out (6-3) to the inning.

6th inning **Score: 6-1 Reds**

3rd at-bat **0 on 1 out**

The Reds knocked Eddie Cicotte out of the box in the 4th inning, scoring five runs to take a 6-1 lead. Eddie Collins makes his first hit of the Series, zapping a ball back to the box that Ruether couldn't handle for a one out infield single (1B). Eddie then moves to 2nd base on Buck Weaver's bloop single (1B) to right-field. Next batter Joe Jackson moves both runners up a base with a ground out (3-U), but Happy Felsch flies out (F-9) to end the frame.

8th inning **Score: 8-1 Reds**

4th at-bat **1 on 1 out**

The game Dutch Ruether was pitching today; there would be no coming back for the Sox. Down 8-1 going into the top of the 8th, Eddie steps into the batter's box with one gone and Fred Mcmullin on 1st after a pinch hit single (1B). Eddie follows with a fly ball to CF Edd Roush, who closes his glove around the ball (F-8) for the 2nd out. Chicago would not score again today, and the Reds win the game 9-1, to take the Series opener.

Game One Summary

Bad start for a good guy.

It was a terrible start for the White Sox and a terrible start to Eddie Collins's World Series. Even though Collins had a single in game one, his first at-bat of the Series set the tone for Eddie's next six ballgames. His poor bunt followed by getting tossed out stealing was not the way Eddie drew up his game plan. It would get much worse before it got better.

Game One Box		Running Total					
		AB	R	H	RBI	AVE	
1st AB	FC 1-6, CS	1	0	0	0	.000	1 LOB (1)
2nd AB	6-3	2	0	0	0	.000	
3rd AB	1B	3	0	1	0	.333	
4th AB	F-8	4	0	1	0	.250	1 LOB (2)

Game Two

LHP Lefty Williams (23-11 2.64) vs LHP Slim Sallee (21-7 2.05)

At Cincinnati, Oh **October 2nd, 1919** **Redland Field**

Attendance-29,698

1st inning **Score: 0-0**

1st at-bat **0 on 1 out**

The Reds winning the opener 9-1, was only a shock to anyone not living in the state of Ohio. A smaller crowd turns up today as the Red rooters take their seats to cheer on the home boys. Eddie Collins takes his turn in the batter's box with one down, and works Sallee for a walk (BB). Eddie's troubles continue as Buck Weaver swats a frozen rope right at SS Larry Kopf (L-6), who snatches the ball and quickly catches Collins charging off 1st base on a hit and run (the only hit and run I can confirm), for an inning ending double play (DP L-6-3).

3rd inning **Score: 0-0**

2nd at-bat **1 on 2 out**

In a scoreless ball game after two innings, the Sox go to work in the top of the 3rd. With Lefty Williams on at 1st base and two out, Eddie pulls Sallee's pitch to 1B Jake Daubert, who scoops up the grounder and tags the bag himself (3-U), ending the 3rd inning.

6th inning **Score: 3-0 Reds**

3rd at-bat **0 on 0 out**

The Reds took a 3-0 lead after a three run 4th inning off Lefty Williams, and the way Sallee was pitching today the Sox were in a deep hole. Leading – off the top of the 6th inning, Eddie laces Sallee's offering on a line straight to SS Larry Kopf, who hangs on for the out (L-6). The Sox won't score in the inning.

8th inning **Score: 4-2 Reds**

4th at-bat **0 on 0 out**

Chicago picked up two unearned runs in the 7th inning, and with the two, three; and four hitters of the order coming up, have their best chance to get something going off Slim Sallee in the late innings. Eddie leads-off the top of the 8th with a routine fly ball to center-field that Edd Roush puts away (F-8) for the 1st out. The Sox will not score again today and lose 4-2, and go down two games to nothing heading home to Chicago.

Game Two Summary

I wish it were 1917!

Eddie Collins had another bad game today, going 0 for three and getting doubled off 1st base on a hit and run play. Eddie did get good wood on the ball once, but his line drive was caught by SS Larry Kopf. Maybe some home cooking will help Collins get back on track, but unfortunately he decides to eat out.

Game Two Box **Running Total**

		AB	R	H	RBI	AVE	
1st AB	BB	4	0	1	0	.250	BB (1)
2nd AB	3-U	5	0	1	0	.200	1 LOB (3)
3rd AB	L-6	6	0	1	0	.167	
4th AB	F-8	7	0	1	0	.143	

Game Three

RHP Ray Fisher (14-5 2.17) vs RHP Dickie Kerr (13-8 2.89)

At Chicago, ILL **October 3rd, 1919** **Comiskey Park**

Attendance-29,126

1st inning **Score: 0-0**

1st at-bat **0 on 1 out**

Game three has now become more important than any White Sox fan could imagine. Losing both games in Cincinnati has put Chicago into a bad rut. Not a rut so deep they can't escape. The longer World Series this year from the usual seven games to nine really helps a team that is behind. All the White Sox need to do is win, and they need to win today. Dickie Kerr held the Reds scoreless in the top of the 1st, and with one out Eddie Collins comes up to bat for the Sox. Ray Fisher entices Eddie to tap back to the mound (1-3), making out number two. The Sox would not tally any runs in the 1st inning.

3rd inning **Score: 2-0 Sox**

2nd at-bat **0 on 0 out**

The Sox took a 2-0 lead after scoring a pair in the bottom of the 2nd inning off Ray Fisher. Leading-off the home half of the 3rd, Eddie drives a single (1B) over SS Larry Kopf's head into left field. This was the type of hit that might get a consistent hitter like Collins going, which would help the Chicago cause immensely. Buck Weaver follows Collins's single with one of his own (1B) to the same spot, with Eddie stopping at 2nd base with still no outs. After that the inning ends quickly with the red hot Joe Jackson, for some reason trying to lay down a sacrifice bunt, pops-up to 1B Jake Daubert (F-3). Next Happy Felsch grounds into a (DP 5-4-3) double play, to end the mini threat.

5th inning **Score: 3-0 Sox**

3rd at-bat **0 on 0 out**

The Sox picked up another run off Fisher in the 4th inning and now lead 3-0, with the rookie Kerr pitching like a seasoned veteran. Eddie leads-off the bottom of the 5th for the Sox, looking to build on his nice single his last at-bat. Ray Fisher has other plans though and gets Collins to hit another come backer to the hill, and throws Eddie out (1-3). Chicago will not score in the inning.

8th inning **Score: 3-0 Sox**

4th at-bat **0 on 0 out**

The bottom of the 8th inning was Eddie's third straight at-bat leading off an inning, and for the third time Eddie hit's a ball very meekly, this time getting out in front of reliever Dolph Luque's (9-3 2.63) pitch and pulling the ball to 1B Jake Daubert who flips the ball to Luque covering 1st base (3-1), making the first out. The Sox would score no more runs today, but they didn't need anymore because Dickie Kerr threw a three-hit shutout at the Reds. This was a huge victory for the Sox in more ways than even they knew. For one, they now trailed Cincinnati only two games to one, for another the win excited the home town fans into coming out in full for tomorrow's game four.

Game Three Summary

Base hits are good for slumps!

In an almost must win game for the White Sox in only the third game of the Series, Dickie Kerr's three-hit shutout was just what the doctor ordered. Eddie Collins collected his second base hit of the Series, but his other two at-bats proved he was still in a deep slump. For the Sox to get back into the World Series, they need Eddie's bat and his leadership. So far though he has shown neither, and it would be too late when he finally does.

Game Three Box		**Running Total**				
		AB	R	H	RBI	AVE
1st AB	1-3	8	0	1	0	.125
2nd AB	1B	9	0	2	0	.222
3rd AB	1-3	10	0	2	0	.200

Game Four

RHP Jimmy Ring (10-9 2.26) vs RHP Eddie Cicotte (29-7 1.82)

At Chicago, ILL October 4th, 1919 Comiskey Park

Attendance-34,363

1st inning Score: 0-0

1st at-bat 0 on 1 out

Yesterday's win helped fill Comiskey Park today. With one gone in the bottom of the 1st, Eddie's hitting woes continue as he pops-up to 2B Morrie

Rath (F-4), making out number two. Chicago didn't score in the inning, and the pitching duel between Cicotte and Ring was on.

3rd inning **Score: 0-0**

2nd at-bat **0 on 1 out**

Tied 0-0 going into the bottom of the 3rd, it was about time for the mighty White Sox to break out with the sticks. Although Eddie didn't get a hit, he did get hit, by a pitch (HBP) to open up the home half of the 3rd. Buck Weaver moves Collins over to 2nd base on a fielder's choice (FC 3-U), and Eddie goes to 3rd on a Morrie Rath's error (E-4). That's as far as Eddie gets though, as Happy Felsch grounds out (5-3) to end the inning.

5th inning **Score: 2-0 Reds**

3rd at-bat **1 on 1 out**

The Reds took a 2-0 lead on a couple of Eddie Cicotte errors that led to two unearned runs, and the Sox weren't getting much offense off of Jimmy Ring. Chicago has Nemo Leibold on at 2nd base with one out as Eddie comes up to the plate. Slicing the ball to 3B Heinie Groh, Eddie might have had an infield hit if Leibold would have kept his base. Nemo wandered off too far off the bag and Groh throws over to 2B Morrie Rath, nailing Leibold (FC 5-4) for the 2nd out. Not many little league teams run the bases as badly as the Sox did in this Series. Buck Weaver grounds out again (3-U) ending the 5th.

7th inning **Score: 2-0 Reds**

4th at-bat **1 on 2 out**

After leading off the bottom of the 7th inning and getting hit by a pitched ball (HBP), Ray Schalk was still on at 1st base with two outs. Eddie hits a hard shot, but it is right at 3B Heinie Groh, who makes the toss over to 1st base (5-3) ending the inning with no runs. The Sox will not score a single run today; in fact they only made three hits off of Jimmy Ring and lost 2-0.

Game Four Summary

Same ol, same ol.

The closest Eddie came to getting a hit today in game four was by the ball, in fact he did get a hit, right in the butt. That was all Eddie could muster today though, as his batting average started looking like a bad stock market account. No one else did much off Jimmy Ring either and the Sox are now in a three games to one hole.

Game Four Box **Running Total**

		AB	R	H	RBI	AVE	
1st AB	F-4	12	0	2	0	.167	
2nd AB	HP	12	0	2	0	.167	HP(1)
3rd AB	FC 5-4	13	0	2	0	.154	1LOB(4) 1 RISP(1)
4th AB	5-3	14	0	2	0	.143	1 LOB(5)

Game Five

RHP Hod Eller (20-9 2.40) vs LHP Lefty Williams (23-11 2.64)

At Chicago, ILL **October 6th, 1919** **Comiskey Park**

Attendance-34,379

1st inning **Score: 0-0**

1st at-bat **1 on 1 out**

Did anybody in their right mind think that Eddie Cicotte and Lefty Williams could lose four games between them in the first five ballgames? That's what Lefty was trying to avoid in today's game five. Cincinnati sends to the hill their fifth different starting pitcher, in righty Hod Eller. Williams held the Reds in check in the top half of the 1st, and Eddie comes up to the plate with Nemo Leibold on 1st base and one out. Collins didn't get much on the ball and taps a slow roller to SS Larry Kopf, who's only play was to 1st base (6-3) moving Nemo to 2nd. Chicago would do no scoring as the game moves on to the 2nd inning.

3rd inning **Score: 0-0**

2nd at-bat **0 on 2 out**

It looked like an old fashioned pitchers dual was in the making after two and a half innings of baseball today. Lefty Williams and Hod Eller both look unhittable. The score is still tied 0-0 going into the Sox turn at the plate. Eller, who struck-out the side in the 2nd inning, K's Eddie Collins (K) also, to strike-out the side in the 3rd, makes it six strikeouts in a row.

6th inning **Score: 4-0 Reds**

3rd at-bat **0 on 1 out**

Hod Eller was still mowing the Sox down, and the Reds broke through with four runs off Lefty Williams in the top of the 6th inning to take a 4-0 lead. In danger of losing game five, also going down four games to one and almost certain defeat in the World Series, the Sox were in crisis mode going into the home half of the 6th inning. Eddie steps up to the plate with one out, and at least gets some wood on Eller's pitch (which wasn't easy today), and lofts a lazy fly ball out to CF Edd Roush (F-8), making out number two. Eller looks incredible today.

9th inning **Score: 5-0 Reds**

4th at-bat **0 on 1 out**

Lefty Williams pitched great before and after the 6th inning, but the four runs he gave up in that inning doomed the White Sox. There still was the 9th inning to play though, and the Sox did have the top of the order coming to bat. With one out, Eddie slices the ball to SS Larry Kopf, who makes the play

(6-3). Eller, after a booming triple by Buck Weaver (3B), finishes off Joe Jackson (6-3) for the victory.

Game Five Summary

Is anyone selling hits?

Not a whole lot to sum up here. Hod Eller followed Jimmy Ring's three-hit shutout with one of his own. The Reds head back home to Hamilton County up four games to one. Eddie Collins drew another 0 for four collar, and has now gone nine at-bats without a base hit; lowering his average to the "outhouse" .111 (just put a little roof on top of the ones). By now a smart fellow like Eddie Collins probably knew what was going on with some (most?) of his teammates, and his low production must have been killing him.

Game Five Box **Running Total**

		AB	R	H	RBI	AVE	
1st AB	6-3	15	0	2	0	.133	1LOB (6)
2nd AB	K	16	0	2	0	.125	
3rd AB	F-8	17	0	2	0	.118	
4th AB	6-3	18	0	2	0	.111	

Game Six

RHP Dickie Kerr (13-8 2.89) vs LHP Dutch Ruether (19-6 1.81)

At Cincinnati, Oh **October 7th, 1919** **Redland Field**

Attendance-32,006

1st inning **Score: 0-0**

1st at-bat **0 on 1 out**

Win or go home, do or die; or any other clique you can think of for the must win game six. As the Series moves back down to Cincinnati, the Reds are looking to end the Series today. The biggest crowd of the three games played so far in Cincinnati showed up today, as the Reds were about to capture their first real Championship since Pop Snyder ran the club back in 1882. With one down, Eddie flies out to CF Edd Roush in straight away center field (F-8). Ruether, who had no problems with the Sox in the opener, had none in the 1st inning either.

3rd inning **Score: 0-0**

2nd at-bat **1 on 2 out**

All square going in the top of the 3rd inning, as Sox catcher Ray Schalk was standing on 2nd base via a walk (BB) and sacrifice bunt (SAC 1-3). Eddie comes to bat with two down and a chance to put Chicago out in front. Poor Eddie Collins can't buy a hit with someone else's money (no, not that money), and flies out this time to LF Pat Duncan (F-7) ending the inning, still tied 0-0.

5th Inning **Score: 4-0 Reds**

3rd at –bat **3 on 1 out**

With two runs in the 3rd inning and two more in the 4th, Cincinnati is in the driver's seat 4-0, half way through game six. The way Dutch Ruether has been handling the Chicago White Sox; it looks like it's all over but the crying. That was about to change in a big way in the next two innings. In the top of the 5th, the Sox finally show signs of life. With the bases loaded and one out, Eddie slugs Ruther's fastball into medium center field, but it was deep enough to score Swede Risberg from 3rd base (SF-8) and putting the Sox on the scoreboard. It was also Eddie's first RBI of the Series (his 23rd at-bat), but no luck Eddie can't catch a break. After CF Edd Roush makes the catch, Dickie Kerr comes running into a 2nd base that is still is occupied by Ray Schalk. Roush made his throw toward 3rd base in case Schalk had any plans to go to that base, and 3B Heinie Groh catches the ball and runs over to 2nd, which now has Schalk and Kerr standing on it. Since the bag was Schalk's, Groh tags out the uninvited guest Kerr for an unusual double play (DP SF-8-5-U), ending what could have been a big inning.

7th inning **Score: 4-4**

4th at-bat **0 on 1 out**

The Sox scored three more runs in the top of the 6th inning, knocking Dutch Ruether out of the ballgame, and in the process bringing game four winning pitcher, Right-hander Jimmy Ring (10-9 2.26) into a relievers roll. Eddie Collins comes to bat with one out and the bases empty in the top of the 7th. For the third time in today's game, Eddie hits a fly ball out to CF Edd Roush in center field (F-8) making the second out of the inning. Ring would not allow the Sox a run in the 7th.

9th inning **Score: 4-4**

5th at-bat **1 on 2 out**

Dickie Kerr was pitching in and out of trouble all game long, but he has also given the Sox a chance to win the game in the top of the 9th inning. With the score tied 4-4 and Nemo Leibold, the potential go ahead run on at 2nd base, Eddie comes up to bat with a chance to put the Sox on top for the first time in today's ballgame, and boy was he due (but so was my horse in the third race at Belmont). Incredibly, Collins hits another fly ball out to CF Edd Roush (F-8), the fourth time he has flown out to Roush in nine innings, ending the visitors half of the inning. The Reds would not score either in the 9th inning and send the game into extra dips. Chicago scored a run in the top of the 10th, and gutsy Dickie Kerr pitched his only perfect inning today to win 5-4. Chicago lives to fight another day.

Game Six Summary

His new buddy? Edd Roush!

Eddie Collins started to show life in game six, putting good wood on the ball all five times up to bat today. That didn't help Eddie's batting average any, because he went 0 for four, but it gave him a new confidence. Eddie's best friend in this game was Reds CF Edd Roush, flying out to Edd four times in five at-bats. I don't know if they keep tract of such things, somebody probably does, but this has to be some kind of record. Eddie did drive in his first run of the Series with a sacrifice fly, but batting out of the number two slot Collins sill has not scored a run yet. At this point Eddie has to get extremely hot just to get above the Mendoza line (a .200 batting average, made famous by George Brett, referring to Mario Mendoza). The win by the Sox kept the Series going 4 games to 2. Eddie left five runners on base today, including four in scoring position.

Game Six Box		**Running Total**					
		AB	R	H	RBI	AVE	
1st AB	F-8	19	0	2	0	.105	1LOB (7) 1 RISP(2)
2nd AB	L-7	20	0	2	0	.100	1 LOB(8) 1 RISP(3)
3rd AB	SF-8	20	0	2	1	.100	2 LOB(10) 1 RISP(4)
4th AB	F-8	21	0	2	1	.095	
5th AB	F-8	22	0	2	1	.091	1LOB(11) 1 RISP(5)

Game Seven

RHP Eddie Cicotte (29-7 1.82) vs LHP Slim Sallee (21-7 2.05)

At Cincinnati, Oh **October 8th, 1919** **Redland Field**

Attendance-13,923

1st inning **Score: 0-0**

1st at-bat **1 on 0 out**

Another game today for the Chicago White Sox with the same stakes, they win this afternoon, or lose the World Series. This might have been a good omen, in a repeat of game one; Shano Collins leads-off the ballgame with a single (1B) to center-field. This time though, Eddie gets his bunt down and it is a good one, moving Shano to 2nd base on the sacrifice (SAC 1-3). Joe Jackson delivers Shano to the plate with an RBI single (1B) to left, giving the Sox a 1-0. Sallee pitches out of the inning with no further runs.

3rd inning **Score: 1-0 Sox**

2nd at-bat **1 on 0 out**

Hanging onto a 1-0 lead, Chicago comes to bat in the top of the 3rd inning. With Shano Collins on at 1st base and one out, Gleason lets Eddie swing away. This time Eddie delivers, slicing a grounder into the hole at shortstop that SS Larry Kopf gloved, but had no play, giving Collins his first base hit (1B) in sixteen at-bats. With the Collins boys on at 1st and 2nd base, Buck Weaver lines a hard shot right at SS Larry Kopf (L-6), Shano froze and gets back to his bag, but Eddie has his head too far up his kazoo to see anything and was doubled off 1st base (DP L 6-3), ending the 3rd inning. This was the second time Eddie was doubled off a bag in the Series (first time was on a hit and run). Joe Jackson picks Eddie up though, with his second RBI single (1B) to left-field in as many at-bats, scoring Shano with the Sox second run. Sallee next retired the side when SS Larry Kopf handles Happy Felsch's grounder to force Jackson at 2nd base (FC 6-4), ending the 3rd inning.

5th inning **Score: 2-0 Sox**

3rd at-bat **0 on 1 out**

Chicago was clinging to a 2-0 lead, as they came to bat in the top of the 5th. One thing that was happening now that hadn't happened yet in the Series, Eddie Collins was beginning to hit. Eddie steps in to bat in the top of the 5th with one out and the bases empty. There were so few people in the stands, and it was so quite; that it reminded some of being in church rather than a ball park. Collins again hits the pill to center field, though this time it was on a line and drops in front of CF Edd Roush for a clean base hit (1B). Then Cincinnati's defense fell apart. Errors by 3B Heinie Groh (E-5) and 2B Morrie Rath (E-4) load the bases, and Eddie scores his first run of the Series, when Happy Felsch drove home two with a single (1B). This rare clutch hit puts the Sox up 4-0.

6th inning **Score: 4-0 Sox**

4th at-bat **1 on 2 out**

Eddie's hitting woes aren't over quite yet though, as the game moves on into the top of the 6th inning. With the hot hitting Shano Collins on 2nd base and two down, Reds relief pitcher Dolph Luque (9-3 2.63), Cincinnati's third pitcher of the game, strikes Collins out (K), to end the inning. This was Eddie's first and only strike out of the Series. Chicago holds on to their 4-0 advantage as Luque quiets the Sox bats.

9th inning **Score: 4-1 Sox**

5th at-bat **0 on 2 out**

Eddie Cicotte gave up one run in the bottom of the 6th making the score 4-1, but Cicotte would budge no more today. Eddie comes to bat for the last time in today's ballgame with two out and the bases empty. Dolph Luque, who was almost unhittable in this Series, entices Collins to ground out to 2B Morrie Rath (4-3), ending the 9th inning. Chicago held on in the bottom of the 9th behind Eddie Cicotte, and win game seven 4-1. The White Sox in winning the last two ballgames head back to Chicago.

Game Seven Summary

Showing signs of life!

You can't keep a great hitter down forever, and Eddie Collins finally snapped out of his funk, by getting two hits in game seven. Plus Eddie dropped down a sacrifice bunt that helped produce a run. After six games, Collins had a game that befits his status as a premier player. It all wasn't gravy, and Eddie still had a monumental blunder on the base paths, getting himself doubled off of 1st base, and he wasn't even the lead runner. The White Sox in sweeping both games in Cincinnati now trail four games to three and brings the Series back to the Windy City, with Lefty Williams going for the Sox, and infamy.

Game Seven Box		**Running Total**					
		AB	R	H	RBI	AVE	
1st AB	Sac 1-3	22	0	2	1	.091	
2nd AB	1B	23	0	3	1	.130	
3rd AB	1B, Run	24	1	4	1	.167	
4th AB	K	25	1	4	1	.160	1 LOB(12) 1 RISP(6)
5th AB	4-3	26	1	4	1	.154	

Game Eight

RHP Hod Eller (20-9 2.40) vs LHP Lefty Williams (23-11 2.64)

At Chicago, ILL **October 9th, 1919** **Comiskey Park**

Attendance-32,939

1st inning **Score: 4-0 Reds**

1st at-bat **1 on 0 out**

Wow! How quickly Lefty Williams (23-11 2.64) blew this game. Now the Sox needed a miracle. When this game was final though, the only miracle left would be if eight players saved their careers. Nemo Leibold is on 1st base with a lead-off single (1B), next Eddie follows with a line shot to left-field and gets some very kind hometown scoring when the ball goes off LF Pat Duncan's glove for a double (2B), moving Leibold to 3rd base. Weaver, Jackson and Felsch all make outs to end the 1st without any Chicago runs being scored.

3rd inning **Score: 5-0 Reds**

2nd at-bat **0 on 0 out**

Cincinnati scored another run in the top of the 2nd inning off Sox reliever Bill James (3-1 2.54) to take a 5-0 lead. The Sox haven't scored a run off Eller in eleven innings, and needed to get something going right now. Eddie leads-off the home half of the 3rd, drilling another shot out to left -field, that LF Pat Duncan hangs onto this time (F-7). Joe Jackson gets the Sox on the board by hitting a deep home run (HR) over the right-field fence, but that was all Chicago would get in this inning to trail 5-1.

5th inning **Score: 6-1 Reds**

3rd at-bat **0 on 2 out**

Cincinnati increased its lead to 6-1 with a single run in the top of the 5th, as shocked Chicago fans wondered how this super team could play so flat. Hod Eller was just rolling along, and the 5th inning was no different. After two quick outs, Eddie comes up knowing that the hitters behind him could score runs very quickly. There would be no rally this inning though, as Collins bounces out to SS Larry Kopf (6-3), ending the 5th.

8th inning **Score: 10-1 Reds**

4th at-bat **0 on 1 out**

With the upset nearly complete, this game has turned into a joke. Knocking Bill James out of the game with three more runs in the top of the 6th, the Reds scored two unearned runs off Roy Wilkenson (1-1 2.05) to take a 10-1 lead. Cincinnati was only six outs away from the World Championship, when the Sox finally showed what they could do (although it was a little late). With one down and the bases clear, Eddie gets things rolling with a sharp single (1B) to center field. Collins then scoots all the way to 3rd base on Buck Weaver's double (2B) to right, and he along with Weaver score when Joe Jackson almost hits another homer, cracking a booming double (2B) to deep right field. The Sox scored four in the inning and trail 10-5 before Eller puts out the Chicago fire.

9th inning **Score: 10-5 Reds**

5th at-bat **1 on 1 out**

Things did get a little tense in the bottom of the 9th inning. Eller plunked pinch-hitter Eddie Murphy (HBP), with a pitch to lead-off the Sox last chance in the 1919 World Series. Then things really would have gotten interesting if Nemo Leibold's drive to deep center-field would have fallen in, but CF Edd Roush made a sensational catch (F-8) for the 1st out. Eddie Collins follows with his third hit (1B) today, again right up the gut into center field sending Murphy to 2nd base. Next up, Buck Weaver almost drove the ball out of the ballpark with a deep blast to right, sending RF Greasy Neale back to the wall to make the grab (F-9), with Murphy tagging and going to 3rd base. Eddie then steals his first base (SB) (in today's scoring it would have been catcher's indifference, with Collins not getting a stolen base), putting runners on 2nd and 3rd. Joe Jackson then grounds out (4-3), ending the game and the World Series.

Game Eight Summary

Too little, too late.

Game eight was almost a repeat of the Series opener. Even with the Sox biggest inning of the Series, four runs in the bottom of the 8th inning, it only made the score closer. Instead of a blowout it was just an old fashion butt whooping. The game was basically over in the 1st, when Lefty Williams just handed the Reds four runs, and you can't just hand Hod Eller four runs. Eddie Collins made three hits today, and along with his two yesterday, still only managed a .226 batting average. Eddie also left twelve runners on base, six in scoring position. Plus his base running stunk, and he didn't field too well either. It all equaled to a lousy World Series, in a Series that proved to be a fixed Series. Bad timing I guess, because Eddie Collins integrity was and always will be above reproach.

Game Eight Box **Running Total**

		AB	R	H	RBI	AVE	
1st AB	2B	27	1	5	1	.185	
2nd AB	L-7	28	1	5	1	.179	
3rd AB	6-3	29	1	5	1	.172	
4th AB	1B, Run	30	2	6	1	.200	
5th AB	1B, SB	31	2	7	1	.226	SB(1)

Chapter Eleven

Charles August Risberg

A hard guy!

Charles August Risberg was born October 13, 1894 in San Francisco, California. Nicknamed Swede, Risberg was signed by the Vernon Tigers of the Pacific Coast League as a pitcher in 1912 at the age of seventeen. In 1913 Swede was sent down to class d ball, where he became a strong armed shortstop with great range. Batting .358 for Ogden of the Union Association in 1914, Swede earned a trip back to the PCL. Risberg was bought by the Chicago White Sox in 1917 and became the starting shortstop. Swede's arrival allowed the Sox to move Buck Weaver over to 3rd base, for a team that won the World Series over John McGraw's New York Giants four games to two. Swede would only see two pinch hitting at-bats in the 1917 Series, as manager Pants Rowland sat Risberg down due to his poor hitting. Something Kid Gleason should have done in 1919. Swede would only hit .203 in his rookie season of 1917 and he almost quit and went home due to homesickness. Risberg was only twenty-two years old and living in the big city on his own for the first time, but Swede stuck it out. In the war shortened 1918 season, Swede raised his batting average to a respectable .256, playing in eighty-two ballgames. Swede then went back home to work in a Navy shipyard in Alameda, California under the "work or fight" order, set down by Secretary of War Newton Baker, of the United States War Department. Returning to regular playing in 1919, Swede again batted .256, along with playing excellent defense that helped Chicago back to the World Series. At only twenty-four years old, Risberg had a bright future in Major League Baseball. The only problem though was that Swede had fallen in with the rough and tumble crowd among the White Sox players that included Chick Gandil. Being fairly tough himself, (Joe Jackson was scared to death of Swede) and not very educated but street wise, Risberg was one of the key players in the fix conspiracy.

Swede absolutely stunk up the field in the 1919 World Series. With an .080 batting average (2-25), and scoring only three runs, with no RBI's in the eight ballgames. Out of all the players who contributed to the fix, Swede was the most blatant. How manager Kid Gleason didn't sit Risberg down after a couple of games is a mystery that has never been explained. Swede didn't get a single hit with runners on base including zero for seven with runners in scoring position. In the field Risberg was a little better but not much, making four errors in key spots, not to mention the plays he could have and should have made. There also were at least five double plays that Swede had a hand in screwing up. Swede had as much to do with the dumping of the World Series with his glove as he had with his bat. It was a complete effort Risberg turned in, an effort of futility. Swede blamed his poor Series on a bad cold but he was more like comatose, and his manager has to shoulder some of the blame too, for giving him the opportunity to keep up the crappy work game after game. Gleason could have moved Buck Weaver over to shortstop and given Fred Mcmullin his chance to chip in to the cause (Fred was Swede's buddy and in on the fix too, but at the time Gleason couldn't have known that).

In 1920 Swede continued to improve, hitting .266, but his season along with seven others would be suspended on September 27th, and then eventually banned for life on August 3 1921, for his involvement in the throwing of the 1919 World Series. At only twenty-five years old, Swede lost at least ten years of Major League Baseball. After his stint in organized baseball was over, Swede continued to play ball in outlaw leagues alongside former teammates. Risberg sued the White Sox in 1924 along with Joe Jackson and Happy Felsch, for wrongful termination and back pay. The White Sox settled out of court with Swede for $288.88. In 1926 Swede testified in the famous Ty Cobb, Tris Speaker hearings on illegal betting on ballgames (I guess Swede was an expert witness), but his testimony was dismissed because Swede was seen as holding a grudge against baseball. Risberg was back in front of Judge Landis in 1927, this time involving alleged pay-offs to Detroit Tiger players for allegedly throwing a four-game Series to the White Sox back in the 1917 pennant race. Nothing came out of this investigation either, as this time Swede was deemed a liar.

After his playing days were over, Swede worked for many years on a Minnesota dairy farm, then retiring back home to California. One of the last of the old Black Sox to pass on, Swede died on his birthday October 13, 1975 in an old folks home in Red Bluff, California at the ripe old age of eighty-one. Charles August Risberg was laid to rest never openly talking about the good (or shall I say bad), old days.

Game One

RHP Eddie Cicotte (29-7 1.82) vs LHP Dutch Ruether (19-6 1.81)

At Cincinnati, Oh **October 1st, 1919** **Redland Field**

Attendance-30,511

2nd inning **Score: 1-1**

1st at-bat **0 on 2out**

Opening day of the 1919 World Series, and the excitement was running high. The Reds touched Cicotte for a run in the bottom of the 1st inning and lead 1-0 going into the 2nd. Chicago tied up the score at one apiece on Chick Gandil's one out bloop single (1B), that plated Joe Jackson from 3rd base. After Gandil was caught stealing (CS 2-4), with two outs Swede Risberg steps up to the plate for the first time in the Series. Swede works Ruether for a walk (BB), and trots down to 1st base. Next hitter Ray Schalk ends the inning, flying out to CF Edd Roush (F-8).

5th inning **Score: 6-1 Reds**

2nd at-bat **1 on 0out**

A five run 4th inning knocked Eddie Cicotte out of the ball game, bringing reliever Roy Wilkenson (1-1 2.05) into the game, giving the Reds a 6-1 advantage. In the top of the 5th, with Chick Gandil on first base after a lead-off single (1B), Swede connects on a high fastball and launched a deep fly ball to right -center field. Reds CF Edd Roush races over into the gap and makes a splendid catch (F-8), robbing Risberg of extra bases. Ruether then retires Ray Schalk and Wilkenson, ending the inning with no runs.

7th inning **Score: 6-1 Reds**

3rd at-bat **0 on 1out**

Still trailing 6-1 heading into the top of the 7th, Chicago needed runs and needs them now. With one out and the bases clear, the right-handed hitting Risberg batted for the third time today. Swede swings a little late on Ruther's offering and grounds out to 2B Morrie Rath (4-3), for out number two. Ruether would only give up one more hit today and Cincinnati scored three more runs to take game one 9-1.

Game One Summary

Not too terrible!

Not a good start for the Sox today. After tying the game at 1-1 in the top of the 2nd inning, the Reds scored eight unanswered runs. In three at-bats today off Reds starter Dutch Ruether, Swede had two good ones. Drawing a walk in his first Series plate appearance and sending CF Edd Roush deep into the right -center alley in the 5th. The Reds kicked the crap out of the Sox though 9-1, and leads one game to nothing in the Series.

Game One Box **Running Total**

		AB	R	H	RBI	AVE	
1st AB	BB	0	0	0	0	.000	BB (1)
2nd AB	F-8	1	0	0	0	.000	1 LOB (1)
3rd AB	4-3	2	0	0	0	.000	

Game Two

LHP Lefty Williams (23-11 2.64) vs LHP Slim Sallee (21-7 2.05)

At Cincinnati, Oh **October 1st, 1919** **Redland Field**

Attendance-29,698

2nd inning **Score: 0-0**

1st at-bat **1 on 2out**

Cincinnati fans will be the first to tell you that the only people stunned by the Reds 9-1 victory in game one, were Chicago fans and some media. Joe Jackson led–off the top of the 2nd inning with a double (2B) off Sallee, and was now standing on 3rd base with two gone. Swede gets a small piece of the ball and lifts a lazy fly out to RF Greasy Neale (F-9), ending the inning with no runs.

4th inning **Score: 0-0**

2nd at-bat **2 on 2out**

Scoreless through three innings, Chicago had something brewing in the top of the 4th. Buck Weaver was on at 3rd base and Joe Jackson at 2nd , after back to back singles (1B) and a sacrifice bunt (SAC 1-3), by Happy Felsch. Then Buck Weaver was nailed at home plate on a nice play by 1B Jake Daubert (FC 3-2), on Chick Gandil's grounder. Chick then stole 2nd base (SB), and the Sox had two in scoring position again. In his first clutch situation, Swede takes a weak swing at the ball, that results in a weak pop-fly to 1B Jake Daubert (F-3), putting an end to a good scoring threat.

7th inning **Score: 4-0 Reds**

3rd at-bat **0 on 1out**

By the top of the 7th inning the Reds held a 4-0 lead. Cincinnati scored three runs in the bottom of the 4th, and added another in the 6th. Swede picks up his first hit of the Series with a one out single (1B) to left field. Risberg then scores on a really weird play which started with a single (1B), off the bat of Ray

Schalk. On Schalk's base knock to right field, Greasy Neale fielded the ball on one hop and fires the pill to 2nd base. His throw goes over SS Larry Kopf's head (E-9) all the way to the left- field fence, scoring Risberg. As Ray circled the bases the relay throw from LF Pat Duncan to 3B Heinie Groh, whose throw to the plate hits Schalk in the back (E-5) allowing Ray to score also. The question is, why did RF Greasy Neale have to throw the ball so hard to 2nd base that the ball carried all the way to the left field wall? Was it that Schalk's hit was really a double, and Neale was trying to nab Ray going into 2nd base? If you look at the 1919 World Series composites, Ray Schalk had seven hits but none of them were for extra bases. So it had to be that Swede either was waiting to see if Neale caught the ball and got a bad jump when it dropped in or Risberg delayed on purpose and was running slow enough that Greasy had a play on him at 2nd base. Also picture the angle it would take for a throw from right-field to end up at the left-field wall. In either case, it was definitely a curious play.

9th inning **Score: 4-2 Reds**

4th at-bat **1 on 0out**

The Sox trailed Slim Sallee and the Reds 4-2 going into their last at-bat. Chick Gandil leads-off the 9th with a single (1B) into right field. Batting next, Swede bounces into a (DP 4-6-3) double play. Chicago would not score any runs in the 9th, and lose again to the Reds. Dropping games one and two in Cincinnati and being down two games to zero with Cicotte and Williams losing, must have been hard for some of the players to swallow. I don't believe Swede was one of them though.

Game Two Summary

In losing 4-2 and going down two games to zip, Swede had three at-bats in which he could have done some damage today. Instead he left four runners on base, three in scoring position. In the 2nd inning he left Joe Jackson stranded on 3rd, in the 4th Swede left runners on 2nd and 3rd; and in the 9th he hit into a 4-6-3 double play. Risberg did get his first base hit, and scored a run on that crazy play in the 7th, but I think Swede was trying to get himself thrown out at 2nd base and the Sox lucked into him scoring. Was Swede doing all he could to help his club win ballgames?

Game Two Box		**Running Total**					
		AB	R	H	RBI	AVE	
1st AB	F-9	3	0	0	0	.000	1 LOB(2) 1 RISP(1)
2nd AB	F-3	4	0	0	0	.000	2 LOB (4) 2 RISP(3)
3rd AB	1B, Run	5	1	1	0	.200	
4th AB	4-6-3 DP	6	1	1	0	.167	1LOB(5)

Game Three

RHP Ray Fisher (14-5 2.17) vs RHP Dickie Kerr (13-8 2.89)

At Chicago, ILL **October 3rd, 1919** **Comiskey Park**

Attendance-29,126

2nd inning **Score: 2-0 Sox**

1st at-bat **2 on 0 out**

Chick Gandil, of all people, gets the Sox the early lead with a two RBI single (1B), in the bottom of the 2nd inning. Still with no outs, Swede comes up to the plate and draws a free pass (BB) from Fisher moving Chick to 2nd base. Next batter Ray Schalk then lays down a perfect bunt, and it would have gone for a base hit, but Chick Gandil lollygagged his way to 3rd base and Fisher has time to force Chick (FC 1-5). Next hitter Dickie Kerr taps back to the mound and Fisher again throws to 3B Heinie Groh (FC 1-5), to force Swede at 3rd also.

Nemo Leibold grounds out (5-3) as Fisher pitches out of the jam, but the Sox have a 2-0 lead.

4th inning **Score: 2-0 Sox**

2nd at-bat **0 on 1 out**

With the game moving into the bottom of the 4th inning, the Sox are still holding onto a two run lead behind the brilliant pitching of little Dickie Kerr. Swede Risberg walks up to bat with one down and no one on base. Swede hits what should have been just a clean single into right field, but the ball takes a bad hop and bounces over RF Greasy Neale's glove and rolls toward the wall. Swede flew around the bases and ends up with a stand-up triple (3B). Ray Schalk again drops down a perfect drag bunt, this time scoring Swede for an RBI single (1B) giving Chicago a 3-0 advantage. Fisher gets out of the inning without giving up any more runs.

7th inning **Score: 3-0 Sox**

3rd at-bat **0 on 0 out**

Leading-off the bottom of the 7th inning with the Sox still leading 3-0, Swede hits a bouncer to 3B Heinie Groh who makes the toss over to 1B Jake Daubert (5-3) for out number one. Both teams will not do any more scoring today, and the Sox win behind Dickie Kerr's three- hitter. Chicago is now on the winning end of a baseball game.

Game Three Summary

Nice game!

Dickie Kerr was the story of game three, pitching a three-hit shut-out and winning 3-0. Swede had a real good game at the plate today too, with a bad hop triple and a run scored. He also walked once in three at-bats. The problem was Swede didn't much feel like playing after this game, and must have figured that you can't play your worst by hitting triples and scoring runs.

Risberg won't come even close to getting another base hit for the next three games.

Game Three Box		**Running Total**					
		AB	R	H	RBI	AVE	
1st AB	BB	6	1	1	0	.167	BB (2)
2nd AB	3B, Run	7	2	2	0	.286	
3rd AB	5-3	8	2	2	0	.250	

Game Four

RHP Jimmy Ring (10-9 2.26) vs RHP Eddie Cicotte (29-7 1.82)

At Chicago, ILL **October 4th, 1919** **Comiskey Park**

Attendance-34,363

2nd inning **Score: 0-0**

1st at-bat **1 on 2 out**

Chicago's victory in game three, guaranteed the Series will move back to Cincinnati for game six. Still tied 0-0, after an inning and a half, Chicago has Ring on the ropes in the home half of the 2nd. Joe Jackson doubled (2B) to lead-off the inning and moved to 3rd base on Happy Felsch's sacrifice bunt (SAC 1-3). Chick Gandil showed no desire to bring Jackson home though, as he popped-up to 1B Jake Daubert (F-3), making the 2nd out. Next up Swede waits Ring out for a walk (BB), and then steals 2nd base (SB). Ray Schalk also works a walk (BB) to load the bases. Ring then gets Eddie Cicotte, after working the count full, to ground out to 2B Morrie Rath (4-3) to end what turned out to be the Sox best chance at scoring today.

4th inning **Score: 0-0**

2nd at-bat **0 on 1out**

In what was shaping up to be a classic pitchers dual, Cicotte and Ring were matching each other pitch for pitch. The White Sox did not capitalize on another scoring chance in the 3rd inning, and came to bat in the 4th tied 0-0. With one out, Swede swats a fly ball to left that LF Pat Duncan puts in his hip pocket (F-7). The Sox would go out with no runs in the 3rd.

6th Inning **Score: 2-0 Reds**

3rd at-bat **1 on 2 out**

The Reds got two gift runs from Eddie Cicotte in the top of the 5th inning on two Cicotte errors, to take a 2-0 lead. It was a lead Cincinnati would not relinquish. In the bottom of the 6th, with Chick Gandil on 1st base after a two out single (1B), Swede comes up to bat, trying or not, to keep the inning alive. Swede raps a can of corn fly ball out to RF Greasy Neale (F-9), killing the inning.

9th inning **Score: 2-0 Reds**

4th at-bat **0 on 0 out**

Leading-off the bottom of the 9th, Ring gets Swede to hit a little come-backer to the mound (1-3) for the 1st out. Chicago had their chances today off Ring even though Jimmy only gave up three hits, and would not score any runs.

Game Four Summary

An effort in futility!

The White Sox were three-hit today by Jimmy Ring and lost 2-0. Swede drew the collar going 0 for three, with a walk and a stolen base. The other three times up Risberg didn't come close to a base hit. Why Kid Gleason keeps sending Swede back out there is beyond me (he isn't playing much better in the field either). Tomorrow's game now has become huge, in fact it is a must win for the Sox to avoid being down four games to one.

Game Four Box		Running Total					
		AB	R	H	RBI	AVE	
1st AB	BB, SB	8	2	2	0	.250	BB (3),SB(1)
2nd AB	F-7	9	2	2	0	.222	
3rd AB	F-9	10	2	2	0	.200	1 LOB (6)
4th AB	1-3	11	2	2	0	.182	

Game Five

RHP Hod Eller (20-9 2.40) vs LHP Lefty Williams (23-11 2.64)

At Chicago, ILL **October 6th, 1919** **Comiskey Park**

Attendance-34,379

2nd inning **Score: 0-0**

1st at-bat **0 on 1 out**

Game five was scheduled to be played October 5th, but was rained out. So game five will be played today in front of a near capacity crowd. Pitching out of a 1st inning jam, Eller strikes out the side in the 2nd including Swede (K), who is out number two.

5th inning **Score: 0-0**

2nd at-bat **0 on 1 out**

Williams and Eller were hooked up in a classic, so far anyway with the score tied 0-0. Eller was setting down the South Cook County boys in record fashion. Striking out the side in both in 2nd and 3rd innings for six consecutive K's, plus in the 4th he recorded a K and two comebackers, Eller had a hand in getting everybody out in the order by himself. With one out in the 5th, Swede grounds out to 3B Heinie Groh (5-3) making the second out. The Sox didn't score in the inning

8th Inning **Score: 4-0 Reds**

3rd at-bat **0 on 0 out**

For the second game in a row, Chicago would be shutout on only three hits. Swede leads-off the bottom of the 8th lifting Eller's pitch into medium right field where RF Greasy Neale corrals the ball (F-9). Chicago has not scored in twenty-two straight innings and loses game five, 5-0.

Game Five Summary

P-U!

Trailing now four games to one after getting only three hits today off of Hod Eller, The Sox were shutout for the second game in a row. Swede might just as well stayed home today, not hitting anything hard with a strikeout in three at-bats. It didn't really matter though as nobody with the exception of Buck Weaver, who had two of Chicago's three hits, and Ray Schalk bothered to show up.

Game Five Box		Running Total					
		AB	R	H	RBI	AVE	
1st AB	K	12	2	2	0	.167	K(1)
2nd AB	5-3	13	2	2	0	.154	
3rd AB	F-9	14	2	2	0	.143	

Game Six

RHP Dickie Kerr (13-8 2.89) vs LHP Dutch Ruether (19-6 1.81)

At Cincinnati, Oh **October 7th, 1919** **Redland Field**

Attendance-32,006

2nd inning **Score: 0-0**

1st at-bat **0 on 2 out**

Back in Cincinnati, a huge crowd came out to see the Reds try to close out the Series. Both Pitchers handled the other team with ease, so this matchup looks to be a thriller. After a scoreless 1st inning, Ruether sets the Sox down in order in the 2nd, with Swede making the final out, flying to RF Greasy Neale (F-9).

5th inning **Score: 4-0 Reds**

2nd at-bat **0 on 0 out**

Winning 4-0 going into the top of the 5th inning, Reds fans could sense the victory within their grasps. Chicago needed to find the heart of a champion, and in the 5th they started to show a pulse. Swede leads-off with a walk (BB) (His fourth of the Series), and trots to 2nd base when Ruether started having trouble finding the strike zone and also walks Ray Schalk (BB). Dickie

Kerr then lines a single (1B) off SS Larry Kopf's glove, loading the bases with no one out. Though the ball may have been deep enough, Swede holds his bag at 3rd on Shano Collins fly ball to CF Edd Roush (F-8) for the 1st out. Next Hitter Eddie Collins does drive Risberg home on a sacrifice fly to almost the same spot (SF-8), making the score 4-1. Dickie Kerr then runs the Sox out of the inning trying to take 2nd base already occupied by Ray Schalk. Heinie Groh tags out Ker for an unusual double play (DP 8-5-U).

6th inning **Score: 4-3 Reds**

3rd at-bat **1 on 1 out**

Buck Weaver led-off the Sox biggest inning of the Series so far, with a bloop double (2B) to left field off Dutch Ruether. Joe Jackson followed with an RBI single (1B) and then Happy Felsch also delivered a RBI double (2B) to make the score 4-3 Reds, chasing Ruether out of the ballgame. That brought game four winner right-handed Jimmy Ring (10-9 2.26) into the game but also brought up old unreliables Chick Gandil, who popped-up to 1B Jake Daubert (F-3) and Swede Risberg, who grounds out to SS Larry Kopf (6-3), making the 2nd out but moves Felsch to 3rd base. Ray Schalk ties the game up at four apiece with an RBI single (1B) into left-field. Ring then gets Dickie Kerr to bounce out to 3B Heinie Groh (5-3) ending the inning.

8th inning **Score: 4-4**

4th at-bat **2 on 1 out**

Swede almost came through with a big hit, almost. Jimmy Ring walked both Joe Jackson and Chick Gandil (BB) to start the 8th, with a Happy Felsch fly out in between. With one out Risberg hits what looks like extra bases and two runs, but CF Edd Roush makes the play of the game, an incredible catch in left- center field (F-8). Joe Jackson, who could have crawled home if the ball had fallen in, runs for the plate anyway and was doubled off 2nd base (DP F-8-4), making Swede's drive an inning ending double play.

10th inning **Score: 5-4 Sox**

5th at-bat **2 on 1 out**

Chicago took a 5-4 lead in the top of the 10th inning, when Chick Gandil delivered his second game winning hit with Dickie Kerr pitching, an RBI single (1B) into right-field scoring Buck Weaver. Gandil's unlikely hit moves Joe Jackson up to 2nd base and sets up another, you had to see it to believe it play. With one out, Swede steps into the batter's box and hits into another inning ending double play involving Jackson. Like Eddie Collins, Joe must have liked the view from inside his kazoo, because he kept putting his head in there. Risberg lines a shot right at SS Larry Kopf (L-6), and there goes Joe halfway to 3rd base for an easy (DP L-6-4) double play. The second time in three innings Swede hits a ball hard, only to see Jackson get doubled up. Kerr held Cincinnati in the bottom of the 10th and the Sox win this crucial game 5-4.

Game Six Summary

Better than yesterday.

In one of the most gut wrenching pitching performances in World Series history, Dickie Kerr pitched ten roller coaster innings for a 5-4 victory and kept the White Sox from elimination. Now trailing four games to two, the Sox did get a run scored from Swede. Drawing a lead-off walk in the 5th, Swede moved around the bases on another walk and an infield hit. Risberg then scored on Eddie Collins's sac fly. Swede swung the bat better today, although his best at-bats resulted in double plays, thanks to Joe Jackson. He is now hitting the outhouse (.111).

Game Six Box **Running Total**

		AB	R	H	RBI	AVE	
1st AB	F-9	15	2	2	0	.133	
2nd AB	BB, Run	15	3	2	0	.133	BB (4)
3rd AB	6-3	16	3	2	0	.125	1 LOB(7) 1 RISP(4)
4th AB	F-8-4, DP	17	3	2	0	.118	2 LOB (9) 1 RISP(5)
5th AB	L-6-4, DP	18	3	2	0	.111	2 LOB (10) 1 RISP(6)

Game Seven

RHP Eddie Cicotte (29-7 1.82) vs LHP Slim Sallee (21-7 2.05)

At Cincinnati, Oh **October 8th, 1919** **Redland Field**

Attendance-13,923

1st inning **Score: 1-0 Sox**

1st at-bat **1 on 0 out**

The few fans who bothered to show today saw Eddie Cicotte continue his great pitching, and their own teams poor fielding. Of the four runs starting left-hander Slim Sallee gives up this afternoon, only two were earned. After the Sox took a 1-0 lead in the top of the 1st, Swede leads-off the 2nd inning by rolling out to SS Larry Kopf (6-3). Sallee held the Sox to no runs in the 2nd.

4th inning **Score: 2-0 Sox**

2nd at-bat **0 on 1 out**

The Sox scored another run off Sallee in the 3rd inning to take a 2-0 lead, and Cicotte held up his end in the bottom half. Swede comes to bat in the top of the 4th inning without a hit in fourteen at-bats in a row, which include two walks. In fact Risberg will never get another hit in World Series play again. Why Kid Gleason didn't sit Swede down at the far end of the bench by now is anyone's guess. With one down Swede fouls-out to 1B Jake Daubert (FO-3), who makes a daisy of a play leaning over the rail and into the sparse crowd for the second out. Sallee stifles the Sox in the 4th.

5th inning **Score: 4-0 Sox**

3rd at-bat **2 on 2 out**

The Sox scored two unearned runs in the 5th thanks to some shoddy fielding on the Reds part, to go up 4-0. Cicotte is taking no prisoners today. Ray Fisher (14-5 2.17), came in for the Reds to replace Sallee with one out in the top of the 5th inning. Swede has a great chance to maybe putting the game in the bag for the Sox. With two down Swede strikes-out (K), leaving runners on 2nd and 3rd. With his batting average dipping below .100 to .095, Risberg should have been run out of Cincinnati after being tarred and feathered, by his own team. Kid Gleason should have moved Buck Weaver to shortstop and put the bat boy on 3rd base three games ago. Or at least Fred McMullin, Gleason couldn't have known Fred was just dying to get in and help blow a game or two.

8th inning **Score: 4-1 Sox**

4th at-bat **0 on 0 out**

In the bottom of the 6th inning the Reds finally scored off Eddie Cicotte, but only one run. The Sox took a 4-1 lead into the top of the 8th. Dolph Luque (9-3 2.63) who came into the game for the Reds in the top of the 6th inning, was again having no trouble getting the White Sox out. With the bases empty and one out in the bottom of the 8th, Risberg hits a high pop-fly to CF Edd Roush who should have caught the ball blindfolded. Well, he looked like he was blindfolded because he drops the ball (E-8). Swede wasn't happy just getting on and tries for 2nd base but was out by a country mile (E-8-6), for the second out of the 8th. Chicago and Cicotte would keep their 4-1 lead and win game seven, sweeping the Reds in Cincinnati and closing the gap.

Game Seven Summary

Risberg, you stink!

If anybody had never seen Swede Risberg play before, they would have sworn he stunk like yesterday's diapers. Swede looked like a no field, no hit bum who wouldn't have even made a high school JV team. Risberg's average would fall below .100 in game seven, and it will get worse before this Series is over. Which is basically just five more batters. The thing is, Swede was a very capable big league shortstop, and he was getting better every year. You know, Swede could have played much better and still did his part in the fix, but let's get back to today's game. Behind Eddie Cicotte's superb pitching, the Sox won 4-1 to extend the Series back to Chicago. No thanks to Risberg though, as Swede went hitless again with an 0 for four. The only time Swede got on base today was when CF Edd Roush dropped his fly ball for an error, and Risberg even screwed that up. So on to Chicago we go, and a 1st inning that will never be forgotten.

Game Seven Box **Running Total**

		A	R	H	RBI	AVE	
1st AB	6-3	19	3	2	0	.105	
2nd AB	F-3	20	3	2	0	.100	
3rd AB	K	21	3	2	0	.095	K (2) 2 LOB (13) 2 RISP(8)
4th AB	E-8-6	22	3	2	0	.091	

Game Eight

RHP Hod Eller (20-9 2.40) vs LHP Lefty Williams (23-11 2.64)

At Chicago, IL L　　October 9th, 1919　　Comiskey Park

Attendance-32,939

2nd inning　　Score: 5-0 Reds

1st at-bat　　0 on 1 out

After only five batters Lefty Williams was done, and so was the White Sox as they would not recover. Down 5-0 going into the bottom of the 2nd, Chicago needed a lot of runs in a hurry. Following Chick Gandil who had lined out, Swede works game five winning pitcher righty Hod Eller for a free pass (BB, his 5th walk of the Series). Next batter Ray Schalk then singles (1B) Swede to 2nd base. Kid Gleason's managing in this Series was about on par with most of his players, and he should have been fired on the spot after this game. Down 5-0 in only the 2nd inning and with a small rally brewing, Kid Gleason lets reliever Bill James (3-1 2.54) bat for himself. James fouls-out to 3B Heinie Groh (FO-5) for the 2nd out, and Eller then K's Nemo Leibold to stop the threat right in its tracks.

4th inning　　Score: 5-1 Reds

2nd at-bat　　0 on 1 out

The Sox get on the scoreboard with a run in the bottom of the 3rd on Joe Jackson's blast out of the ballpark (HR). That gave the 32.000 plus fans something to cheer about, but it was short lived. Winning the last two Series games gave the faithful a false sense of hope, that a miracle comeback was in the cards, but Chicago was only four-flushing. With one out in the bottom of the 4th, Eller strikes-out Swede (K) and then retires Ray Schalk (5-3), ending the inning.

7th inning **Score: 9-1 Reds**

3rd at-bat **0 on 0 out**

It was all over but the crying. After giving up one run in the 5th, Bill James and his relief Roy Wilkenson (1-1 2.05) give up three more in the 6th; and Chicago was now trailing 9-1 going into the bottom of the 7th. Swede leads-off the bottom of the 7th inning, popping out to 2B Morrie Rath (F-4) in short right field. Eller sets the Sox down in order, again.

8th inning **Score: 10-4 Reds**

4th at-bat **1 on 2 out**

The Reds had scored another unearned run off Roy Wilkenson in the top of the 8th inning to take a 10-1 lead. In the bottom half, Chicago has one out when it erupts like the great fire of 1871. The Sox scores four runs on four hits in their biggest inning of the World Series, but it was way too little, way too late. The four spot brought the score to 10-5, and that's where the game ended. Swede receives another gift from CF Edd Roush, who couldn't seem to hold on to a Risberg fly ball. Big Edd drops Swede's fly again (E-8), scoring Chick Gandil with the Sox fourth run of the inning, though no RBI for Risberg. Eller, after a little excitement in the 9th gets the last out and Cincinnati was Champions of the World.

Game Eight Summary

That's just terrible!

Criminal, that's the only way, well I guess there are a lot of ways, to describe Swede Risberg's play in the 1919 World Series, but that may be the best one. Swede did make some really nice plays in the field, but his poor ones overshadowed them. And at the plate, the only good thing you can say is that he hit higher than his I. Q. Overall Swede should have been shot at dawn without a blindfold, and his manager Kid Gleason should have been shot in the leg for giving him the opportunity. Kid had to of been suspicious after the first two games, and should have pulled Risberg right off the field after the fourth. Game eight was no different than any other for Risberg, another 0-for, making his hitless streak reach eighteen. Other players have had poor World Series before, including some great ones. At least they were trying, Swede wasn't. Risberg did draw his fifth walk of the Series in game eight, and he also got on base when CF Edd Roush dropped another of his fly balls. That's about all you can say positive about Swede's World Series. In less than a year, Swede and the boys would have to pay the piper for their actions. First suspended, then banned from the game they loved. Was it worth it?

Game Eight Box			**Running Total**				
		AB	R	H	RBI	AVE	
1st AB	BB	22	3	2	0	.091	BB (5)
2nd AB	K	23	3	2	0	.086	K (3)
3rd AB	F-4	24	3	2	0	.083	
4th AB	E-8	25	3	2	0	.080	

Chapter Twelve

George Daniel Weaver

A raw deal.

George Daniel Weaver was born on August 18, 1890 in Pottstown, Pennsylvania. From early on Buck was something special in all sports, but especially in baseball. After high school (something some his pals on the White Sox would never see the inside of), Buck got his start in professional baseball at the age of seventeen, while playing semi-pro ball for Mt. Carmel, Pennsylvania in the outlaw Atlantic League in 1908. Buck then moved on to Northampton, Massachusetts of the Connecticut State League in 1909. And for the 1910 season Charlie "Red" Dooin, manager of the Philadelphia Phillies, signed Buck to a contract calling for $175 dollars a month to play for the York, Pennsylvania White Roses. Buck showed enough promise with the White Roses that Ted Sullivan, super scout for the Chicago White Sox, bought up Buck's contract for $750 and signed Buck to a Pacific Coast League contract to play for the famous San Francisco Seals for the 1911 campaign. Buck hit .280 for the Seals and when Charles Comiskey took notice of Buck, he was on his way to the Big Leagues.

Buck made his Major league debut on April 11, 1912 as the twenty-one year old starting shortstop for the Chicago White Sox. Playing in one hundred and forty-seven games, Buck didn't do very much hitting, batting just .226. He also didn't do a whole lot of fielding either, committing a whooping seventy-one errors. What he did do was show incredible range and a strong arm. During the winter and spring months Buck taught himself to switch hit, and what a difference it made. In 1913 Weaver improved his batting average to .272, although he still had his problems in the field, making another seventy errors at short. The 1914 campaign saw his errors drop to fifty-nine; still a staggering number, but his hitting also lapsed at a .246 pace. Buck improved again in 1915 with a respectable .268 average with a career high eighty-three runs scored, and his season error total also dropped another ten to a still high total of forty-nine.

Buck was moved over to 3rd base for the 1916 season, with Zeb Terry taking over at shortstop. But when Terry couldn't cut the mustard, manager Pants Rowland had to shift Buck back to short. The back and fourth hurt Weaver's hitting, and he finished the season with a .227 average. His fielding was much improved to career low thirty-six errors, though he made most of theses at shortstop. Buck did manage to score seventy-eight runs with such a low average, and showed so much promise at 3rd base that owner Charles Comiskey set out to find a capable shortstop so Buck could become the permanent 3rd sacker. That capable shortstop arrived in the form of Swede Risberg, and the switch occurred for the 1917 season. The move solidified the Sox infield, and with Buck able to concentrate on one position, his overall play improved to the point where Buck batted a career high .284. He also made only twenty-one errors, and with Risberg's steady play at short (though he didn't hit much), the pair was a big help in the White Sox winning the AL pennant and 1917 World Series over the New York Giants four games to two.

The World War I shortened 1918 season saw Buck hit .300 for the first time in one hundred and twelve games, while playing most of his games at shortstop, as Swede was regulated to a utility role. Buck also chose to work with most of his other teammates in the Navy shipyards under the work or fight order as set down by Secretary of War Newton Baker. With the war over the 1919 season was only scheduled for one hundred and forty games, due to the fact that the owners were concerned that with the economy the way it was, and that baseball did not do to well financially in 1918 that attendance might suffer. Was they ever wrong, as attendance soared to record heights, and so did Buck Weaver. Playing in all one hundred and forty games Buck hit a solid .296, and set career highs in runs (89), hits (169), doubles (33), RBI's (75), and Buck also made his fewest errors (20). Buck led the American League in games played (140) and at-bats (571). Buck sure liked to swing the bat too, walking only eleven times (his second year in a row with only eleven), and didn't strikeout much either with the low total of twenty-one. All this added up to was another AL pennant for the White Sox. Then it all fell apart.

Buck really shined in the World Series against the Cincinnati Reds, Champions of the National League. Batting .324 with eleven base hits in the eight games, while tying the Series record for doubles with four to go along with a triple, and Weaver also scored four runs. Although Buck failed to drive in a runner in the Series, he didn't bat too many times with runners on base, even though he batted in the number three slot. Buck also played a stellar defense, handling all twenty-seven chances without an error and making several fine plays in the field. All Buck Weaver got for his efforts in the Series was a lifetime ban from baseball. Seems Buck attended at least one meeting, maybe two (but this has never been confirmed), where the plot to throw the Series was discussed. As I'll get into in-depth in the next chapter, I believe Buck had an injustice done to him that just makes me sick to my stomach when I think about it. I believe you will too when you're finished reading about it.

Buck came of age in 1920, even with the rumors of scandal concerning the 1919 World Series lurking throughout the season. Batting a robust .333 with two hundred and ten base hits, Buck also scored one hundred and four runs while driving in another seventy-five. Buck cracked thirty-five doubles to go along with his eight triples and two homers. Buck showed a little more patience at the plate too, with twenty-eight walks, and struck out only twenty-three times in six hundred and thirty at-bats. Weaver was now the premiere 3rd baseman in the game, and he looked to skyrocket in the live ball era of the 1920's. But the plug was pulled on Buck and seven other teammates on September 27th, when the indictments were handed down from the Cook County Grand Jury. Immediately suspended by club owner Charles Comiskey, Buck would never wear a big league uniform again. Buck was formally banned from baseball by Commissioner Landis on August 3, 1921, a day after being acquitted on all charges by a jury. Weaver was only thirty years old.

Like most of his ousted teammates, Buck would scratch out a living playing in outlaw leagues and semi-pro ball. Weaver even managed a women's softball team, anything to stay in the game he loved so much. In 1927 Buck was managing an outlaw team in, of all places, the remote outback US-Mexico border town of Douglas, Arizona. But unfortunately for Buck, Chick Gandil somehow got the job of running the ball club. Chick's first order of business was to get his old pal Buck booted from the league (how he did this is unknown). The reason for this was probably over Weaver not testifying for Chick and Swede Risberg, a few weeks earlier, in Judge Landis's investigation over allegations that the White Sox in 1917, made pay-offs to members of the

Detroit Tigers to throw a four-game series to the Sox that September during the pennant race. Nothing came out of the investigation (which doesn't mean it wasn't true?), because Chick and Swede had no credibility. This made the second time Chick had a hand in getting Buck tossed out of baseball. What a guy Gandil was.

Buck ended up running a drug store for many years, until the business went bankrupt during the Great Depression. After that Buck made a living as a painter and doing other odd jobs, then settling in as a betting clerk at a racetrack. Would Buck have been a Hall of Famer? I don't know, but what I do know is that Buck was the best 3rd baseman in all of baseball at the time he was banned, and he was getting better every year. He also had a true love for the game. The whole situation involving Buck Weaver is a crying shame, and he is the only member of the black sox who deserves clemency. Baseball owes it to his family to clear his name, to put him back as a retired player in good standing. Buck Weaver died of a massive heart attack on January 31, 1956 in Chicago at the age of sixty-five. Buck tried every year until his death to clear his name, to no avail.

Game One

RHP Eddie Cicotte (29-7 1.82) vs LHP Dutch Ruether (19-6 1.81)

At Cincinnati, Oh **October 1st, 1919** **Redland Field**

Attendance-30,511

1st inning **Score: 0-0**

1st at-bat **0 on 2out**

Welcome to Redland Field in Cincinnati for the opening game of the 1919 World Series between the hometown Reds and the Chicago White Sox. When switch-hitting Buck Weaver stepped into the right-handed batters box against the left-handed throwing Ruether, there is two outs with the bases empty. Buck gets all of a Ruether pitch and sends a bullet into the left-center field gap; it looks for sure like extra bases. The quick CF Edd Roush gets a great jump on the ball, and makes a sensational one-handed grab (F-8) ending the 1st inning.

4th inning	**Score: 1-1**
2nd at-bat	**0 on 0out**

Tied 1-1 going to the top of the 4th inning, Buck leads-off the frame, dropping a drag bunt down the 3rd base line. Reds 3B Heinie Groh is not fooled and makes a fine play (5-3), robbing Weaver of a base hit for the second at-bat in a row. Ruether would retire the Sox in the 4th as the score remains tied.

6th inning	**Score: 6-1 Reds**
3rd at-bat	**1 on 1out**

Cincinnati broke the tie and Eddie Cicotte's back with five runs in the bottom of the 4th inning to take a 6-1 lead. The powerful Sox though have four innings to get the runs back, and with one down and Eddie Collins on at 1st base, Buck loops a bloop single (1B) into right-field as Collins stops at 2nd base. That is as far as the runners make it though, as Ruether sets down Jackson and Felsch to end the small uprising.

8th inning	**Score: 8-1 Reds**
4th at-bat	**1 on 2out**

By the top of the 8th, the game has turned into a laugher. The Reds have scored two more runs in their half of the 7th inning to take an 8-1 lead, and were not looking back. Fred McMullin leads-off the 8th with a pinch-hit single (1B), and was still there with two out. Buck ends the inning with a high lazy fly ball to CF Edd Roush (F-8). Ruether had no problems with the Sox in the 9th, and the Reds, who had scored one more run in the bottom of the 8th inning, take game one by the whopping score of 9-1. This game made a lot of people a lot of money, which included some members of the Chicago White Sox.

Game One Summary

Better start than most.

Excitement reigned supreme today, exciting from the Cincinnati stand point anyway, as the Reds took game one, behind ace pitcher Dutch Ruether 9-1. Buck hit the ball really well today, although he only had one hit to show for it. Buck was robbed twice of base hits, once by CF Edd Roush and the other by 3B Heinie Groh. The Sox look tomorrow to Lefty Williams to tie up Series, and split the two games played in Cincinnati.

Game One Box **Running Total**

		AB	R	H	RBI	AVE	
1st AB	L-8	1	0	0	0	.000	
2nd AB	5-3	2	0	0	0	.000	
3rd AB	1B	3	0	1	0	.333	
4th AB	F-8	4	0	1	0	.250	1 LOB(1)

Game Two

LHP Lefty Williams (23-11 2.64) vs LHP Slim Sallee (21-7 2.05)

At Cincinnati, Oh **October 1st, 1919** **Redland Field**

Attendance-29,698

1st inning **Score: 0-0**

1st at-bat **1 on 1out**

The Reds 9-1 victory in game one was a shock only to true White Sox fans and the poor bastards who were dumb enough to bet on the Sox. The Sox are now looking for a split of the two games in Cincinnati. In the top of the 1st inning, Eddie Collins was on 1st base after a walk (BB) and with one out Buck climbs in to bat against Sallee. Buck pulls a sizzling liner right at SS Larry Kopf, who hangs on for dear life (L-6). Eddie Collins, who was off to second base on a hit and run, was easily doubled off at 1st base (DP L-6-3), ending the top of the 1st inning.

4th inning **Score: 0-0**

2nd at-bat **0 on 0out**

Leading-off the visitors half of the 4th inning, Buck lines a single (1B) into right-field over 2B Morrie Rath's head. Weaver then takes 2nd base on a Joe Jackson single (1B), and the Sox are in business. With no outs Happy Felsch drops down a perfect sacrifice bunt (SAC 1-3) moving both runners up a bag. Buck is cut down at the plate on a nice play by 1B Jake Daubert (FC 3-2), on a grounder by Chick Gandil for the 2nd out. Sallee then retires Swede Risberg to stop the rally in its tracks.

6th inning **Score: 3-0 Reds**

3rd at-bat **0 on 1out**

Buck Weaver is just pounding the living daylights out of the baseball right now. With the Reds up 3-0, after a three spot in the bottom of the 4th inning, when control specialist Lefty Williams couldn't find the strike zone and walked three batters. When he did find the zone, he got shelled. With one gone in the top of the 6th, Buck's blast off Sallee short hops the left field wall for a stand up double (2B). After a Joe Jackson strike-out (K), Sallee balks Weaver to 3rd base (B). Happy Felsch though fails to get Buck home, when he flies out to CF Edd Roush (F-8) ending another good scoring chance for the Sox.

8th inning **Score: 4-2 Reds**

4th at-bat **0 on 1out**

The Reds held a 4-0 lead, after they scored another run off Lefty Williams in the 6th inning. The Sox cut the lead in half on a goofy play in the 7th, when they scored two runs on the same base hit as Ray Schalk circled the bases, scoring Swede Risberg and himself thanks to two Reds errors. With the score 4-2 Reds, going into the top of the 8th with one out, Buck drills a sharp grounder that SS Larry Kopf scoops up with no trouble (6-3) for the 2nd out. Slim Sallee would have no more problems with the Sox the rest of the way and win by the score of 4-2.

Game Two Summary

Hitting it on the nose!

The score was closer today but the result was the same, as the Reds won 4-2 behind the pitching of Slim Sallee. Chicago is now trailing two games to zero, after the nightmare in Cincinnati. Buck was on fire in game two, getting two base hits including a double. Even his outs were hard hit. In Buck's first eight at-bats of the Series, seven were hit on the button (including his drag bunt in game one). The Sox had plenty of base runners off Sallee (ten hits), but when they needed a clutch hit nobody could come through. Game three in Chicago now has become very important for the Sox.

Game Two Box		**Running Total**					
		AB	R	H	RBI	AVE	
1st AB	L-6-3 DP	5	0	1	0	.200	1 LOB(2)
2nd AB	1B	6	0	2	0	.333	
3rd AB	2B	7	0	3	0	.429	2B(1)
4th AB	6-3	8	0	3	0	.375	

Game Three

RHP Ray Fisher (14-5 2.17) vs RHP Dickie Kerr (13-8 2.89)

At Chicago, ILL **October 3rd, 1919** **Comiskey Park**

Attendance-29,126

1st inning **Score: 0-0**

1st at-bat **0 on 2 out**

Only the third game of the Series, but it is now a big game for the White Sox. About 5,000 empty seats greet the Sox for their first game at Comiskey Park, no doubt upset at their team's lackluster play so far. Also those dirty rumors just won't go away. Dickie Kerr held Cincinnati in check in the 1st inning, and Chicago now comes to the plate for the first time today. After Fisher recorded two quick outs, Buck bats, hitting left-handed for the first time in the Series. Weaver turns on a fat pitch, but gets under the ball and pops-up to 1B Jake Daubert (F-3), ending the inning.

3rd inning **Score: 2-0 Sox**

2nd at-bat **1on 0 out**

The Sox took an early 2-0 lead when they scored a pair in the bottom of the 2nd inning. Eddie Collins led-off the bottom of the 3rd with a single (1B), and moves to 2nd base on Buck's liner over SS Larry Kopf's head (1B) into left-field. Then the inning ends very quickly when Joe Jackson pops-up a terrible bunt attempt (F-3), even though he was as hot as Weaver, and Happy Felsch grounds into a (DP 5-4-3) double play.

5th inning **Score: 3-0 Sox**

3rd at-bat **0 on 2 out**

Chicago now held a 3-0 advantage with another run in the 4th inning, and Dickie Kerr was pitching like a seasoned pro. The Reds Ray Fisher wasn't throwing too badly either, as the game moves to the halfway point. Fisher has a rather easy 5th inning, after getting the first two Sox batters; Buck ends the inning by tapping back to the box, as Fisher handles the play (1-3).

8th inning **Score: 3-0 Sox**

4th at-bat **0 on 2 out**

The Reds had pinch-hit for starter Ray Fisher in the top of the 8th, and the right-handed reliever Dolph Luque (9-3 2.63), was now pitching in the bottom of the 8th. Luque retired Nemo Leibold and Eddie Collins, as Buck comes up to bat for the fourth time today and bounces out to 2B Morrie Rath (4-3) to end the home half of the 8th inning. Dickie Kerr was without a doubt the story of today's game. The Sox pulled to within a game, now down only two games to one.

Game Three Summary

Still swinging a good bat.

The Sox needed a victory in the worst way, and Little Dickie Kerr delivered. Buck only hit one ball out of the infield today, but it was a line drive single to left-field. The Sox didn't need very much this afternoon, as Kerr threw a three-hit shutout and won 3-0. Buck was in the beginning of a slump, and the rest of the team will follow suit.

Game Three Box **Running Total**

		AB	R	H	RBI	AVE
1st AB	F-3	9	0	3	0	.333
2nd AB	1B	10	0	4	0	.400
3rd AB	1-3	11	0	4	0	.364
4th AB	4-3	12	0	4	0	.333

Game Four

RHP Jimmy Ring (10-9 2.26) vs RHP Eddie Cicotte (29-7 1.82)

At Chicago, ILL **October 4th, 1919** **Comiskey Park**

Attendance-34,363

1st inning **Score: 0-0**

1st at-bat **0 on 2 out**

Now that the Sox were on the tally board with a win in game three, the seats were filled for game four. Cicotte held the Reds to a scratch single in the top of the 1st inning, as the Sox came up to bat in the bottom half. Jimmy Ring had a rather easy inning also, with Buck making the third out on a fly ball to RF Greasy Neale (F-9).

3rd inning **Score: 0-0**

2nd at-bat **1 on 1 out**

A pitcher's duel was shaping up in Chicago today, as Eddie Cicotte and Jimmy Ring were mowing down hitters like high grass. The game has moved to the bottom of the 3rd inning, still tied 0-0. Eddie Collins, hitting with one out, gets plunked (HBP) with a Ring fastball. On a hit and run play, Buck hits the ball to the right side but it was too close to 1B Jake Daubert. Daubert fielded the ball and made the play himself (3-U), for the second out with Collins taking 2nd base. Chicago would not score.

5th inning **Score: 2-0 Reds**

3rd at-bat **1 on 2 out**

In the top half of the 5th inning, Cincinnati had taken a 2-0 lead courtesy of two Eddie Cicotte errors (maybe one was Joe Jackson's?). Missing out on scoring chances in the 2nd and 3rd innings, the Sox had another chance to get on the boards in the bottom of the 5th. The only problem was, with Nemo Leibold on at 2nd base and one out, Nemo managed to get himself thrown out when he ventured too far off 2nd base on a grounder by Eddie Collins (FC 5-4) for the 2nd out. Now Collins was on 1st base but with two down. For the 2nd time in as many at-bats, Buck grounds out to 1B Jake Daubert (3-U), as Daubert makes the play by himself again, ending the 5th. This was the last chance Chicago would have to score off Ring today.

8th inning **Score: 2-0 Reds**

4th at-bat **0 on 0 out**

Eddie Cicotte was good today but Reds pitcher Jimmy Ring was better. The Sox were still trailing 2-0 going into their next to last ups. Buck leads-off the 8th pulling a Texas leaguer into right field that looks like it was going to drop for an easy double. Out of nowhere 2B Morrie Rath races over to make a beautiful one-handed catch (F-4), near the 1st base foul line for the first out. Jimmy Ring completed the inning with no damage, as well as the 9th, throwing a spectacular three-hit shutout at the White Sox and winning the ballgame 2-0.

Game Four Summary

Slump!

The Sox were hoping to even up the Series today, with their ace Eddie Cicotte back on the mound. But that wasn't to be, as the Reds Jimmy Ring tossed a three-hit shutout at them. The Sox were slipping into a team slump of extraordinary magnitude. If they thought Jimmy Ring was good today, just wait until they get lode of Hod Eller tomorrow. Buck had his first game of the Series without a base hit, but he was robbed by 2B Morrie Rath of extra bases. Other than that at-bat, he suffered the same fate as most of his other teammates. The Sox are now trailing the Reds by a count of three games to one, with Lefty Williams on the hill for game five. Could it be possible that the Sox might lose four of the first five ballgames, with Cicotte and Williams taking all four losses?

Game Four Box **Running Total**

		AB	R	H	RBI	AVE	
1st AB	F-9	13	0	4	0	.308	
2nd AB	3-U	14	0	4	0	.286	1 LOB(3)
3rd AB	3-U	15	0	4	0	.267	1 LOB(4)
4th AB	F-4	16	0	4	0	.250	

Game Five

RHP Hod Eller (20-9 2.40) vs LHP Lefty Williams (23-11 2.64)

At Chicago, ILL **October 6th, 1919** **Comiskey Park**

Attendance-34,379

1st inning **Score: 0-0**

1st at-bat **1 on 1 out**

Another big crowd today as the Sox is in a crisis mode, needing to come out on top today or face a humiliating four games to one deficit. Yesterday's rainout was a very welcome day of rest for the weary Sox pitcher's going on only two days rest. Williams threw a goose egg at the Reds in the top of the 1st inning, and the Sox are looking for a fast start. They get it when Nemo Leibold drew a lead-off walk (BB), and moved to 2nd base on Eddie Collins ground out to SS Larry Kopf (6-3). Batting left-handed against the right-handed throwing Eller, Buck belts a smash right back up the box that hits Eller in the behind, and caromed far enough away for an infield single, but Eller saved a run. Weaver is now on 1st base and Leibold on 3rd after the base hit. Unfortunately for the Sox, neither Joe Jackson nor Happy Felsch could give the home team the lead. It was too bad, because it would be a long time before the Sox will have another runner in scoring position.

4th inning **Score: 0-0**

2nd at-bat **0 on 0 out**

The way Williams and Eller were working the hitters today, the first team to score could be the winner. In fact, when Buck taps back to the mound (1-3) to open the bottom of the 4th inning, it snapped a string of six straight strikeouts for Hod Eller. Eller also retires Joe Jackson on another comebacker (1-3), and then strikes out Happy Felsch (K) to end the easy frame.

3rd inning **Score: 4-0 Reds**

6th at-bat **0 on 2 out**

Williams was just cruising along with a one- hitter going, then his pitches suddenly flattened out and he was pounded for four runs, giving the Reds a 4-0 lead. The bottom of the 6th inning, Eller kept his two-hitter going when Buck ends the frame by grounding out to SS Larry Kopf (6-3).

9th inning **Score: 5-0 Reds**

4th at-bat **0 on 2 out**

The game was all but over after the Reds scored another run in the top of the 9th off reliever Erskine Mayer (1-3 8.25), to take a 5-0 lead. Buck Weaver has no quit in him though. After Eller retires the first two Sox in order, Buck breaks out the lumber and launches a booming triple (3B), all the way to the fence in right-center field. This was the Sox last hurrah though, as Joe Jackson hits a two hopper to Larry Kopf (6-3), ending the game.

Game Five Summary

Breaking-out again.

This time it was Hod Eller's turn to throw a three-hit shutout (the third game in a row that ended in a three-hit shutout). Nobody in their right mind would have predicted that the Sox would lose four of the first five games, and all four of the losses would be credited to Eddie Cicotte and Lefty Williams, and that their only win would be by a rookie (Dickie Kerr). That was an inconvenient truth howeve. Buck Weaver snapped out of his slump today in a big way, getting two of the Sox three hits, including a triple. It all went to waste though as the only other Sox to get a base hit off Eller was Ray Schalk, and he was tossed out of the game in the 6th inning after losing his mind on a close play at the plate. The Series now shifts back to Cincinnati, and the prospects of the Series coming back to Chicago are slim and none, and slim was looking for a cab.

Game Five Box **Running Total**

		AB	R	H	RBI	AVE	
1st AB	1B	17	0	5	0	.294	
2nd AB	1-3	18	0	5	0	.278	
3rd AB	6-3	19	0	5	0	.263	
4th AB	3B	20	0	6	0	.300	3B (1)

Game Six

RHP Dickie Kerr (13-8 2.89) vs LHP Dutch Ruether (19-6 1.81)

At Cincinnati, Oh **October 7th, 1919** **Redland Field**

Attendance-32,006

1st inning **Score: 0-0**

1st at-bat **0 on 2 out**

A full house turned out today at Redland Park as the Cincinnati Reds look to close out the World Series. After Ruether sets down the first two batter's Buck, batting from the right side, continues his hot hitting with a frozen rope into left-field for a single (1B). Ruether then gets Joe Jackson to pop-up (F-5) to 3B Heinie Groh, ending the 1st inning.

4th inning **Score: 2-0 Reds**

2nd at-bat **0 on 0 out**

The Sox have not scored a run now in the last twenty-five innings, and when the Reds take a 2-0 lead with a pair of runs in the bottom of the 3rd inning, things couldn't have been much worse. Is there anybody other than Weaver, Schalk and Kerr (occasionally Joe Jackson), who feels much like playing this game? Well, not in this inning. Buck leads-off the top of the 4th by hitting a lazy fly ball out to LF Pat Duncan (F-7), who gloves the ball for the first out. Ruether would only give up a scratch single (1B) to Happy Felsch before retiring the Sox, and keeping the score 2-0 Reds.

6th inning **Score: 4-1 Reds**

3rd at-bat **0 on 0 out**

The Reds have increased their lead to 4-0 when the Sox ended their scoreless streak at twenty-six innings with a run off Ruether in the top of the 5th, making the score 4-1. Time is running out on Chicago. Buck Weaver is back in the groove and greets Ruether leading-off the top of the 6th, looping the ball over the head of SS Larry Kopf into left-field, hustling into 2nd base for a lead-off double (2B). For only the second time in six games, Joe Jackson follows a Weaver base hit with one of his own, driving Buck home with an RBI single (1B) to center-field (Buck's first run scored in the Series), making the score 4-2. Chicago would score two more runs in the inning and tie the game up at four apiece, knocking Dutch Ruether out of the game in the process, bringing game four winner Jimmy Ring (10-9 2.26) into the ballgame. For the first time in this Series, we now have a ballgame.

7th inning **Score: 4-4**

4th at-bat **0 on 2 out**

Dickie Kerr was pitching the gutsiest ballgame in the history of the World Series. In and out of trouble all afternoon, Kerr had not retired the Reds in order yet today. With the score still tied at 4-4, Buck was now batting left-handed against right- handed Jimmy Ring with two out. Buck pulls a hard shot but it was right at 2B Morrie Rath, who scoops up the ball on one hop, and tosses out Weaver (4-3) putting an end to the top of the 6th inning.

10th inning **Score: 4-4**

5th at-bat **0 on 0 out**

You couldn't ask for more, extra innings in the World Series. In a must win game for the Sox non-the-less. Buck starts-off the top of the 10th inning against Jimmy Ring and laces a stinging double (2B) down the left-field line (Buck's second double and third hit of the game). Joe Jackson then lays down his curious bunt (see 10th inning of game six in chapter four), that goes for a base hit (1B) advancing Weaver to 3rd base. Buck then scores what turns out to be the winning run; when Chick Gandil singles (1B) into right-field (Chick had the game winning hits in both of Dickie Kerr's wins, go figure). Ring would get out of the 10th with no more runs but Dickie Kerr recorded his only perfect inning of the ballgame in the bottom half, and Chicago has a 5-4 victory. The win gives the Sox a stay of execution, at least for one more game, with the Series standing at four games to two, still in favor of the Reds.

Game Six Summary

POW!

What a ballgame! The Sox were trailing 4-0 after four innings, and it looked like their miserable World Series was going to end today. The hometown Reds looked to wrap it all up in front of 32,000, as starter Dutch Ruether was in total command and the Sox Dickie Kerr was struggling every inning. That started to change in the top of the 5th, when the Sox scored their first run in twenty-six innings. By the 6th, Ruether was out of the game and the Sox had tied up the score at four all. Dickie Kerr still struggled like the dickens, but he held the Reds scoreless the rest of the way, and Chicago had a 5-4 victory in 10 innings. You just can't say enough about Kerr's performance, or about Buck Weaver's. Buck had three hits today, including two doubles and scored the tying and winning runs. If anybody could have gotten on in front of Buck, he batted all five times with the bases empty, the Sox might of won big instead of a nail biter. Kid Gleason prayed to the baseball Gods that the Sox can carry this win over into tomorrow, trying to hold serve in match point number two.

Game Six Box		**Running Total**					
		AB	R	H	RBI	AVE	
1st AB	1B	21	0	7	0	.333	
2nd AB	F-7	22	0	7	0	.318	
3rd AB	2B, Run	23	1	8	0	.348	2B(2)
4th AB	4-3	24	1	8	0	.333	
5th AB	2B, Run	25	2	9	0	.360	2B(3)

Game Seven

RHP Eddie Cicotte (29-7 1.82) vs LHP Slim Sallee (21-7 2.05)

At Cincinnati, Oh **October 8th, 1919** **Redland Field**

Attendance-13,923

1st inning **Score: 0-0**

1st at-bat **1 on 1out**

Shano Collins led-off the game by singling (1B) up the gut into center field and made it to 2nd base on Eddie Collins's sacrifice bunt (SAC 1-3), with a red hot Buck Weaver coming up to bat. Buck puts good wood on the ball but it's an at-um ball straight to CF Edd Roush (F-8) for out number two. Sallee then gives up an RBI single (1B) to Joe Jackson, giving the Sox an early 1-0 lead before getting out of the 1st inning.

3rd inning **Score: 1-0 Sox**

2nd at-bat **2 on 0out**

As the ballgame heads into the top of the 3rd inning, the Sox held a slim 1-0 lead. Chicago jumps out to a quick start in the inning, with the Collins boys on at 1st and 2nd base via lead-off singles (1B). Slim Sallee then gets two even quicker outs when Buck lays into the ball and shoots it like a cannon to SS Larry Kopf who catches the ball in the air (L-6). Shano Collins froze on the line drive but Eddie Collins got caught inexplicably too far off of 1st base and was doubled off (DP L-6-3). This was one game where Joe Jackson felt much like playing, as he delivered another RBI single (1B) scoring Shano, putting the Sox up 2-0. Sallee made it out of the inning when Happy Felsch forced Jackson at 2nd base (FC 6-4), to end the inning.

5th inning **Score: 2-0 Sox**

3rd at-bat **1 on 1out**

Chicago was still holding onto a 2-0 lead as the Sox came to bat in the top of the 5th inning. With Eddie Collins on at 1st base after a one out single, Buck pulls a scorcher that 3B Heinie Groh cannot handle (E-5), with Collins taking 2nd base. Cincinnati's defense was falling apart as 2B Morrie Rath muffs Joe Jackson's grounder (E-4) for another Reds error loading the bases. Happy Felsch next decided to get into the act when he delivers a huge two RBI single (1B), scoring Collins and Weaver and giving the Sox a 4-0 advantage. Cincinnati manager Pat Moran pulled the plug on Slim Sallee and brought in game three losing pitcher, right-hander Ray Fisher (14-5 2.17) into the ballgame. Fisher gets out of the 5th without giving up anymore runs, but the damage was already done. Eddie Cicotte would take care of the rest.

7th inning **Score: 4-1 Sox**

4th at-bat **0 on 0 out**

The game moves into the 7th inning with the Reds right-handed reliever Dolph Luque (9-3 2.63) now pitching. Good thing the Sox had the 4-1 lead (Cincinnati scored one run in the 6th), because they could not hit Luque to save their lives. Leading-off and batting left-handed against the hard throwing Luque, Buck strikes-out (K). Luque would strikeout five in his four innings of work, but Cicotte needed no more help and wins 4-1. Completing the two game sweep in Cincinnati, the Sox are now within a game, four to three, as the Series unbelievably is headed back to the Windy City for game eight. Too bad Kid Gleason didn't put Lefty Williams on a raft and send him down the Ohio River before they left for home, but I doubt if anybody downstream wanted Lefty either.

Game Seven Summary

A tough o-fer.

Kid Gleason's prayers for game seven were answered by Eddie Cicotte. Showing the Reds how he won twenty-nine games during the 1919 season, Cicotte was in total command throughout the ballgame, winning for the only time in the Series 4-1. The Reds fielding finally caught up with them in game seven also, making four errors. Buck left four runners on base today (his first of the series) including two in scoring position, although he hit the ball well except for his last at-bat. This was only the second game Buck failed to get a base hit. Now it is on to Chicago, and a date with infamy.

Game Seven Box **Running Total**

		AB	R	H	RBI	AVE	
1st AB	F-8	26	0	9	0	.346	1 LOB(5),1 RISP(1)
2nd AB	L-6-3 DP	27	0	9	0	.333	2 LOB(7),1 RISP(2)
3rd AB	E-5, Run	28	3	9	0	.321	1 LOB(8)
4th AB	K	29	3	9	0	.310	K(2)

Game Eight

RHP Hod Eller (20-9 2.40) vs LHP Lefty Williams (23-11 2.64)

At Chicago, ILL **October 9th, 1919** **Comiskey Park**

Attendance-32,939

1st inning **Score: 4-0 Reds**

1st at-bat **2 on 0 out**

A huge crowd of faithful White Sox fans came to Comiskey Park today to witness their hometown hero's on a roll. Winning the last two games in Cincinnati to force a game eight, no one on the Southside could believe the game would be more or less over in the first five batters. Before a cat could lick its chops, Chicago was down 4-0 and Lefty Williams was headed for the showers. Lefty just didn't feel much like pitching today, if you can call that pitching? The White Sox who did feel much like playing, and there wasn't many, tried to get the Sox back into the game in the bottom of the 1st. With runners on at 1st and 2nd base and no outs, Buck comes to the plate facing Reds starter Hod Eller, the tall right-hander who controlled everybody but Buck Weaver in winning game five. This time though it was Eller doing the controlling, as he strikes Buck out looking for the 1st out (K). As hard as I tried, this is the only at-bat in the eight games you can point to and say Buck might have tanked it. If you are looking for at-bats where throwing a game is evident, then taking a third strike with two runners in scoring position does not look too good. Buck Weaver did not tank it though, he just got fooled. Eller then retires Joe Jackson and Happy Felsch to get out of the 1st inning unscathed. And the rout was on.

3rd inning **Score: 5-1 Reds**

2nd at-bat **0 on 1 out**

The Reds were now up 5-0 after another run in the top of the 2nd inning. Hod Eller, who pitched out of a big jam in the 1st inning, and a small one in the 2nd, faces Buck in the bottom of the 3rd with one out. Eller wins this battle also as Weaver just gets under the ball and sends a high pop-up to 2B Morrie Rath (F-4) making the 2nd out. Joe Jackson did put the Sox on the board with a deep home run (HR) to right but that's all Chicago would score in the inning and trail 5-1.

6th inning **Score: 9-1 Reds**

3rd at-bat **0 on 0 out**

By the bottom of the 6th inning, Chicago was getting their butts kicked 9-1 and needed a miracle. The Reds had scored one run in the 5th inning off relief pitcher Bill James (3-1 2.54) and three more in the 6th off James and Roy Wilkenson (1-1 2.05). The baseball Gods must have been watching football today, as no *Angels in the Outfield* showed up for game eight. There was no quit in Buck Weaver though, leading-off the bottom of the 6th. Weaver shoots a bullet into right-field for a single (1B), but he dies there on 1st base as no one could even move him up a base.

8th inning **Score: 10-1 Reds**

4th at-bat **1 on 1 out**

With Hod Eller holding a 10-1 lead, the fat lady was warming up her voice. Embarrassed and probably crazy mad, Buck comes to bat with Eddie Collins on 1st base and one out. Buck takes out his frustrations out on the baseball, drilling a double (2B) over 1B Jake Daubert's head into right field with Collins stopping at 3rd base (besides Jackson in game six, no other Sox scored from 1st base on any of the ten doubles Chicago hit in the Series). Joe Jackson next smashes another double (2B) to the wall in right-field, driving home Collins and Weaver, making the score 10-3. In their last hurrah, the Sox would score two more runs in the 8th inning to close within 10-5.

9th inning **Score: 10-5 Reds**

5th at-bat **2 on 1 out**

The Sox had another rally going in the bottom of the 9th, with Eddie Murphy on at 2nd base and Eddie Collins at 1st and one out. Next up, Buck cracks what looks like a three run homer, but the ball falls into RF Greasy Neale's glove at the wall in right-field (F-9) for the 2nd out, as Murphy tagged up and went to 3rd base. A moment later Joe Jackson grounds out (4-3) and the fat lady started singing her song. The Reds were the champions of baseball, winning game eight 10-5, and the Series five games to three.

Game Eight Summary

This is the thanks I get?

Five batters, four runs and one disgraced pitcher equals a humiliating defeat at the hand of the Cincinnati Reds 10-5. The game wasn't even that close however, as the Reds at one time held a 10-1 lead. Hod Eller doesn't blow 10-1 leads. The Reds were baseball kings, and the Sox could look forward to scandal at the end of the following season. Buck finished with a pretty good ballgame, though he missed a big chance in the bottom of the 1st when he K'd looking with runners on 2nd and 3rd with no outs, putting the only blemish on Buck's otherwise stellar World Series. Buck did have two hits including his record tying fourth double of the Series, and he just missed a three run homer that would have made the game interesting. Although Buck didn't drive in any runs in the Series, he didn't have many chances until the last two ballgames. Buck left eight runners on base in games seven and eight including five in scoring position. With the exception of his 1st at-bat in game eight, Buck put good wood on the ball in those scoring chances. Buck had a great World Series, and contributed in no way to any of the Sox five losses, and only Dickie Kerr, Ray Schalk and Shano Collins can also make that claim.

Game Eight Box **Running Total**

		A	R	H	RBI	AVE	
1st AB	K	30	3	9	0	.300	2 LOB(10),2 RISP(4)
2nd AB	F-4	31	3	9	0	.290	
3rd AB	1B	32	3	10	0	.313	
4th AB	2B,Run	33	4	11	0	.333	2B(4)
5th AB	F-9	34	4	11	0	.324	2 LOB(12), 1 RISP(5)

Chapter Thirteen

Making a case for Buck Weaver

When pleading Buck Weaver's case for reinstatement, where do you begin? I think first you have to start with the history of players being banned from baseball. Before there was a Commissioner of baseball (which started with Commissioner Landis in 1921), and even back before the Major Leagues was run by a three member National Commission (which started in 1903 with the signing of an agreement allowing the American League be recognized as a second Major League. This Commission consisted of, the head of the Commission Cincinnati Reds owner Garry Herrmann, President of the American League Byrun "Ban" Johnson and National League President John A. Heydler). The players policed their own actions (called the National Association of Professional Base Ball Players, or the NAPBBP). This lasted until Chicago promoter William A. Hulbert, in 1876 staged a coup that replaced the NAPBBP with a league controlled by the games owners.

As far back as 1865, three players off the New York Mutuals were banned from baseball. Thomas Devyr, Ed Duffy, and William Wansley were expelled for accepting $100 to throw a game on September 27th (fifty-five years to the day of the Black Sox Indictments), to the Brooklyn Eckfords. All three players were reinstated on November 30, 1870. In 1876, George Bechtel of the Louisville Grays got himself into hot water after sending a wire to teammate Jim Devlin, saying that they could make $500 apiece if they threw a game on June 10. When Louisville officials got wind of the plot, Bechtel was given the choice of resigning or being expelled. He just couldn't bring himself to resign and was banned from the game, never to play again (and having the dubious distinction of being the first man ever permanently tossed out of baseball). That same Louisville team was also the subject of the first big scandal to rock the game of baseball. In 1877 (under William A Hulbert and the owners watch) three players off the Grays were expelled from baseball on December 5, when they were charged with dumping baseball games during the preceding season (another player Bill Craver was also banned in 1877, not for the dumping of the games, but for not cooperating with the investigation). Jim

Devlin (who escaped punishment in the George Bechtel case), George Hall, and Al Nichols were accused by the National League of accepting money to throw ballgames on August 31, and September 1, 1877. Another player on the Louisville team Oscar Walker, though not involved with the scandal itself, was banned for contract jumping.

Even umpires were not immune from prosecution from the powers of baseball. In 1882, Richard Higham was working with a well known gambler in Detroit. Higham was confronted by the angry team owners of Detroit after a number of bad calls went against their team. Higham spilled the beans and was banned from umpiring for the rest of his life. He is the only umpire ever banned from baseball. In 1908 a team doctor was kicked out of baseball and asked never to return. Dr. Joseph Cramer, team doctor of the New York Giants, was caught offering $2,500 to Hall of Fame umpire Bill Klem. Cramer asked Klem to help the Giants in the famous play-off between the Giants and the Cubs.

The first owner to get into hot water and bounced from the game was Horace Fogel, owner of the Philadelphia Phillies. In 1912 Fogel, who was also a long time sportswriter, was given a pink slip (the first and only banishment by the National Commission) for accusing the National League and its umpires of favoring the New York Giants. He also made an accusation that the pennant race that season was crooked. It seems also at this time that baseball had turned a blind eye to gambling. Rumors of thrown ballgames ran rampant, and even players were not above placing bets on the outcome of games. After the World Series of 1919, baseball was in serious trouble. The public confidence that the games were not being played fair and square, and that gamblers were running baseball, was ruining the game and something had to be done before baseball came crashing down. Two things happened that changed this path to destruction. One was the immergence of a baseball God (without a doubt the biggest reason), whose home run hitting put people into the stands in record numbers- Babe Ruth. The other was the hiring of a single Commissioner to replace the three members of the National Commission which consisted of; Garry Herrmann (President), John Heydler (National League President), and Ban Johnson (American League President). It should be noted that the breakup of the National Commission and the hiring of a Commissioner was starting to take place during the winter of 1919-1920, almost 10 months before the black sox scandal even broke. This upset Ban Johnson off immensely, because it basically took away his one-man show in the American League. On January 12, 1921 baseball signed as their new Commissioner, federal Judge Kenesaw Mountain Landis, to a $50,000 a year lifetime contract. Landis's first order of business was to clean up baseball, anyway he could.

Judge Landis had to deal right off the bat with the White Sox player's accused of throwing the 1919 World Series. The eight ballplayers included Joe Jackson, Eddie Cicotte, Lefty Williams, Buck Weaver, Happy Felsch, Swede Risberg, Chick Gandil and Fred McMullin. Since they were already suspended from the White Sox since September 27, 1920, when the indictments were handed down by the Cook County Grand Jury, Landis had the luxury of waiting until the trial of these player's was over before taking any action. The trial started in July and lasted about a month, ending on August 2, 1921 with the player's being acquitted on all charges. But it didn't matter to the new Commissioner. The very next day Landis gave his verdict:

"Regardless of the verdict of juries, no player who throws a ball game, no player that undertakes or promises to throw a ball game, no player that sits in conference with a bunch of crooked players and gamblers where the ways and means of throwing a game are discussed and does not promptly tell his club about it, will ever play professional baseball!"

It was all over for the black sox, all eight players were banned for life, and there would be no pardons. Then Judge Landis got really busy. From 1920 to 1924, Landis banned ten ball players from Major League baseball. Of the ten, six were for gambling offenses, three for contract disputes, and one for auto theft. The players given the boot for gambling offenses were Lee Magee 1920, Joe Gedeon 1921, Eugene Paulette 1921, Phil Douglas 1922, Johnny O'Connell 1924 and Cozy Dolan also in 1924. Contract disputes were dealt with very harshly too, the irony being that they all played in the 1919 World Series. First Heinie Groh and Ray Fisher of the Cincinnati Reds were banned in 1921 for refusing to sign their contracts. Heinie Groh gave in, signed his contract and was reinstated two days later. It took Fisher almost 60 years before Commissioner Bowie Kuhn reinstated Ray as a retired person in good standing.

The White Sox Dickie Kerr was banned by Judge Landis in 1922, for refusing to take a $500 pay cut. Kerr wasn't reinstated until 1925. The reserve clause was a wonderful thing for the owners. Where was Marvin Miller when these players needed him? An interesting case involved Benny Kauff, who was picked up for auto theft in 1919. Later acquitted in a court of law, Landis banned Kauff anyway in 1921. As Landis said, "Kauff was no longer a fit companion for other ball players." The Philadelphia Phillies lost another owner in 1943 when William Cox became Judge Landis's last expulsion, for placing bets on the Phillies.

It would be another thirty-five years before another was banned from baseball, and he was a biggy. In 1979 Commissioner Kuhn sacked Willie Mays from our National Pastime. Willie had accepted a job as a greeter from an Atlantic City casino. In 1983 Kuhn also banned Mickey Mantle for the same offense. What a joke that was, considering the number of owners that had stakes in horse racing and tracks over the years (John McGraw himself once owned a track in Cuba). New Commissioner Peter Uberroth reinstated our national hero's Willie and Mickey in 1985. On a sad personal note, in 1989 my childhood hero Pete Rose was banned for life, after placing bets on his own Cincinnati Reds. Pete was the last man kicked out of baseball for gambling. In 1990 New York Yankee owner George Steinbrenner was forced to give up running the team by Commissioner Fay Vincent, for paying known gambler Howie Spira $40,000 to dig up dirt on Dave Winfield during a contract dispute. The Boss was later reinstated by Vincent on March 1, 1993. Two other players were banned for drug related offenses. Hall of Famer Ferguson Jenkins was banned fourteen days after an arrest for illegal drugs on August 25, 1980 by Commissioner Bowie Kuhn. Jenkins was reinstated by an arbitrator on September 22, 1980. And last but not least, the sad saga of Steve Howe. The talented left-hander was suspended on six different occasions before finally being banned by Commissioner Fay Vincent after an arrest for cocaine possession on July 24, 1992. Incredibly Howe was also reinstated by an arbitrator in November 1992.

Not a history that baseball is very proud of. As we get back to Buck Weaver, it was well known by all players that if you helped throw baseball games prior to 1919, you were probably not going to play Major League baseball again. Yet just gambling on a game by a player was not a capital offense until Judge Landis's landmark decision in 1921. But Buck Weaver did not gamble on baseball games, nor did he help in any way to throw the 1919 World Series. No player on either team played better than Buck did in the Series. Two players hit for a higher average than Buck's .324, Joe Jackson at .375 and the Reds Greasy Neale at .357. And only Jackson had more hits than Weaver with twelve, to Buck's eleven. Buck didn't drive in any runs in the Series, but it's hard to drive in runs when nobody is on base in front of you. Out of Buck's thirty-four plate appearances, he batted twenty-one times in the Series with the bases empty. Buck did leave twelve runners on the bases in the eight games (eight in the last two games) but out of the twelve, two were left on when Buck lined into double plays and two more were left on base when Weaver almost belted a three run homer in his final at-bat of game eight. Of the six runners Buck left on in scoring position, one was on one of the lineout double play, and two more on the near miss home run. No one can match Buck's hitting in this Series, not even Joe Jackson with all his fantastic stats. In the field Buck handled twenty-seven chances without an error, the only regular infielder on either team who didn't make one. In fact, while researching this book, I looked very hard to pin something, anything on Buck's play to help support a case of his helping in any way to throw even one game in this Series. I could only come up with one example. In game eight with runners on at 2nd and 3rd base with no outs in the very 1st inning, Hod Eller struck Buck out looking. But Eller struck out fifteen in his two starts. This was the only at-bat in thirty-four trips to the plate that you could remotely point your finger at, and Weaver had no shady plays in the field.

So why was Buck Weaver banned for life by Commissioner Landis? It certainly wasn't his overall stellar play in the 1919 World Series, and it wasn't because he accepted money from anyone either. What Buck did was admit that he sat in on at least one, maybe two of the meetings where the fix was discussed. The first meeting you could argue that Buck went along not really knowing where he was going, just hanging around with his pals, wrong place at the wrong time. So check that one off. You can't make any argument for Buck attending another meeting though, if in fact he went to another meeting, other than the fact that these player's were his friends and he didn't want to snitch on his friends. All right, morally it was wrong, but in 1919 there was no policy set down by the National Commission concerning ratting out your fellow ball players. In fact, if there was one Buck certainly would have spilled the beans, not wanting to risk his career for anyone. Weaver proved this by not accepting money and telling his dirty teammates to go to hell, playing nothing less than his very best every second he was on the field. Judge Landis in his banishment decree included this sentence especially for Buck, "that no player who sits in conference with a bunch of crooked ballplayers, where the ways and means of throwing games are discussed and does not immediately report this, will ever play professional baseball again." This was added to make an example of Buck Weaver. But what kind of retroactive crap was this, a policy made two years after the fact. Even though this was a well thought out and much needed rule of baseball law, and one that I truly believe in, this should not have applied to Buck Weaver (if anything at all, Buck should have received no more than a short suspension). Like I said, if this was a written rule of baseball at the time, there is no way Buck would have kept his silence. You can see where Judge Landis believed this would discouraged others from not telling what they knew when something crooked was about to go down, and it has worked. But when Judge Landis died on November 25, 1944, Buck's lifetime ban should have died with him.

In succession Happy Chandler, Ford Frick, William Eckert, Bowie Kuhn, Peter Uberroth, A. Bartlett Giamatti, Fay Vincent and current Commissioner Bud Selig have all passed on Buck Weaver. It's about time Commissioner Selig does something for baseball that doesn't involve a dollar sign. Do something for the real baseball fans who don't like interleague play. Who would like to see both leagues go back to east and west divisions, and getting rid of four teams who don't deserve to be in the play-offs. That's what made baseball special, when a game in April meant as much as a game in September. And who would also like to see a 90 year injustice removed from a ball player who died in 1956. I can close my eyes and see Buck Weaver walking around in limbo just like Jacob Marley in Charles Dickens classic, *A Christmas Carol*. Buck has the chains of his former life, weighing him down as he screams out for the justice that has never come. Commissioner Selig now holds the keys to those chains. The point has been made, no one in the history of baseball has ever been banned for the same offense Buck was banned for, and I doubt if anyone ever will be again. Buck Weaver broke no rules of baseball when he was banned, and the only player ever expelled for something similar to Weaver's case was Bill Craver, who in the scandal of 1877, refused to cooperate with the investigation. Well, Buck Weaver cooperated with Landis's investigation and was banned anyway.

Consider this also, everyone on both teams had to of known what was going on in this World Series. Especially after the second game, they had to of known. As close knit as the teams of that era were, even if they couldn't stand each other, as the different cliques on the White Sox were, you still would have known what everybody else was doing. It wasn't like today when after the game, all the players scatter to the winds and don't see one another until the next game. Back then they traveled on trains together, roomed together, ate together and saw who came and went in the hotels. Even if one group hated the other group's guts, which was the case on the White Sox, there's no way they didn't know what the others were up to. And none of them reported that they heard a fix was about to go down. Even if someone had, I doubt they would have gotten anymore action out of American League President Ban Johnson other than a big @#*! You!

Enough is enough Commissioner Selig; it is time to set Buck Weaver free. It is time to make him a retired player in good standing. He is the only player involved in the black sox scandal who deserves it.

Section Three

Throwing a series by the numbers

Chicago White Sox 88-52 .629
1919 American League Champions
Team Roster

Ht	Wt	Name	Pos	B	T	Age	Gms	AB	R	H	2B	3B	HR	RBI	SB	Ave	BB	K	S/Ave	TB
6' 1 1/2	190	Charles Gandil Chick)	1B	R	R	32	115	441	54	128	24	7	1	60	10	0.290	20	20	0.383	169
5' 9	175	Edward Collins (Eddie)	2B	L	R	33	140	518	87	165	19	7	4	80	33	0.319	68	27	0.405	210
6' 0	165	Charles Risberg (Swede)	SS	R	R	24	119	414	48	106	19	6	2	38	19	0.256	35	38	0.345	143
5' 11	170	Geirge Weaver (Buck)	3B	B	R	29	140	571	89	169	33	9	3	75	22	0.296	11	21	0.401	229
5' 6 1/2	157	Harry Leibold (Nemo)	RF	L	R	27	122	434	81	131	18	2	0	26	17	0.302	72	30	0.353	153
5' 11	175	Oscar Felsch (Happy)	CF	R	R	28	135	502	68	138	34	11	7	86	19	0.275	40	35	0.428	215
6' 1	200	Joseph Jackson (Shoe-less Joe)	LF	L	R	30	139	516	79	181	31	14	7	96	9	0.351	60	10	0.506	261
5' 9	165	Raymond Schalk (Cracker)	C	R	R	27	131	394	57	111	9	3	0	34	11	0.282	51	25	0.320	126
6' 0	185	John Collins (Shano)	RF	R	R	33	63	179	21	50	6	3	1	16	3	0.279	7	11	0.363	65
5' 11	170	Fredrick McMullin (Fred)	3B	R	R	27	60	170	31	50	8	4	0	19	4	0.294	11	18	0.388	66
5' 9	155	John Murphy (Honest Eddie)	OF	L	R	28	30	35	8	17	4	0	0	5	0	0.486	7	0	0.6	21
5' 11	165	Byrd Lynn	C	R	R	30	29	66	4	15	4	0	0	4	0	0.227	4	9	0.288	19
5' 11	170	Joseph Jenkins (Joe)	C	R	R	29	11	19	0	3	1	0	0	1	1	0.158	1	1	0.211	4
5' 9 1/2	143	Harvey McClellan (Little Mac)	INF	R	R	25	7	12	2	4	0	0	0	1	0	0.333	1	1	0.333	4

Ht	Wt	Pitcher	Pos	B	T	Age	Gms	GS	CG	W	L	Pct.	ERA	Inn	ER	Hits	BB	K	SHO	SV
5' 9	175	Edward Cicotte (Eddie)	P	B	R	35	40	35	30	29	7	0.806	1.82	307	62	256	49	110	5	1
5' 7	155	Richard Kerr (Dickie)	P	L	L	25	39	17	10	13	7	0.650	2.89	212	68	208	64	79	1	0
5' 9	160	Claude Williams (Lefty)	P	L	L	26	41	40	27	23	11	0.676	2.64	297	87	265	58	125	5	1
6' 1	170	Roy Wilkenson	P	R	R	25	4	1	1	1	1	0.500	2.05	22	5	21	10	5	1	0
6' 4	195	William James (Big Bill)	P	B	R	32	5	5	3	3	1	0.750	2.54	39	11	39	14	11	2	0
6' 4	190	Grover Lowdermilk (Slim)	P	R	R	34	27	11	5	5	5	0.500	2.78	109	30	101	47	49	0	0
6' 0	168	Erskine Mayer	P	R	R	30	6	2	0	1	3	0.250	8.25	24	22	30	11	9	0	0
6' 2	180	Urban Faber (Red)	P	B	R	31	25	20	9	11	9	0.550	3.83	162	69	185	45	45	0	0
5' 11	165	John Sullivan (Lefty)	P	I	I	25	4	2	1	0	1	0.000	4.20	15	7	24	8	9	0	0

Cincinnati Reds 96-44 .686

1919 National League Champions

World SeriesTeam Roster

Ht	Wt	Name	Pos	B	T	Age	Gms	AB	R	H	2B	3B	HR	RBI	SB	Ave	BB	K	S/Ave	TB
5'10 1/2	160	Jacob Daubert (Jake)	1B	L	L	35	140	537	79	148	10	12	2	44	11	0.276	35	23	0.350	188
5' 8 1/2	160	Morris Rath (Morrie)	2B	L	R	32	138	537	77	142	13	1	1	29	17	0.264	64	24	0.298	160
5' 9	160	William Kopf (Larry)	SS	B	R	28	135	503	51	136	18	5	0	58	18	0.270	28	27	0.326	164
5' 8	158	Henry Groh (Heinie)	3B	R	R	30	122	448	79	139	17	11	5	63	21	0.310	56	26	0.431	193
6' 0	170	Alfred Neale (Greasy)	RF	L	R	27	139	500	57	121	10	12	1	54	28	0.242	47	51	0.316	158
5' 11	170	Edd Roush (Eddie)	CF	L	L	26	133	504	73	162	19	12	4	71	20	0.321	42	19	0.431	227
5' 9	170	Louis Duncan (Pat)	LF	R	R	26	31	90	9	22	3	3	2	17	2	0.244	8	7	0.411	37
5' 10	168	William Rariden (Bedfor Bill)	C	R	R	31	75	218	16	47	6	3	1	24	4	0.216	17	19	0.284	62
5' 10	160	Ivey Wingo	C	L	R	29	76	245	30	67	12	6	0	27	4	0.273	23	19	0.371	91
5' 11	179	Sherwood Magee (Sherry)	OF	R	R	35	56	163	11	35	6	1	0	21	4	0.215	26	19	0.264	43
5' 9	158	James Smith (Jimmy)	INF	B	R	24	28	40	9	11	1	3	1	10	1	0.275	4	8	0.525	21
6' 0	187	Raymond Bressler (Rube)	OF-P	R	L	24	61	165	22	34	3	4	2	17	2	0.206	23	15	0.309	51
5' 11	165	Henry Schreiber (Hank)	INF	R	R	28	19	58	5	13	4	0	0	4	0	0.224	0	12	0.293	17
6' 0	180	Artemus Allen (Nick)	C	R	R	31	15	25	7	8	0	1	0	5	0	0.320	2	6	0.400	10
5' 10 1/2	175	Charles See (Charlie)	OF	L	R	22	8	14	1	4	0	0	0	1	0	0.286	1	0	0.286	4
Ht	Wt	Pitcher	Pos	B	T	Age	Gms	GS	CG	W	L	Pct.	ERA	Inn	ER	Hits	BB	K	SHO	SV
5'11 1/2	185	Horace Eller (Hod)	P	R	R	25	38	30	16	20	9	0.690	2.40	248	66	216	50	137	7	2
6'1 1/2	180	Walter Ruether (Dutch)	P	L	L	26	33	29	20	19	6	0.760	1.82	243	49	195	83	78	3	0
6' 1	170	James Ring (Jimmy)	P	R	R	24	32	18	12	10	9	0.526	2.26	183	46	150	51	61	2	3
6' 3	180	Harry Sallee (Slim)	P	L	L	34	29	28	22	21	7	0.750	2.05	228	52	221	20	24	4	0
5' 11 1/2	180	Raymond Fisher (Ray	P	R	R	32	26	20	12	14	5	0.737	2.17	174	42	141	38	41	5	1
5' 7	160	Adolpho Luque (Dolph	P	R	R	29	30	9	6	9	3	0.750	2.63	106	31	89	36	40	2	3
6' 0	187	Raymond Bressler (Rube)	P	R	L	24	13	4	1	2	4	0.333	3.46	42	16	37	8	13	0	0
5' 9 1/2	170	Albert Mitchell (Roy)	P	R	R	34	7	1	0	0	1	0.000	2.32	31	8	32	9	10	0	0
5' 8 1/2	175	Edwin Gerner (Lefty)	P	L	L	22	5	1	0	1	0	1.000	3.18	17	6	22	3	2	0	0

Position	Player	1919 Salary	Promised Pay-off	Actual Pay-off
Pitcher	Eddie Cicotte	$5,500	$30,000	$10,000
Pitcher	Lefty Williams	$3,000	$20,000	$5,000
Pitcher	Dickie Kerr	$1,100	not involved	no
Left-field	Joe Jackson	$6,000	$20,000	$5,000
Center	Happy Felsch	$4,000	$20,000	$5,000
Right	Shano Collins	$1,200	not involved	no
Right	Nemo Leibold	$1,100	not involved	no
Catcher	Ray Schalk	$3,500	not involved	no
1st-base	Chick Gandil	$4,000	$20,000	$35,000
2nd-base	Eddie Collins	$15,000	not involved	no
Short	Swede Risberg	$1,400	$20,000	$20,000
3rd-base	Buck Weaver	$6,000	not known if offered	Nothing
Utility	Fred McMullin	$1,000	$10,000	Nothing
Total	Total	$52,800	$140,000	$80,000

Bone Head and General Poor Play

Total	Game	Inning	Outs	Player Involved
1	1	1	0	E. Collins(1)- Bad bunt forcing S.Collins at 2nd base
2	1	1	1	E. Collins(2)- Caught stealing on very next play
3	1	1	0	E.Cicotte (1)- Hit Morrie Rath on purpose
4	1	1	0	Gandil (1) - Caught stealing
5	1	4	2	Risberg (1) - Couln't make play on Neale's infield single
6	1	4	2	S. Collins(1)- Missed cut-off man allowing Wingo to take 2nd base
7	1	4	2	S. Collins(2)- Missed cut-off man allowing Daubert to take 2nd base
8	1	7	0	Gandil (2) - Dropped Weaver's throw
9	2	1	1	E. Collins(3 - Doubled-off 1st on Weaver's liner
10	2	2	1	Jackson(1) - Should have tried to score on Gandil's grounder to short
11	2	4	1	Felsch(1) - Missed cut-off man allowing Groh to take 3rd base
12	2	5	1	Risberg (2) - Missed pop-fly behind mound, sure double-play
13	3	2	0	Gandil(3) - Jogged into 3rd base force on sure Schalk in-field single
14	3	3	0	Jackson(2) - Popped up sacrifice bunt attempt when red hot
15	3	4	1	Schalk(1) - Caught stealing
16	3	6	0	Jackson(3) - Caught stealing
17	3	6	1	Felsch(2) - Caught stealing
18	4	5	1	Cicotte(2) - Threw ball into stands allowing Duncan to take 2nd base
19	4	5	1	Jackson(4) or Cicotte(2)- either could have gotten error on Jackson's throw
20	4	5	1	Jackson(5) - Playing way too shallow on Neale's double
21	4	5	1	Leibold(1) - Groh caught Leibold napping off 2nd base
22	5	4	2	Risberg(3) - Muffed Roush's grounder
23	5	4	2	Schalk(2) - Passed ball on Roush stolen base
24	5	6	0	Felsch(3) - Poor throw back to infield on Eller's double,Hod taking 3rd
25	5	6	1	Felsch(4) - Should have caught Roush's long drive, scored a triple
26	5	6	1	Jackson(6) - Poor throw to plate as Roush scored
27	5	6	2	Byrd(1) - Dropped Jackson's poor throw, might have had play at plate
28	5	9	0	E. Collins(4)- Booted Roush's grounder
29	6	2	0	Risberg(4) - Bobbled Duncan's grounder
30	6	4	1	Risberg(5) - Hit Ruether in back with throw to 3rd base,Dutch scored
31	6	7	2	Felsch(6) - Dropped Duncan's Fly ball foe 3 base error
32	6	7	0	Felsch(7) -Lolligagged on Rath's bloop single, could have caught ball
33	6	8	1	Jackson(7) - Caught off 2nd base for inning ending double play
34	6	8	2	Gandil(4) - Should have made play on Neale's single
35	6	10	0	Jackson(8) - Bunted for base hit with winning run on 2nd base
36	6	10	1	Jackson(9) - Doubled off 2nd base again, 2x in 3 innings
37	7	1	2	Jackson(10)- After RBI single, caught between 1st and 2nd base, was lucky to get back to 1st
38	7	1	0	E. Collins(5)- Booted Rath's grounder
39	7	3	1	E. Collins(6)- Head up ass on Weaver's liner,not lead runner
40	7	8	1	Risberg(6) - Out trying to take x-tra base on Roush's error
41	8	1	1	Williams(1) - Every pitch he threw in 1st inning
42	8	1	0	Weaver(1) - K'd looking with two in scoring position,only time in this category
43	8	1	1	Jackson(11)- Weak pop-up with two runners in scoring position
44	8	1	2	Felsch(7) - K'd with two runners in scoring position
45	8	2	2	Gandil(5) - Should have made play on Groh's grounder with two out
46	8	2	2	Jackson(12) - Should have caught Roush's RBI double that went off glove
47	8	4	1	E.Collins(7) - Should have made play on Roush's grounder scored base hit
48	8	5	2	Risberg(7) - Should have made play on Neale's RBI single
49	8	6	0	Schalk(3) - Low throw to Weaver on bunt by Daubert
50	8	6	1	E.Collins(8) - Should have made play on Roush's grounder that went off glove
51	8	6	1	E.Collins(9) - Another ball scored base hit that he should have fielded by Duncan
52	8	6	1	Leibold(2) - Roush and Duncan moved up a base after slow throw to infield
53	8	6	1	Kid Gleason- Should have removed Leibold from game after shitty throw
54	8	8	1	Kid Gleason- Should have had pitcher nail Kopf with pitch after Duncan's Sac bunt with 9-1 lead
55	8	8	2	Jackson(13)- Missed cut-off with no chance to get Roush at plate, Rariden taking 2nd base
56	8	9	0	Risberg(8) - Should have made play on Rath's infield hit

Great Plays and Double Plays Turned

Total	Game	Inning	Outs	Player Involved
1	1	5	2	Risberg(1 - Great stop and throw on Kopf
2	1	6	1	Risberg(2) - Caught liner by Rath and doubled-off Neale at 2nd
3	1	7	1	Risberg(3)&E,Collins(1)- Double play on Kopf grounder
4	2	1	2	S.Collins(1) - Nice catch to rob Groh of x-tra bases
5	2	2	0	E.Collins(2) - Caught Daubert's liner and doubled-off Roush
6	2	8	1	Felsch(1) - Great catch and throw on Roush to double-off Groh
7	3	4	1	Risberg(4) - Caught Duncan's liner and doubled Groh off 2nd
8	4	1	0	E.Collins(3) & Risberg(5)- double play on Daubert grounder
9	4	7	1	Weaver(1) - Great stop and throw on Duncan
10	4	8	1	Cicotte(1) & Risberg(6)- Turn double play on Ring
11	6	1	2	Risberg(7) - On Roush hit, turned and nailed Groh at 3rd
12	6	4	1	Jackson(1) - Caught Daubert's fly and threw out Rath at plate
13	6	7	1	Risberg(8) & E.Collins(4)- Double play on Roush grounder
14	8	3	1	Weaver(2) - Great stop and throw on Kopf
15	8	4	1	Leibold(1) - Nails Eller at plate on Daubert single
16	8	6	1	Weaver(3) - Fields Neale's grounder and forces Roush at plate
17	8	6	2	Schalk(1) - Picked Kopf off 2nd base to end inning

Not Hitting in Clutch							
Total	Game	inn	Outs	1st Base	2nd Base	3rd Base	Total in Parenthesis
1	1	6	1	Weaver	E. Collins		Jackson (1) 4-3
2	1	6	2		Weaver	E. Collins	Felsch (1) F-9
3	2	2	1			Jackson	Gandil (1) 6-3
4	2	2	2			Jackson	Risberg (1) F-9
5	2	4	1		Jackson	Weaver	Gandil (2) FC 3-2
6	2	4	2		Gandil	Jackson	Risberg (2) F-3
7	2	6	1		Weaver		Jackson (2) K
8	2	6	2			Weaver	Felsch (2) F-8
9	2	8	2		Jackson		Felsch (3) 5-3
10	3	2	0	Risberg	Gandil		Schalk (1) FC 1-5
11	3	2	1	Schalk	Risberg		Kerr (1) FC 1-5
12	3	2	2	Kerr	Schalk		Leibold (1) 5-3
13	3	3	0	Weaver	E.Collins		Jackson (3) F-3
14	3	3	1	Weaver	E.Collins		Felsch (4) DP 6-4-3
15	4	2	1			Jackson	Gandil (3) 6-3
16	4	2	2	Schalk	Risberg	Jackson	Cicotte (1) 4-3
17	4	3	2		E. Collins		Jackson (4) E-4
18	4	3	2	Jackson		E. Collins	Felsch (5) 5-3
19	4	5	1		Leibold		E. Collins (1) FC 5-4
20	5	1	1	Weaver		Leibold	Jackson (5) F-5
21	5	1	2	Weaver		Leibold	Felsch (6) F-7
22	5	9	2			Weaver	Jackson (6) 6-3
23	6	5	0	Kerr	Schalk	Risberg	S.Collins (1) F-8
24	6	6	0		Felsch		Gandil (4) F-3
25	6	6	1		Felsch		Risberg (3) 6-3
26	6	6	2		Schalk		Kerr (2) 5-3
27	6	8	1	Gandil	Jackson		Risberg (4) DP F-8-4
28	6	9	2		Leibold		E. Collins (2) F-8
29	6	10	0	Jackson		Weaver	Felsch (7) K
30	6	10	1	Gandil	Jackson		Risberg (5) DP L-6-4
31	7	1	1		S.Collins		Weaver (1) F-8
32	7	1	2	Felsch	Jackson		Gandil (5) FC 4-6
33	7	3	0	E.Collins	S.Collins		Weaver (2) DP L-4-3
34	7	5	1	Felsch	Jackson		Gandil (6) 1-3
35	7	5	2		Felsch	Jackson	Risberg (6) K
36	7	6	2		S.Collins		E.Collins (3) K 2-3
37	8	1	0		E.Collins	Leibold	Weaver (K) Looking
38	8	1	1		E.Collins	Leibold	Jackson (7) F-6
39	8	1	2		E.Collins	Leibold	Felsch (8) K
40	8	2	1	Risberg	Schalk		James (1) F-5
41	8	2	2	Risberg	Schalk		Leibold (2) K
42	8	8	1		Jackson		Felsch (9) F-3
43	8	9	1	E.Collins	Murphy		Weaver (4) F-9
44	8	9	2		E.Collins	Murphy	Jackson (8) 4-3

Double Plays Not Turned

Total	Game	Inning	Outs	Players Involved	Reason not turned
1	1	4	1	Cicotte to Risberg	Risberg (1) - Slow turn
2	1	7	0	Risberg to E,Collins	E.Collins(1) - Late with throw
3	2	5	1	Risberg	Risberg (2) - Dropped Rath's pop-up
4	3	2	1	Risberg	Risberg (3) - Didn't try for lead runner
5	3	5	0	Risberg	Risberg(4) - Again didn't try for lead runner
6	3	5	1	Gandil to Risberg	Risberg (5) -No throw back to 1st base
7	5	5	0	E.Collins	E.Collins(2) - Didn't try for lead runner
8	6	2	1	Risberg to E,Collins	E.Collins (3)- Slow relay to 1st base
9	6	3	1	E.Collins to Risberg	E.Collins (4)- Fumbled Rariden grounder
10	6	9	1	Schalk to Risberg	Schalk (1) - After K, Daubert stole 2nd
11	7	3	1	Risberg to E,Collins	E.Collins (5)- Late with relay to 1st
12	7	3	1	Risberg to E,Collins	Risberg (6) - Late with throw to Collins
13	8	4	1	E.Collins	E.Collins (7)- Rath singled off glove
14	8	6	1	E,Collins	E.Collins (8) -Roush singled off glove
15	8	6	1	E.Collins	E.Collins (9) -Daubert singled past Eddie

Bibliography

Baseball Encyclopedia, McMillan Publishing Company, New York- 1984

Coen, Richard M., Neft, David S., and Johnson, Roland T., *World Series*, The Dial Press, New York-1976

Curren, William, *Big Sticks The Batting Revolution of the Twenties*, William Morrow and Company, Inc., New York-1990

Dickey, Glen, *The History of the American League Baseball*, Stein and Day Publishers, New York-1980

Musial, Stanly, and Broeg, Robert, *Stan Musial-The Man's Own Story*, Doubleday & Company, Inc., Garden City, New York-1964

Ritter, Lawrence S., *The Glory of Their Times*, The McMillan Company, New York-1966

Rosenberg, John M., *The Story of Baseball*, Random House, New York-1966

Seymour, Harold Ph. D., *Baseball the Golden Age*, Oxford University Press, New York-1971

Smith, Ron, *The Ballpark Book*, Sporting News Books, St. Louis-2003

Spink, J. G. Taylor, *Judge Landis and Twenty-Five Years of Baseball*, Stein and Day Publishers, New York-1947

About the Author

Kelly Cleaver is the son of Washington, NJ Star and Easton, PA Express sports writer Hunce Cleaver and wife Joan. He grew up in the world of sports in Washington, New Jersey and Yuma, Arizona. Kelly was an all-state shortstop at Yuma High School where he has the distinction of holding a state and national record that can never be broken, only tied. He did not strike-out his senior year. Kelly continued his baseball at Arizona Western College and Fort Hays State University (Kansas). Kelly will be inducted this year into the first class of the Yuma softball Hall of Fame. He currently resides in Levering Michigan with his wife Linda and sons Kelly Jr. and Maxwell and daughter Katie.